T0305382

Cost Control, College Access, and Competition in Higher Education

Cost Control, College Access, and Competition in Higher Education

Robert E. Martin

Ewing T. Boles Professor of Economics,
Department of Economics, Centre College, Danville, Kentucky

Edward Elgar
Cheltenham, UK · Northampton, MA, USA

© Robert E. Martin 2005

All rights reserved. No part of this publication may be reproduced, stored in a retrieval system or transmitted in any form or by any means, electronic, mechanical or photocopying, recording, or otherwise without the prior permission of the publisher.

Published by
Edward Elgar Publishing Limited
Glensanda House
Montpellier Parade
Cheltenham
Glos GL50 1UA
UK

Edward Elgar Publishing, Inc.
136 West Street
Suite 202
Northampton
Massachusetts 01060
USA

A catalogue record for this book
is available from the British Library

ISBN 1 84376 953 0

Printed and bound in Great Britain by MPG Books Ltd, Bodmin, Cornwall

Contents

Figures

Tables

Acknowledgements

This book is dedicated to Josef Hadar. I am forever grateful to Joe and to the rest of the faculty at Southern Methodist University for showing me the path and then turning on the lights so I might see. I am also grateful to Michael Rizzo for numerous comments and suggestions, to Will Young for his most excellent research support, and to Kacie Powell for her professional manuscript formatting. Centre College provided inspiration and financial support for this project.

My wife endured months of obsessive/compulsive behavior as this book was in preparation and for that she deserves special thanks. I would also like to acknowledge my children, their spouses, and my grandchildren, since it is out of concern for their future that I wrote this book.

Foreword

I have several related objectives in mind for this book. The first is to present an integrated model of the representative higher education institution where the institution's objective is the maximization of quality reputation. Sound public policy comes with a clear understanding of the institution's objectives and the institution's internal incentive structure. In the absence of a clear model of the representative institution public policy may have unintended consequences or inefficient results. The robust industrial organization literature rests on a well crafted theory of the profit maximizing firm. The literature that might be described as the 'college organization' literature is sparse and under-developed at best. An important reason for this lack of development is the absence of an enterprise model for higher education institutions.

The second objective is to explore the relationship between the college access problem and college cost control. College attendance and completion rates among minority students are less than the rates for white students and attendance and completion rates are less for low income students than for high income students. The lower rates are due to financial constraints, lack of preparation, and cultural differences. The financial aspects of college access are almost always discussed in terms of the need for more subsidies to higher education, while the direct contribution that college cost control makes to the financial access issue is ignored or given passing acknowledgement. The evidence suggests that tuition increases, net of scholarships, are a rising burden for students and their families, that there are multiple causes for these cost increases, and that the higher education community bears a significant responsibility for not controlling these costs.

The third objective is to frame a particular public policy issue: what type of competition among higher education institutions is socially optimal? Since cooperation is a necessary condition for the private provision of public goods, does this suggest that something other than unconstrained pure competition among institutions is optimal? If pure competition is preferred, why do we encourage cooperation among charities? Should colleges be encouraged to practice more price discrimination in order to reallocate public subsidies away from merit aid to more need based aid? Do endowments have anticompetitive effects? There are more questions than answers in this last part of the book.

AN ENTERPRISE MODEL

In the modern economy, production takes place within a variety of different types of institutions. Clearly, the profit maximizing firm is the most famous and extensively studied type of producer institution. However, there are more types of producing institutions than just the traditional profit maximizing firm, and the variety is greater than the simple distinction between the commercial, non-profit, and government sectors. Charities, group professional practices, share cropping, franchising, producer cooperatives, and a variety of government organizations are examples of producer institutions that account for a considerable share of annual GDP. Obviously, higher education institutions represent one form of producer institution that differs significantly from the traditional profit maximizing firm and they make a substantial annual contribution directly and indirectly to GDP. If the set of all producer institutions is the enterprise set, then the theory of the firm is the enterprise model for-profit maximizing firms.

Some of the alternative forms may behave as if they are profit maximizing institutions, but others do not. The incentive structures within these institutions are different and it follows that they respond differently to economic influences. Therefore, it does not follow that public policies designed for-profit maximizing firms or industries are appropriate for charities, health care, or higher education.

A common feature among all types of institutions that survive for any extended period of time is that they have some optimal properties. Their actions are consistent with some objective rather than being simply the product of random actions and reactions. The survivor principle provides strong evidence that these institutions have rational foundations. Hence, the first step in understanding any of the alternative sectors is to correctly specify their objective function. A robust industry theory cannot be developed before an enterprise model[1] is developed. One cannot model the industry, either in a neoclassical or game theoretic model, until one has a coherent enterprise model for the representative institution. The enterprise model for the representative institution is the foundation on which industry models are constructed.

The economic theory of higher education is relatively under-developed as compared to, say, the theory of the profit maximizing firm. The complex nature of the higher education governance structure causes abundant ambiguity about higher education objective functions. My intention here is not to develop an industry model. At this point, I am only interested in an integrated model of the representative institution, and even that is incomplete, since I make no attempt to model the research function of major universities.

The foundation for the development of a model is laid in Chapter 2, where I explore the similarities between the profit maximizing firm and the typical higher education institution. There are many similarities and many differences. The most significant similarity is that both types of institution must balance their cash outflows with cash inflows in the long-run. This means they are both subject to very similar economic forces, such as risk, transactions cost, production technology, and the distribution of asset ownership. These are the same forces that help us understand the origin and internal structure of the profit maximizing firm. They also have implications for the economic origin and internal structure of higher education institutions. This discussion has little to do with the historical or cultural foundations of colleges and universities; it is entirely in terms of the economic foundations of colleges and universities.

Chapters 3, 4, and 5 represent component parts of the enterprise model for the representative institution. In Chapter 3, I present a production and cost model where the institution's cost function is derived from a human capital production technology where students are both customers and inputs. Since the output is human capital, the implicit cost is a function of the number of students enrolled and the quality of the human capital imparted to the average student. The long-run cost function depends on enrollment and the institution's quality reputation. The quality adjusted cost function implies that minimum efficient scale occurs at a lower enrollment level than one would observe in a cost function that does not control for quality, and this explains why most private institutions do not exploit all returns to scale available from enrollment.

In Chapter 4, I consider the charity market and its impact on subsidies for higher education. Donors may contribute to higher education because they wish to subsidize the production of human capital or because they wish to signal wealth. Institutions seek to accumulate endowments in order to produce more human capital and in order to provide a hedge against both systematic risk and institution-specific risk. In a model where donors wish to signal wealth or status, I demonstrate that the implicit net revenue function from fundraising is a function of the institution's quality reputation as well as the cost of fundraising inputs. In the long-run, endowment revenues depend on the institution's quality reputation.

Chapter 5 contains an intergenerational model for the representative institution. The long-run cost function used in this model comes from Chapter 3 and the long-run net revenue function from fundraising comes from Chapter 4. The institution's objective is to maximize its quality reputation. During the annual enrollment cycle the institution enrolls the highest quality students it can support and during the following production cycle it maximizes the human capital it imparts to students. In the long-run, the institution's quality reputation depends on the success of its alumni. Long-run stationary state equilibrium is derived and a number of useful pricing hypotheses are derived.

COLLEGE COST AND COLLEGE ACCESS

The prices paid for college by students are like automobile and housing prices, they are composed of a list price and, in most cases, a negotiated transaction price. The differences lead to considerable confusion among journalists who report on higher education and this leads to confusion among the public. The average transaction price is equal to tuition and fees less scholarships and discounts. The real transaction price is the correct measure of the financial burden imposed on students and their families over time. The historical record explored in Chapter 1 reveals that the real transaction price for college increased steadily over the past three decades, although there is some recent evidence that the real transaction price at public institutions declined during the last three years.

The real price of many products and services increased during the last three decades, so the relevant question for college costs is: were those cost increases excessive? The record reveals that the rate of college cost increases has exceeded virtually every other rate of cost increase, including health care costs, when compared to the cost of private higher education. Costs appear to have risen because of the demand for new services from higher education, unfunded government mandates, mission creep[2], lower productivity, excessive overhead, resistance to new technology, and inflated administrator salaries. While administrator salaries compose a small fraction of each institution's total cost, their size relative to faculty and staff salaries precludes any serious conversation about cost control between administrators and the rest of the campus. Campus leaders who ask others to sacrifice while they are handsomely compensated have no credibility. All of the foregoing cost increases threaten the three-way social contract between succeeding generations and the education community.

Since there are no residual claimants, agency problems are more severe in higher education than they are in the typical publicly held profit maximizing firm. The pursuit of agency rents causes expenditures to rise as soon as revenues rise. This is the commonly noted budgetary slack model, or what Ron Ehrenberg calls the higher education 'cookie monster' that gobbles up resources wherever they may be discovered. The evidence in Chapter 6 suggests that revenue increases tend in time to precede increases in college costs; whenever revenues increase, a budgetary slack is created and that slack is filled by increases in expenditures. In the perfectly competitive profit maximizing industry, increasing costs tend to drive prices higher, while increasing demand and rising prices cause costs to rise only if it is an increasing cost industry.

The lack of effective cost control in higher education, the importance of third parties who pay for a significant share of each student's education and the budgetary slack phenomenon significantly limit the ability of public subsidies to resolve the college access problem. Whenever public subsidies increase, the student's 'ability to pay' for higher education increases, and colleges and universities move to capture part of that subsidy by increasing tuition and fees. An increase in expenditures soon follows the increase in tuition and fees. The increase in tuition and fees offsets at least part of the gains in access and the increase in expenditures is used to justify further increases in tuition and fees. In other words, a permanent fix for the financial constraints aspect of the college access problem is not possible until the higher education cost control problem is resolved. The college access problem is discussed in detail in Chapter 7.

COOPERATION AND COMPETITION

Public attitudes towards cooperation and competition among higher education institutions have changed significantly since the end of World War II. The change in attitudes culminated in the Justice Department's action against the 'Overlap Group' in the early 1990s. In the early 1950s the elite east coast institutions began to meet to consider students whose applications overlapped several institutions, the purpose being to set scholarship awards for these students such that the net price to the student was the same for each institution. They defended this practice by arguing the student could then choose which institution to attend on the basis of the quality of their programs. The Overlap Group sought to limit price competition and to promote quality competition. The settlement with the Justice Department was followed by aggressive tuition discounting throughout private higher education. The most vigorous competition was for gifted students, and as a result merit financial aid increased at the expense of need based aid. Since list prices were increasing and need based aid was decreasing during this period, college completion rates among low income and minority students stagnated and fell. These trends are discussed in more detail in Chapters 2 and 7. Since the representative institution's long-run objective is to maximize its reputation and that reputation depends on the accomplishments of its alumni, these results are predictable.

It is ironic that the public and the Justice Department tolerate and encourage cooperation among professional sports teams where the purpose of that cooperation is to limit salary competition for the best athletes, even though professional sports teams are clearly for-profit institutions and they do not produce public goods or services. The justification given for this differential treatment is that cooperation is required to promote 'competitive balance' among the teams. The argument is that without cooperation, the wealthiest teams would dominate the leagues. It is clear, however, that free entry into franchised areas would render the wealth of incumbent teams a temporary advantage at best.

Alternatively, consider the issue of 'competitive balance' and entry conditions among higher education institutions. Higher education institutions compete for the best students just as professional sports teams compete for the best athletes. However, colleges and universities provide services with significant spillover effects, while the public good character of professional sports teams is dubious at best. Even with a substantial endowment, it is improbable that a new entrant could crack the top ranks of higher education institutions, since status as an academic institution is conferred by successful alumni and that normally takes decades. Therefore, the threat of entry is impotent and competitive balance among institutions is an appropriate public policy issue. The exclusivity of the elite institutions increases as time passes, as their number and size remain the same and as the domestic population continues to grow. These trends lead to tournament-style results in the income distribution, and the rising income inequality leads to dynastic wealth and to dynastic poverty.

NOTES

1. The competitive and monopoly firm models represent enterprise models for the profit maximizing firm, just as output maximization subject to a budget constraint represents the enterprise model for the Soviet style enterprise, and public choice models are enterprise models for government institutions.
2. The term mission creep refers to the tendency of all higher education institutions to change their mission. Two-year institutions want to become four-year institutions, baccalaureate institutions want to add graduate programs, and those with graduate programs want to become research institutions. This leads to a proliferation of mediocre programs and rising cost.

1. The social contract

Whoso neglects learning in his youth,
Loses the past and is dead for the future.

Euripides (480? – 406 BC)
Phrixus

1.1 INTRODUCTION

The responsibility one generation feels toward those that follow is a valuable public asset. It shapes public and private behavior in subtle and significant ways. The degree to which the current generation is willing to sacrifice for the benefit of future generations is the measure of this sense of responsibility. It shapes public policy on the environment, education, and economic security. Some argue that this commitment is weaker today than in the past. For instance, it is possible to interpret the rise in real Social Security benefits, the looming fiscal crisis in that program and the lack of political will to fix the problem as a weakening of the social commitment between generations. The current elder generation seems prepared to lead a more comfortable life at the expense of today's young adults and their children. Some may also argue that high government deficits[1] are also evidence of a weaker commitment.

It appears the social commitment between generations with respect to higher education is at least strained and at worse may be coming undone. The principal reason why this commitment is in trouble is because higher education costs have been rising faster than costs in every other sector of the economy, with the possible exception of health care. The public burden imposed by the dual cost trends in education and health care is substantial. Rising tuition rates place a higher burden on students, their families, and the public who supply the subsidies that are an important part of higher education financing.

Our understanding of what causes systemic real increases in education costs is incomplete and the education establishment all too frequently denies there is a problem. It is a fact that productivity growth is slower in the service sector than in manufacturing industries, but the rate of productivity growth in higher education appears to have lagged far behind even the rest of the service economy. An important factor in the higher education cost control problem is an under-developed theory of enterprise behavior. An integrated model of the

1

representative institution does not exist and this makes it difficult to identify the source of the cost control problems, to effectively manage institutions, and to design public policies that enhance productivity growth and control cost. The models in this book are designed to address the lack of goal oriented models of institutional behavior in the economics of higher education. They are offered as management, research, and policy tools to help employ resources more efficiently in higher education.

Higher education faces rising enrollments and these new students are increasingly arriving with greater financial need and weaker academic preparation. Rising global competition is fueled by better educated workers and workers that continue to learn throughout their lifetime. Any country that allows a significant proportion of its population to fall behind in the race for education is committing itself to a smaller middle class, less social mobility, and a highly skewed income distribution. A renewed public commitment to universal access to education at all levels is needed. At the moment, the public has lost trust in higher education's ability to employ resources effectively. Without a change in attitude and a real commitment to reform on the part of higher education, it seems unlikely that the public will be willing to provide the resources required to effectively educate all of the next generation. It is in our collective best interest to find a solution to this dilemma.

1.2   THE TRANSFER OF KNOWLEDGE

Each generation invests in the education of the generation that follows. Historically, society's total investment exceeds the private investments made by parents on behalf of their children. This intergenerational social contract is the source of steady improvement in the human condition. The contract is simple: the older generation subsidizes the education of the younger generation with the implicit agreement that the younger generation will do the same for the generation that follows. As population and wealth grow, the contract ensures that a rising stock of human capital will be passed from one generation to the next. Without this commitment the transfer of knowledge and skills from one generation to the next may not take place, since the human capital accumulated by each generation dies with that generation. Without written records and a concerted effort to impart the knowledge to those that follow, the knowledge can be lost. The bonds between parents and their children and between society and its collective children are the bedrock upon which every successful civilization rests. Secular trends in real living standards are driven by the strength of this intergenerational commitment. The historical record is clear; the social contract has produced steady growth in real wealth and in the quality of life in the United States.

At this moment, the social contract is in trouble. Each year, the electronic and the print media contain articles and air reports on the high and rising cost of post-secondary education. These stories have titles such as 'College Tuition Rises 4%, Outpacing Inflation' (Bronner, 1998), 'Cost of four-year Degree Passes $100,000 Mark' (Honan, 1994), 'Why Colleges Cost Too Much' (Larson, 1997), and 'College Tuition Outpaces Inflation Again' (Mabry, 1999). Polls indicate that while the public believes the quality of post-secondary education is high, it costs too much (Crawford, 2003). In response to the public's concern, Congress and President Clinton passed Public Law 105-18 in 1997, which established the National Commission on the Cost of Higher Education. The Commission released its report entitled 'Straight Talk About College Costs and Prices' in 1998. The Commission members state they are

> convinced that if the public concern continues, and if colleges and universities do not take steps to reduce their costs, policymakers at the Federal and state levels will intervene and take up the task for them...continued inattention to issues of cost and price threatens to create a gulf of ill will between institutions of higher education and the larger society. (1998, 1)

The Commissioners also conclude:

> This Commission, therefore, finds itself in the discomfiting position of acknowledging that the nation's academic institutions, justly renowned for their ability to analyze practically every other major economic activity in the United States, have not devoted similar analytic attention to their own internal financial structures. (1998, 17)

It is important to note that the individual Commission members are sympathetic to higher education; they are not individuals with an axe to grind.

The National Commission's report was preceded by a report from the Council for Aid to Education entitled 'Breaking the Social Contract: The Fiscal Crisis in Higher Education', where the Commission on National Investment in Higher Education's recommendation was

> a two-pronged strategy: increased public investment in higher education and comprehensive reform of higher education institutions to lower costs and improve services. The second of these, institutional reform, is in fact a prerequisite for increased public funding. Unless the higher education sector changes the way it operates by undergoing the kind of restructuring and streamlining that successful businesses have implemented, it will be difficult to garner the increases in public funding needed to meet future demands. (1997, 3)

The Council for Aid to Education also states:

> Now that there are stringent fiscal limits on public resources, the government is beginning to ask the same kinds of questions of colleges and universities that it has asked the health care industry – questions about cost, productivity, efficiency, and effectiveness. Until institutions of higher education can provide good answers to such questions, it will be difficult to increase public support and to regain the priority formerly given to higher education in federal, state, and local budgets. (1997, 11)

Other studies followed the National Commission's report and the Council for Aid to Education's report. In 2002, the Lumina Foundation published a study entitled 'Unequal Opportunity: Disparities in College Access Among the 50 States' that concluded college access varies substantially by geography and that very few private institutions were accessible to low income students without incurring burdensome debt that neither they nor their families could afford (Kipp et al., 2002). This study received a sharp reaction from lobbying groups who represent private higher education institutions (Burd, 2002). Still another report was issued by the US House Committee on Education and the Workforce entitled 'The College Cost Crisis' in which one will find some of the harshest criticism yet voiced about the problem of cost control in higher education (Boehner and McKeon, 2003). Recently, spring 2004, rising college costs became a component of Democratic presidential candidate John Kerry's redefinition of the economic 'misery index' and a new commission was established. This new commission is called the National Commission on Accountability in Higher Education and was organized by the State Higher Education Executive Officers association and funded by the Ford Foundation.

Writing for *Business Week*, William C. Symonds observes that

> The democratization of its higher education system was one of America's great 20th century achievements. Before World War II, college was reserved for an elite minority. Since then, generous financial aid programs, coupled with large taxpayer subsidies of public universities and community colleges, helped to usher in a tenfold increase in enrollments. The US became the first nation to embrace mass higher education, gaining an enormous advantage in a world economy that puts increasing value on knowledge workers.
>
> But suddenly, this cornerstone of the US economy is threatened by escalating costs, diminished revenues, and a troubling inability to manage the crisis. (2003, 74)

David Longanecker, who is the executive director of the Western Interstate Commission for Higher Education, observes that 'American higher education is confronting a perfect storm of more limited public resources, increasing demand, and an increasingly difficult-to-serve customer base of poor and minority students' (Symonds, 2003, 74). Unfortunately, as Symonds notes since 'a larger share of these (new students) are from poor, immigrant, and minority families, they require additional financial aid and often cost more to educate because they arrive at college generally less well-prepared academically' (2003, 74). Without an effort to provide access to these students, social mobility will decline and we are in danger of creating a class of permanently disadvantaged citizens. Richard B. Freeman claims these trends may lead to an apartheid economy that is more reminiscent of third world economies if we continue to neglect the disparities that arise from declining access to higher education (1996, 118).

It is not clear how these cost trends influence public support for higher education, but one can reasonably guess that they are not helpful. What is apparent is the shift in taxpayer perceptions that has taken place in the last three decades. The proportion of the public who view education as a private good rather than a public good appears to be increasing. As is evidenced by the declining share of higher education expenditures in state budgets, the public is less willing to subsidize education through government support. Once a sufficient proportion of any generation becomes convinced that education is a private good, the contract will be broken and succeeding generations will have to provide for themselves.

Faced with this volume of criticism and concern, a prudent education establishment would move to fix the problem as quickly as possible and undoubtedly there are many educators who are ready to admit, in a quiet private moment, that we are responsible for a lot of the cost problems in higher education. Unfortunately, most of the public response from the education establishment has been defensive and some of the responses by individual members of the academe have been both offensive and irrational.[2] An 'intervention' with the education establishment may be required before a solution is found. The issue is too important to let things continue the way they are for very much longer. The nation's economic prosperity is at risk.

1.3 THE THIRD PARTY TO THE SOCIAL CONTRACT

In reality, there are three parties to the social contract: the adult generation, the younger generation that follows, and the education establishment. The education establishment is responsible for safeguarding education quality, educating the required number of students, and controlling higher education costs. Since the public is asked to provide the subsidies for education, all parties are accountable to those who pay for education. If there is a problem with quality, quantity, or cost, the public has the right to an explanation. The notion that education is entitled to unlimited financial support with no questions asked is the attitude responsible for the secular decline in primary and secondary education. The same notion is taking hold in higher education. The social contract is not an open ended commitment to provide subsidies no matter what the outcome might be. The obligation to be accountable is particularly important in higher education since the public has no direct control over the decisions taken by the higher education establishment. The tradition of academic freedom limits the ability of governing boards to take a hand in academic decisions, so the public's control is even more limited. The privilege bestowed by academic freedom contains an obligation to be responsible stewards of the nation's higher education institutions.

Thus, it is perfectly reasonable to ask if the education establishment has been a good steward of the social contract. The fact that higher education in the United States continues to be the preferred choice for a significant proportion of the world's best and brightest students suggests we are doing some things right. These gifted foreign students continue to vote with their feet. The objective evidence regarding cost leads to a mixed result, however. It appears that public higher education is doing a better job of managing its costs than is private higher education; but both types of institutions have issues with respect to cost control (Martin, 2002). This result is curious since private institutions are less regulated and tend to engage in more competition than public institutions.

The Real Price of Higher Education

As with other expensive consumer durables like housing and automobiles there is a difference between the list price and the transaction price in higher education. The posted tuition and fees represent the 'sticker price', which is the price most frequently reported by the press.[3] Generally, these list prices are reported as a simple average of all types of institutions, so the tuition and fees charged by a public university with 50 000 students is averaged with the tuition and fees charged by a small college with 1000 students. Clearly, this gives too much weight to the more expensive small college in the calculation of average tuition and fees. In order to avoid this misleading effect it is necessary to consider the public and private higher education institutions separately. More importantly, the sticker shock caused by these reports is overdone since they do not represent actual transaction prices. The average student receives a scholarship; therefore, tuition and fees less the average scholarship is a better indicator of the real price paid by students for higher education. If the scholarships increase faster than tuition and fees, then, net tuition will fall even though list price is increasing. The data reveals that net tuition and fees increased significantly during the period from 1976 through 1996 for both public and private institutions. Hence, scholarships did not increase enough to offset the rise in list price.

The critical issue is not that net tuition increased but whether or not those increases are 'excessive'. In order to come to some judgment about this, the net tuition increase has to be compared with other price increases in the economy. It is important to note that I am ignoring the investment good properties of higher education by making this comparison of price increases in higher education with other consumer prices in the economy. The point of this particular exercise is to come to some judgment about how 'burdensome' higher education costs may appear to the representative family, and their only frame of reference is going to be the prices they pay for other consumer goods. The conclusion one comes to regarding the size of the problem we face depends on which price increases are used for comparison. The most common comparison is made with respect to general price increases such as the GDP deflator. Figure 1.1 contains the difference between the net tuition indexes for public and private institutions less the GDP deflator. The base year for all three indexes is 1976. The differences represent the changes in the real burden imposed on families relative to the burden they carried in 1976. In both cases the burden imposed on families has increased during the period, although the burden implied by net tuition at private institutions is more than double the increase for public institutions. No doubt, families are familiar with the struggle required to finance higher education and the data in Figure 1.1 are not news to them.

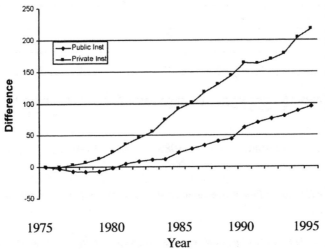

Source: NCES, Digest of Education Statistics, 2002, Tables 173, 312, 347, and 348; BEA, National Accounts.

Figure 1.1   How tuition has outpaced inflation: 1976–1996

One can argue that it is more appropriate to compare net tuition increases with the service-sector Consumer Price Index (CPI),[4] since higher education is a service and the rate of inflation in services is traditionally higher than in the rest of the economy. The increases in net tuition relative to the service-sector price index for public and private institutions from 1976 to 1996 are presented in Figure 1.2. The base year for each of these relative indexes is 1976 and the series plotted represent the net tuition index for that type of institution less the service-sector price index. For example, the service-sector price index increased from 100 in 1976 to 293 in 1996, while the public institution index for net tuition increased from 100 in 1976 to 325 in 1996. Hence, the rate of increase in the public institution index was 30 points faster than the service-sector price index. The relative rate of increase for private institutions was from 100 in 1976 to 447 in 1996. The increase in net tuition at private institutions is over 150 points higher than the increase in the CPI service index.

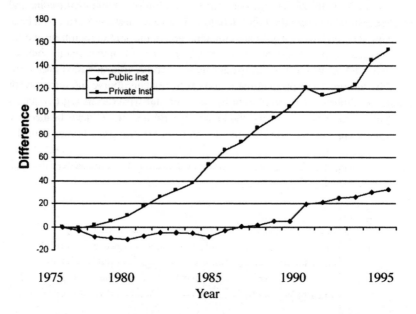

Source: NCES, Digest of Education Statistics, 2002, Tables 173, 312, 347, and 348; BEA, National Accounts.

Figure 1.2   How tuition has outpaced service–sector inflation: 1976–1996

Health care is another sector where higher real prices are a growing burden to families. Indeed, health care and higher education have similar characteristics: they provide services, they are labor intensive, and they have third party payees (insurance companies in health care and subsidy providers in higher education). Clearly there are important differences; two differences are the rate of technological change and the degree to which each sector has been restructured during the past three decades. There has been rapid technological change in medicine and the industry has undergone repeated restructuring. The organizational structure of higher education is essentially the same as it was three decades ago. There have been important structural changes in higher education, however. As Michael J. Rizzo notes the 'center of gravity' in higher education has changed significantly during the last three decades (2004). First, the number of graduate students enrolled continues to increase as a proportion of the total student body, and graduate education is more expensive than undergraduate education. Second, the number of first generation students, minority students, and students who are less well prepared has grown as a proportion of the student body. Again, the cost of educating these students is higher. Finally, the rising emphasis on science and technology, at the expense of the humanities, and the increased emphasis on research also raise the cost of higher education. These shifts in the composition of the student body and in curriculum emphasis would raise costs even if college and universities had their costs firmly under control.

Figure 1.3 contains the difference between the net tuition indexes for each type of higher education institution and the Consumer Price Index for health care expenditures for the period from 1976 through 1996. The net tuition index for private institutions increased more rapidly than the CPI for health care throughout the period, finishing the 20-year period 20 points higher than the CPI for health care. Net tuition for public institutions did not increase as fast as the CPI for health care. It actually finished the period 100 points lower than the health care index.

Net Prices and Costs in Higher Education

From the foregoing, it is fair to conclude that students and their families have been asked to shoulder an increasing financial burden and public concern about these burdens is justified. What is not clear is whether the increased burden comes from declining public/private support for higher education or from increasing costs.

In competitive industries prices rise when costs rise. In higher education, prices can rise even if costs are constant or falling. This can happen when public subsidies and/or private charity are reduced significantly. Since the average student receives a subsidy in both private and public institutions, average net tuition is less than average cost. A permanent increase in enrollment that is not accompanied by an increase in subsidies means either the average subsidy must go down (raising the net price) or the sticker price must rise (raising the net price).

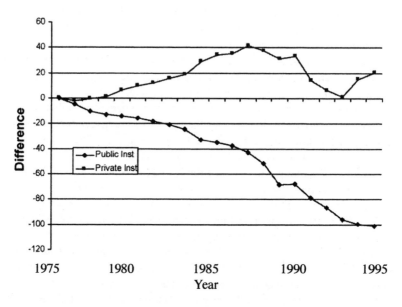

Source: NCES, Digest of Education Statistics, 2002, Tables 173, 312, 347, and 348; BEA, National Accounts.

Figure 1.3   Net tuition and health care inflation: 1976–1996

In an imperfect for-profit industry with stable costs, prices can rise as the firm's market power increases. The higher prices lead to higher profits in this case. While higher education does not earn profits that can be distributed to owners, it can earn surpluses that are appropriated as rents by the agents who control the institution. The institution's accounting budgets will be balanced, but their economic budgets will be in surplus. Hence, net tuition in higher education can rise due to one of three reasons: declining public support, agency problems, or increases in cost. Separating the effect of agency problems and real cost increases is empirically very tricky. The accounting costs reported by higher education are a function of both real cost variables and agency rents.

If the institution's cost per student rises faster than other prices, this may suggest cost increases are excessive and are the result of agency problems. Consider the cost indexes for both public and private institutions using total education and general expenses (E&G expenses) less scholarships on a per student basis. The data covers the years from 1976 through 1996. The real E&G costs per student for public and private institutions are plotted in Figure 1.4. The costs for both public and private institutions increased faster than the service-sector CPI from 1976 to 1996.

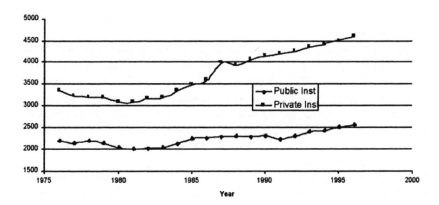

Source: NCES, Digest of Education Statistics, 2002, Tables 173, 347, and 348; BEA, National Accounts. Deflated by service–sector CPI.

Figure 1.4   Real E&G cost per student

Research Associates of Washington computes higher education price indices, and those indices are published by the US Census Bureau in the Statistical Abstract of the United States. There are individual indices for personnel, services, supplies, and equipment as well as an index for the total cost of inputs for higher education. The service-sector CPI and the total higher education input price index are virtually identical, which implies that the cost of resources required for higher education services are essentially the same as in the service sector. Therefore, whatever is causing E&G costs to rise faster than the service-sector CPI, it is not the prices paid for resources. The difference is explained by how those resources are employed in higher education relative to how resources are employed in the rest of the service economy. Hence, I assume the service-sector CPI index is an appropriate base line for cost increases during the period from 1976 through 1996. In other words, it is reasonable to expect cost to rise at that rate during the period.

One may justify this assumption by observing that if higher education exercises the same control over its costs as was exercised by the representative firm in the service sector, then cost per student should rise at pace with the service-sector CPI index. Then the service-sector CPI index is the appropriate deflator for net tuition, E&G cost per student, and external support per student. Let the deflated net tuition series be the variable *tuition*. Given a balanced budget, the real increases in net tuition may be the result of declining real external support per student or it may be the result of variations in real cost per student. The real E&G cost per student is the variable *cost*. The real external support per student is the variable *exsup*. External support per student is the sum of federal aid, state/local appropriations, private gifts/grants, and endowment income divided by enrollment.

Table 1.1 contains the results from regression models where *tuition* is the dependent variable and *cost* and *exsup* are the independent variables. The results from three models are reported in Table 1.1. The first model is the consolidated model for both public and private institutions. This model indicates that net tuition is an increasing function of cost per student and a decreasing function of external support per student. All variables including the intercept are significant at the 0.01 or better level. The second model contains dummy shift variables for public institutions.

The second model is the unrestricted model. The dummy variables are for the intercept and the slopes with respect to cost per student and external support per student at public institutions. In this model, the intercept term for private institutions is not significant. The cost coefficient and the external support coefficient for private institutions are significant at least at the 0.03 level. However, the coefficient for external support in private institutions is positive. The coefficient for external support in public institutions is negative and significant at least at the 0.02 level. The fact that the signs for external support are opposite each other and they are both significant implies that net tuition responds differently to changes in external support at public institutions than it does at private institutions. This conclusion is consistent with the Wald test on the restricted versus the unrestricted model, where the F statistic is 7.20 which is significant at the 0.01 or better level. The shift coefficient for cost per student at public institutions is not significant, suggesting that the cost coefficient for public institutions is the same as the cost coefficient for private institutions.

The third model is the same as the second model except the shift variable for cost per student at public institutions has been omitted. This model assumes the effect of rising cost per student is the same in both types of institution. In this case all of the remaining slope variables are significant at least at the 0.01 level and the net slope value for external support at public institutions is negative, while the slope value for external support at private institutions is positive. The elasticity of net tuition with respect to cost at public institutions is 0.74 and the elasticity of net tuition with respect to cost at private institutions is 0.52.

Due to the limited degrees of freedom, caution must be used when interpreting the results. The small number of explanatory variables may also be a cause for concern. However, a Ramsey RESET test was run on the third model and the results suggest the model does not suffer from major omitted variable problems. This conclusion is consistent with theory. Changes in real net tuition should be driven by variations in costs and variations in external support in a not-for-profit enterprise. The results reveal that variations in the net tuition index are positively related to variations in real cost per student for both public institutions and private institutions. The uniform cost coefficient is positive and significant at better than the 0.01 level.

Table 1.1   Net tuition, cost, and external support*
(Dependent variable = Tuition)

Variable	Model 1	Model 2	Model 3
Intercept	6.98	−4.04	−3.81
	(3.08)	(−1.18)	(−1.31)
Cost	0.86	0.42	0.43
	(23.50)	(2.82)	(4.41)
Exsup	−0.88	2.14	2.05
	(−8.91)	(2.39)	(3.30)
pub		16.41	16.21
		(2.14)	(2.19)
pubcost		0.03	
		(0.13)	
pubexsup		−2.71	−2.60
		(−2.67)	(−3.95)
Total R^2	0.98	0.99	0.99
N	41	41	41

Note: * t - values are in parentheses.

A significant difference in the two types of institutions appears in the effect of external support per student. The coefficient estimate for public institutions is negative and significant at better than the 0.01 level, while the coefficient for private institutions is positive and significant at better than the 0.01 level. A decline in external support per student will cause an increase in net tuition for public institutions. The elasticity of net tuition with respect to external support at public institutions is −0.60 and the elasticity of net tuition with respect to external support at private institutions is 0.59.

The difference in external support at public and private institutions is revealed by Figure 1.5, where real external support per student is plotted for both types of institutions. Throughout the period, real external support per student at public institutions has been approximately constant, while real external support per student at private institutions was approximately constant until the mid-1980s when it began to rise. Except for a short period around 1980, real external support per student at private institutions has grown. Recall from Figure 1.4 that the cost per student index at both public and private institutions has been rising faster than the service-sector index throughout the period. Therefore, the decline in external support that is frequently reported as the primary reason for rising net tuition is true only for public institutions and that is only accurate in the sense that external support failed to grow at the same rate as did real E&G cost per student. The public did keep the real external support per student constant; what it did not do was keep external support a constant proportion of a rising real E&G cost per student. The trend in external support for private institutions has been more generous by comparison. These results suggest that the relationship between costs, external support, and net tuition is significantly different for public institutions and for private institutions. From a public policy perspective, it would be a mistake to treat them as if they are the same.

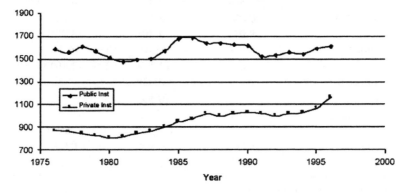

Source: NCES, Digest of Education Statistics, 2002, Tables 173, 330, and 331; BEA, National Accounts. Deflated by the service–sector CPI.

Figure 1.5   Real external support per student

The preceding analysis suggests that rates of increase in net tuition have not been contained within the norms that a prudent person would expect. Hence, the rise in the cost of higher education to students and their families is a legitimate public policy issue for all of higher education. The first question that immediately follows is: are there special or extenuating circumstances beyond the control of those taking the decisions in higher education that can explain the net tuition increases? If the answer to this first question is no, then the next question is: what factors are responsible for these excessive increases and how can those factors be eliminated?

Since real external support per student is constant at public institutions and rising at private institutions, the source of the problem appears to be the increases in real E&G cost per student. The decline in external support at public institutions has occurred in only one sense, in that the public has not kept external support a constant proportion of E&G cost per student. If E&G cost per student had risen at the same rate as the service-sector CPI, which is the appropriate benchmark for rising E&G cost, then the real burden imposed by net tuition would have been constant. Therefore, E&G cost control is a problem in both public and private institutions, although the problem appears to be more acute in private institutions.

Given that children of wealthy families are more likely to attend private institutions than are the children of minority and lower income families, these diverse trends in external support for public and private institutions have some unpleasant economic and social implications. From an economic perspective, society's interests are best served if the children of minority and lower income families receive more support than the children of wealthy families. Indeed, it can be argued that external support for wealthy students crowds out private investment in education. Given that the total available external support is finite, crowding out lowers total private and public investment in human capital. The theory of economic growth, capital market constraints, and income distribution reveals that this allocation will create separate human capital dynasties between wealthy families and poor families. The social implications of those dynastic differences are chilling at best.

1.4 TUITION AND COST DRIVERS

In order to untangle the factors that cause tuition to rise, Michael Mumper surveyed public officials, staff, faculty, and administrators regarding public higher education in 11 states during the period from 1995 to 1999 (2001). From these survey results he created a 'causal narrative' which represents the opinions of those parties with an interest in and responsibility for higher education. The focus of the interviews was why public sector tuition is rising so rapidly.

Mumper classified the responses he received into five narrative explanations for rising tuition (2001). The first narrative claims the state governments are responsible for rising tuition since they failed to increase state support at the same rate at which costs per student were rising. This is a little misleading since the real question is whether state support per student declined in real terms, and the data reveal that real support per student was approximately constant. The second narrative is related to the first since it claims tuition rose because states had other severe budgetary problems in programs where legal mandates required their support. Medicaid, prisons, and court ordered primary/secondary school reforms are cited as examples. Since higher education is one of the very few state agencies that has its own external source of revenues, state politicians withheld financial support, knowing that the colleges and universities would raise tuition in order to cover their cost. This policy by state government constitutes a stealth tax increase on students and their parents. Since tax revenues are fungible, any reduction in the obligation to higher education could be used to support other programs and the colleges and universities would take the blame. As we have seen in the preceding section, declining external support is only part of the answer at public institutions and has no bearing on private higher education. The real culprit is the rising cost per student.

The third narrative reported by Mumper is that 'quality programs cost money' (2001, 51–53). This narrative comes from the institutions themselves, where administrators claim that the cost of quality is out of their control. The factors most frequently mentioned here were technology and deferred maintenance. Since higher education input prices rose at the same rate as the service-sector CPI and cost per student increased at a faster rate than the rest of the service economy, it would be logical to expect to see a measurable increase in higher education quality. The following data do not suggest that higher education quality has been rising over the last three decades.

Mumper's fourth narrative blames the colleges themselves for the rise in tuition (2001, 53–58). He describes this position as follows:

> This story is built on the assumption that one job of campus leaders is to make choices about where to spend their limited funds. In this view, as the goods and services that colleges must purchase increased in price, the institutions should have been more responsible; they should have reexamined their spending priorities rather than simply continuing past purchasing patterns. Colleges' proper response to rising prices was not simply to pay but to reexamine their expenditures. Like all public agencies, colleges should find a way to live within their budgets by changing priorities, improving efficiency, or increasing productivity. (2001, 53–54)

He cites evidence that suggests expenditures for research and administration at public institutions increased from 1985 to 1995, while expenditures for instruction actually fell.

The fifth narrative encountered by Mumper is the denial narrative (2001, 58–60). Here it is argued that since enrollments are rising and the proportion of the college age population attending college is also rising in the face of ever higher tuition, there is no problem. People can still afford higher education so that must mean higher tuition/fees are not preventing access. In fact, this is a story about inelastic demand. For all but the very wealthiest in our society, higher education is an indispensable input in the production of a middle class life style. In that sense, the demand for higher education is like the patient's demand for kidney dialysis. Rather than a reason for apathy, the inelastic demand for higher education is a cause for serious concern about controlling costs.

Factors that Drive Costs Higher

A variety of explanations for rising cost in higher education have been suggested. Some of these explanations can be considered extenuating circumstances and others indicate problems in higher education that need to be addressed. The primary cost drivers are thought to be rising labor cost per student (primarily expenses associated with faculty), rising administrative costs, increased government regulation, technology, 'mission creep', and agency problems (Martin, 2002). The shifts in the 'center of gravity' alluded to earlier in this chapter are also factors that drive costs higher; more graduate students, less well prepared students, and curriculum composition are factors that may be considered extenuating circumstances.

Mission creep and rising expectations

Mission creep is a major problem for public higher education institutions. Mumper attributes the following comment to a member of the Colorado General Assembly:

> We have a problem here known as 'mission creep'. Every institution aspires to be like the ones that have more status. All the community colleges want to be four years. All the four years want to be research universities. They are all expanding their range of classes and increasing their research capacity. Nobody is happy just being what they are. And it all ends up costing a lot of money. (2001, 57)

The incentives for mission creep are clear. Average salaries for faculty and administrators rise as one moves up the ranks from community college to four-year college, to master's level university, to PhD granting university. Similarly, as one moves up the ladder teaching loads go down. The public plays a role in the mission creep problem by demanding convenient access to specialized courses and graduate programs. This inevitably results in redundant low quality graduate programs with very few students. The higher education governing boards, administrators, and faculty are jointly responsible for the increases in cost due to mission creep.

Rising expectations lead higher education institutions to provide more services to students than in the past and to the extent the cost of these new services are bundled with the traditional education services provided by these institutions, net tuition and cost per student must rise as new services are made available to students. These services include more counseling beyond traditional academic counseling, luxury dormitory accommodations, more variety and higher food quality, state of the art athletic facilities, high quality on-campus entertainment events, and international travel opportunities. Another important contributor to costs in this category is the expansion of remedial courses that are required for students who are not fully prepared for higher education. These costs have been shifted from secondary education to higher education. Since society and students are demanding these new services, the institutions cannot be faulted for satisfying the demand. Therefore, the cost of new services can be construed to be an extenuating factor in the rising cost of higher education.

Government regulation

The National Commission suggests that government regulation may be a significant factor in rising costs (1998, 287). If government regulation is to be considered an extenuating explanation for the rise in E&G cost per student, one has to show that regulation imposes more costs on higher education than does the equivalent regulation in the service sector. The mandates associated with Title IX are one form of government regulation that fits this condition, since they are regulations unique to education. To the extent that any governmental body imposes unfunded mandates on higher education, they are contributing to the excessive rise in E&G cost per student. If government regulation in general is responsible for rising costs in higher education, then the cost problem should be more severe in public higher education than it is in private higher education, and it appears that the reverse is true. Private higher education institutions are subject to substantially less government regulation than are public higher education institutions, yet the cost control problem is more severe in private higher education institutions.

Technology

Information technology is frequently cited as a cause for increasing higher education costs. All institutions struggle to keep up with the demands for new software and hardware, which they must have in order to instruct students using up-to-date systems. Undoubtedly, the initial cost of this new capital is high. On the other hand, new capital also has productivity effects that reduce cost. Manufacturing firms and service firms in the private economy purchase very similar equipment with the intent to capture the productivity benefits they offer. These productivity benefits are not always captured by higher education institutions. If higher education captured the productivity benefits as the rest of the service sector does, this suggests that cost increases in higher education would be more in line with cost increases in services, which they are not. William F. Massy argues that the productivity benefits available to higher education through information technology will not be captured until the cultural barriers to the adoption of those benefits are removed (1998, 89). The National

Commission concludes that 'there is no evidence to date to indicate that the use of technology in higher education has resulted in cost savings to colleges and universities' (1998, 16).

Malcolm Getz et al. conclude that higher education takes three times as long to adopt innovations as does the private sector (1997). One of the more curious results from Getz et al. is the finding that of all the innovations they considered, financial innovations took the longest period of time to be adopted in higher education (1997, 617). This conclusion is curious because financial innovations can be adopted without faculty consent and it is normally thought that faculties are the major obstacle to innovation in higher education. Therefore, if technology is a major cost center rather than a productivity center for higher education, it is at least in part a self-inflicted wound.

Rising labor cost

Higher education is very labor-intensive and faculty members are the most expensive labor component. In the long-run faculty impacts average cost per student in two ways: the average salary paid per faculty member and productivity per faculty member. Average salary per faculty member can increase without raising average cost per student if productivity increases as the average salary increases. Figure 1.6 contains real average faculty salaries for the period from 1976 through 1999. The data reveal that real average faculty salaries at public institutions actually declined over the period, while real average salaries at private institutions rose faster than the service-sector index since the mid-1980s.

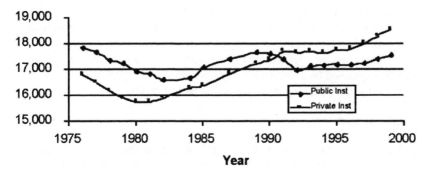

Source: NCES, Digest of Education Statistics, 2002, Table 235; BEA, National Accounts.

Figure 1.6   Real average faculty salaries

While it is not the only measure of faculty productivity, the student/faculty ratio is an obvious measure of productivity. Table 1.2 contains student/faculty ratios for public and private institutions during the period from 1976 through 1999. The student/faculty ratio at both public and private institutions declined over that period. Other things being equal, this trend raises average cost per student at both types of institution. However, other things were not the same at public and private institutions. Average faculty salaries grew faster than the service-sector index at private institutions and did not grow as fast as the service-sector index at public institutions. These data suggest that faculty labor costs are responsible for part of the increase in average cost per student at private institutions, while their impact on average cost per student at public institutions is ambiguous.

Table 1.2 Student/faculty ratios: 1976–1999

Year	1976	1991	1996	1999
Public Institutions	27.8	25.5	23.4	23.7
Private Institutions	20.0	16.9	16.5	15.4

Source: NCES, Digest of Education Statistics, 2002, Tables 173 and 223.

Real incomes paid to knowledge workers have risen steadily during the past two decades. The ratio of highly skilled workers to semi-skilled workers in higher education is higher than any other service sector except possibly health care. The most obvious measure of this effect is the ratio of PhDs or MDs to college educated workers in higher education and health care on the one hand and, say, the financial services industry on the other hand. The knowledge intensive production process in higher education and health care should lead to higher labor cost increases than the representative service sector industry in this environment. Hence, part of the labor cost issue in higher education may be explained by extenuating circumstances, while part of it may also be explained by rent-seeking behavior on the part of faculty.

Overhead costs

Administrative cost increases are another category that made a significant contribution to the historical increase in E&G expenses per student. Leslie and Rhoades conclude:

> By essentially any measure, administrative costs in colleges and universities have risen dramatically during the past two decades, disproportionately more than the costs of instruction and research. Accelerating a four-decade pattern, expenditures for presidents, deans, and their assistants grew 26 percent faster than instructional budgets in the 1980s. (1995, 187)

Leslie and Rhoades also note that rising administrative costs have a perpetuating momentum due to the common practice of 'norming' administrative costs across peer institutions (1995, 206). The business community would call this practice benchmarking. The difference in the way benchmarking is conducted in business versus higher education is revealing. In business, benchmarking is used to identify the lowest cost per unit provider and this is the benchmark to which the firm directs its effort. In higher education, benchmarking is used to identify the average cost per unit provider and this is the benchmark to which the institution directs its effort. The administrative cost per student is compared with the same statistic for peer institutions and judged not to be excessive if the administrative cost is within a comfortable interval around the average for peer institutions. Some members of the higher education establishment will argue that being a high cost provider is an indicator of high quality. The same practice is applied to faculty salaries and teaching loads which tends to perpetuate the momentum in these cost factors as well.

In the past decade presidential compensation in higher education has accelerated significantly. Julianne Basinger reports that the number of presidents of public institutions who earn in excess of $500 000 a year doubled from 2002 to 2003, and four private institution presidents earned more than $800 000 (Basinger, 2003). One of those private institution presidents earns well over $1 000 000 a year. The *Chronicle of Higher Education* reports that two of the top endowment money managers at Harvard earned $35 million each in 2003, prompting one alumnus to ask whether it was appropriate for Harvard to 'pay $35 million to anyone for anything' (February 6, 2004, A23). These trends are not restricted to an elite set of executives. Table 1.3 contains median presidential compensation for private institutions from 1997 through 2001. The rates of increase in median compensation exceed the rate of increase in the service sector index over the same period by a factor of two to three.

Table 1.3   Median presidential compensation at private institutions

Year	Research Universities ($)	Master's Institutions ($)	Liberal Arts Colleges ($)
1997	290,054	155,972	179,389
1998	314,944	160,396	194,640
1999	331,727	163,505	194,407
2000	356,092	173,547	205,323
2001	385,631	184,475	216,170

Source: Basinger, Julianne, 'Closing In on $1 Million.' *The Chronicle of Higher Education*, November 14, 2003.

Table 1.4 contains the relative rate of growth in average salaries for full professors and presidential compensation at five institutions. These data reveal that the rate of growth in presidential compensation at these institutions exceeded the rate of growth in compensation for full professors at their respective institutions by a factor over two at the low end and over ten at the high end. Again, presidential compensation does not cause an increase in cost per student if it is accompanied by a corresponding increase in presidential productivity. Unfortunately, there is nothing in the statistical record displayed above that would suggest that presidential productivity has improved. At least the very similar meteoric rise in executive compensation in the corporate sector can be justified by a measured record of productivity increases and rising profits. No such track record of success is found in higher education.

Executive compensation is set by governing boards in higher education. In a competitive market driven economy, compensation must be strongly correlated with productivity. The trends in compensation among higher education executives can be rationalized only if there is a clear record of rising executive productivity. From the public's perspective, the most important indicator of how productive higher education executives are is how well they control cost and how well they maintain academic quality. The record on cost control is at best miserable and a case can be made that more and more resources are being diverted from academic quality towards peripheral activities. Board-sanctioned compensation trends undercut any hope that higher education executives could ever be effective at controlling costs. Obviously, the governing board's incentives are not properly aligned with the public interest; the question is why?

It is hard to escape the conclusion that this compensation is administered politically rather than on the basis of a careful analysis of presidential productivity. More seriously, these trends in leadership compensation adversely select for the type of leadership that is motivated only by compensation rather than a commitment to public service. After all, does it follow that one should expect to become a millionaire through public service? Finally, any president earning these sums would have no credibility among campus constituents if they were to ask for personal sacrifices to lower costs. Any serious discussion of cost control would not be possible.

An important lesson from the corporate scandals of the last few years is that high executive salaries do not ensure high quality leadership. In fact, one can make a fairly strong case that high salaries adversely select for people whose sole motivation is money. Since senior managers of commercial firms are the agents hired to protect the interest of shareholders, they must feel an obligation to shareholders first and then be motivated by money. If not, the shareholders are sheep to be shorn. This lesson has not been learned by governing boards in higher education. Presidential compensation packages are administered salaries. They are not competitive salaries in the sense that soy bean prices are competitive. The disconnection between presidential compensation and presidential productivity is due to two very anticompetitive effects: the goals of governing boards and the role of executive search firms.

Table 1.4   Ratio of growth rates in presidential compensation and full professor salaries: 1997–2001

Institution	Ratio
Rensselaer Polytechnic Institute	10.5
Vanderbilt University	4.2
University of Pennsylvania	2.4
Rockefeller University	3.3
Johns Hopkins University	2.9

Source: Basinger, Julianne,'Closing In on $1-Million.' *The Chronicle of Higher Education*, November 14, 2003.

Governing boards compete with the governing boards of peer institutions and this competition is for public status, not personal compensation. The more positive press their institution generates and the larger the institution's endowment, the more prestige is conveyed on the members of the governing board. Hence, from the board's perspective jobs one and two for any president are to raise as much endowment as possible and to keep a non-controversial profile. Job two ensures that little will be done about cost control, because any attempt to control cost is going to be controversial no matter how adept the leadership may be.

The gatekeepers for this market are the executive search firms and they have a significant conflict of interest. One cannot become a 'qualified candidate' without the approval of a search firm and the search firms have a financial interest in keeping the list of qualified candidates short, and since they are acutely aware of the governing board's motivation, they will eliminate any candidate with a hint of controversy. Since the search firm's compensation is proportional to the salary paid, they have a clear and obvious incentive to push those salaries higher. Even though the institutions pay the fees, the search firms act as if they are agents for the candidates. The candidates know how the process works, so once hired, they hire the search firms to find 'qualified candidates' for provost and dean positions.

Quality and Productivity

The most charitable thing one can say about accounting and financial practices in higher education is that they are ambiguous; some would say they are Byzantine. It is very difficult to track the source and use of funds in higher education accounting. This characteristic makes 'cost shifting' a temptation and a serious problem when studying the economics of higher education. The national ranking systems, such as *US News and World Report's* annual ranking, encourage these deceptive practices and there have been embarrassing reports of dishonesty in reporting at some prominent institutions.[5] Cost shifting occurs when expenditures are made in one area but booked in another area. This practice distorts two accounts. It is also a common problem in defense contracting. These issues prompted the National Commission to conclude:

> College finances are far too opaque. Higher education has a major responsibility to make its cost and price structures much more 'transparent,' i.e., easily understandable to the public and its representatives. (1998, 19)

The Commission continues by observing that the lack of transparency is undermining public trust, which will lead to decline in these institutions if it is allowed to continue (1998, 20).

Since there is cause to be concerned about the integrity of the financial data, it is important to look at indirect ways to validate what we think we know about higher education cost. One way to do that is through staff to student ratios. Higher education is labor intensive, so labor costs in all areas are the primary drivers of cost per student. Therefore, trends in staff to student ratios in different functional areas are the best real indicators of the source of rising average cost per student. If these ratios decline, they imply that productivity is increasing, and if they rise they suggest that productivity is declining.

Table 1.5 contains staff to student ratio indexes for professional and non-professional staff classifications for public and private institutions. The base year for these indexes is 1976. They are computed by first calculating the number of staff by classification per 1000 students and then using 1976 as the base year to create the index number. The first thing to notice about the staff/student indexes is that all of the professional staff indexes at both public and private institutions are increasing, and some of those increases are very large. By 1999, the number of non-faculty professionals per 1000 students increased by a factor of between two to three times from where it was in 1976. The largest proportional increase, however, was in the instruction and research assistant ratio at public institutions which in 1999 is well over three times what it was per 1000 students in 1976. The only ratios that have stayed constant or declined are those for non-professional staff. Since these indexes are composed entirely of real variables, the number of staff and the number of students, they are impervious to distortion by financial factors.

Faculty resources

There are several possibilities to be considered in interpreting the faculty and instructional assistant results in Table 1.5. The first is that productivity declined significantly during the period from 1976 to 1999. The second is that quality improved during the period, since an increase in the number of faculty per 1000 students might imply that the average class size declined during the period and this can be interpreted as an increase in quality. This does not automatically follow, however, since it is possible that the increase in the number of faculty resulted in a reduction in teaching loads instead. Average class sizes could have increased if teaching loads fell sufficiently, or, class size could have remained constant while lower quality instruction inputs were substituted for higher quality inputs. The third possibility is that the academic preparation of the students who enrolled during the period declined. If student preparation declined, more instructional inputs per student would be required to achieve the same academic outcome. A final possibility is some combination of all three of these possibilities: productivity may have declined, quality increased, and student preparation may have declined.

Table 1.5   Index of staff to student ratios: public and private institutions

Year	1976	1991	1996	1999
Public Institutions				
Professional Staff				
Executive/administrative/managerial	100	108.2	107.4	112.2
Faculty (instruction and research)	100	109.0	118.7	126.8
Instruction and research assistants	100	283.9	303.8	335.2
Non-faculty professionals	100	184.9	197.5	225.6
Non-professional staff	100	100.3	98.5	98.0
Private Institutions				
Professional Staff				
Executive/administrative/managerial	100	117.5	120.1	137.1
Faculty (instruction and research)	100	118.2	121.8	137.7
Instruction and research assistants	100	92.2	123.5	141.6
Non-faculty professionals	100	235.7	238.3	287.6
Non-professional staff	100	110.3	97.5	101.8

Source: NCES, Digest of Education Statistics, 2002, Table 223.

If quality increases, one would expect academic outcomes to improve. The Graduate Record Exams (GREs) are important measures of academic quality. Figure 1.7 reveals that average scores on the verbal part of the exam and the quantitative part of the exam have had different trends since 1965. Average verbal scores are declining and average quantitative scores are increasing. The proportion of students graduating who take the GREs rose over this period while the standard deviation in the test scores in each category remained approximately the same. Since GRE scores are an important part of the documentation required for admission to graduate school, better students are more likely to take the exam. A rise in the proportion taking the exam over time would suggest that the average quality of the students taking the exam is lower. Hence, a constant or rising trend is consistent with improved quality, while a declining trend is an ambiguous indicator. A small decline is consistent with improvement and a significant decline suggests a decline in quality. The overall decline in average verbal scores represents a 12.3 percent decline. Within the subject matter tests, the average test scores for biology, chemistry, engineering, and psychology increased over the period from 1965 to 2000. Average education test scores were approximately constant and average literature test scores declined. Overall, the GRE scores do not send an unambiguous signal regarding the state of academic quality during the period.

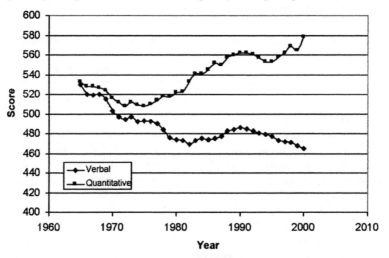

Source: NCES, Digest of Education Statistics, 2002, Table 311.

Figure 1.7   Average GRE scores: 1965–2000

The average hours earned for graduation is one measure of the difficulty of graduation requirements over time. The average number of courses taken in mathematics and the sciences is also an indicator of the rigor imposed on undergraduate students. The average number of hours taken in mathematics, biological sciences, physical sciences, computer science, and engineering is an indicator of the amount of scientific preparation the average graduate receives. Potentially, this is another measure of quality. If the average hours earned for graduation is increasing, requirements for graduation would appear to be increasing and if students are taking a larger proportion of hours in the sciences, one could argue that the rigor of the average degree is increasing. Table 1.6 contains the average number of hours taken for graduation in 1976, 1984, and 1993. It also contains the total number of hours in the sciences and the proportion of those hours taken for graduation. The average number of hours taken for graduation increased from 124 in 1976 to 126.5 in 1993. The average number of hours taken in the sciences did not change during the period, causing the proportion of hours taken in the sciences to decline slightly. From these data, it is hard to make the case that scientific rigor in the representative undergraduate degree increased during the period from 1976 to 1993.

Table 1.6   Average hours earned for graduation and the composition of science courses

Year	Average Hours	Hours in Science	Proportion
1976	124.0	27.3	22.0
1984	123.5	29.7	24.0
1993	126.5	27.0	21.3

Source: NCES, Digest of Education Statistics, 2002, Table 307.

Teaching loads appear to have been declining throughout much of the period in question. Clotfelter conducted a detailed study of four private institutions, Carleton College, the University of Chicago, Duke University, and Harvard University (1996). Regarding teaching loads, he concludes:

One general trend over the period of study was a decrease in measured classroom teaching loads. On the basis of data for three departments in each of the four institutions over the period 1976/77 to 1991/92, the unweighted average classroom teaching load fell by 12 percent in the representative humanities department, 26 percent in the natural science department, and 28 percent in the social science department. The decreases occurred principally in undergraduate teaching, with some departments showing increases in graduate teaching. These declines in classroom teaching loads go hand in hand with the increases observed in the size of the arts and sciences faculty at the institutions. Moreover, this growth definitely contributed to higher spending, although, as the calculations in chapter 5 show, it explains only a small part of the overall increase. No consistent trend was observed in the average size of classes in the sample departments, at either the undergraduate or graduate level. ... Finally, in apparent reflection of the decline in faculty classroom teaching loads, the percentage of undergraduates who were taught in class by regular-rank faculty tended to fall. (1996, 251–252)

A declining proportion of undergraduate students taught by regular-rank faculty and significant increases in the number of instruction and research assistants reported in Table 1.5 are consistent with a pattern of substituting low quality instructional inputs for high quality instructional inputs at both public and private institutions. These trends would not increase the quality of undergraduate instruction.

The academic preparation of college-bound students can be measured by average SAT scores. Figure 1.8 contains the average verbal and math scores for college-bound high school students from 1966 to 2001. After a decline ending around 1980 the average SAT math score remains approximately unchanged from what it was in 1966. There is a secular decline in the average SAT verbal score of approximately 7 percent over the period. The proportion of public institutions offering remedial classes rose from 90.4 percent in 1987 to 92.3 percent in 2001, while the proportion of private institutions offering remedial classes rose from 58.6 to 60.2. These changes are not dramatic, but they do suggest some decline in academic preparation. Overall, these trends do not suggest a significant decline in academic preparation among college-bound high school students, despite the growing proportion of high school students who attended college over this period.

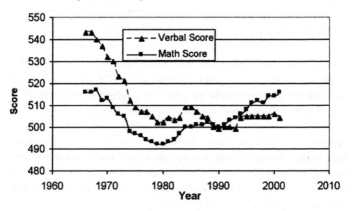

Source: NCES, Digest of Education Statistics, 2002, Table 134.

Figure 1.8   Average SAT scores: 1966–2001

The foregoing data suggest that faculty productivity has declined over the last three decades and this, coupled with rising real salaries, must contribute to cost per student increases that exceed the rate of increase in the service-sector index. The case for an increase in academic quality is weak, while there appears to be some merit to the notion that a slight decline in academic preparation among college-bound high school students has taken place.

Overhead staffing

The rise in the executive and non-faculty professionals ratios per 1000 students in Table 1.5 suggests that both types of institutions not only failed to capture the returns to scale that are known to exist in higher education (see Chapter 5) as their enrollments grew, but they abandoned the returns to scale they had achieved in 1976. These trends suggest significant losses in productivity with respect to the resources employed in overhead functions. There is a sharp contrast in this record and the systemic effort to eliminate overhead in the rest of the economy during the period from 1976 to 1999. It seems likely that advances in information technology should have reduced the need for overhead staff during this period.

In summary, increased demand for new services from higher education and unfunded government mandates have contributed to rising costs in higher education beyond what one might expect from the service sector. Since these requirements are imposed by others, higher education should not be blamed for these cost increases. Declining external support is responsible for part of the net tuition increase in public higher education, while external support in private higher education has been very generous. Cost control problems are more severe in private higher education than they are in public higher education. In both the private and public sector, instruction productivity has declined, and that must contribute to cost increases in excess of the rate of cost increase in the service industry. At best, the evidence that the quality of higher education has increased is weak. In some areas such as the substitution of lower quality instruction inputs for higher quality instruction inputs, quality appears to have declined. A case can be made that average student preparation has declined over the period considered. On balance, these data reveal that the real burden imposed by the cost of higher education has risen faster than other areas of the economy and that the higher education community bears responsibility for the imposition of a significant part of the increased burden. It is not unreasonable to expect higher education to correct these problems before public support for higher education is increased significantly.

1.5   THE OPTIMAL INVESTMENT IN HIGHER EDUCATION

In this subsection, I consider the 'college access controversy'. Despite popular wisdom on this issue, the existence of the access problem, its extent if it does exist, and who might be responsible for the problem are facts still in dispute in the literature. This issue is developed more fully in Chapter 7. My purpose here is to introduce the issue and to place it in context with the social contract. The college access problem is a complex combination of the private/public good characteristics of human capital, the existence of binding financial constraints, student preparation for college, and the role of the education establishment in this problem.

Elements of the Controversy

If capital markets are complete, each student can choose her own optimal private investment in human capital. If capital markets are imperfect, then credit constraints may prevent the student from choosing her optimal investment in human capital. If human capital also has public good characteristics and capital markets are perfect, then, the optimal private investment is still not the social optimal investment in human capital, and the optimal social policy calls for the subsidization of human capital accumulation. It follows that the optimal social policy calls for the subsidization of human capital accumulation if it is a public good and it calls for larger subsidies if capital markets are imperfect and credit constraints are binding. As we will see in the following subsection, the evidence from studies of economic growth strongly suggests that human capital has important public good characteristics.

The preparation issue refers to where those subsidies should be applied. Suppose human capital is a pure private good and there are no credit constraints, but suppose some students arrive at their high school graduation unprepared to do college work. Since they are unprepared for college work, borrowing to go to college (or being subsidized to go to college) will set them up for failure. A secondary effect from this policy would be to introduce large numbers of unprepared students into the post-secondary education system, where they will undoubtedly lower the quality of that experience for all of those who attend those institutions. Furthermore, they will incur debts they cannot repay because they cannot graduate from college. If it is lack of preparation that prevents students from going to college, then the primary problem appears to be too little private/public investment at the primary/secondary school level and/ or significant quality issues at the primary/secondary school level. If this is the case, then the college access problem is in reality a quality/investment problem at the primary/secondary school level and increasing public subsidies that go to colleges and universities will have little impact on the access problem. What is needed in this case is improvement in primary/secondary schools.

The awareness of opportunity issue is simple; it suggests that low income students may not know that opportunities to finance their education are available to them (Kane, 1994). The relationship between education and income across generations of individual families has dynastic characteristics. Different generations within families tend to persist in their family's tradition of relative education and income (Bowles and Gintis, 2002). A partial explanation for this persistence is a lack of understanding of the opportunities that are available. Lower income students may not have access to adequate counseling or their family culture may not place much value on education. Again, increasing access subsidies will be of little material benefit in this case.

The traditional popular understanding of the access problem is that credit constraints prevent lower income students from making an optimal private investment in human capital. It is important to note that this conventional view does not consider the public good characteristics of human capital. If human capital is a public good, then high income students (who do not face credit constraints) will choose private investments in human capital that are below their social optimal investment in human capital. In other words, the issue of academic subsidies is not just restricted to lower income families. The need may be the greatest for low income families, but the public interest is served when all students receive academic subsidies if human capital is a public good.

The empirical evidence demonstrates that enrollment demand is sensitive to price and that the enrollment decisions made by lower income students appear to be more price sensitive than are the enrollment decisions made by students from higher income families (Kane, 1994; Dynarski, 2003). Bhashkar Mazumder states 'there is some common ground in this literature, in that all of these studies find that an increase in college costs of $1000 in 2001 dollars is typically found to translate into a decline in enrollment of about 4 percentage points' (2003). Therefore, every $1000 increase in the price of higher education beyond what is absolutely necessary to provide a quality experience reduces access by 4 percentage points. Therefore, to the extent that the education establishment has not been a good steward of the social contract, it is partly responsible for the college access problem.

Capital Markets and Public Goods

The education social contract evolved as a solution to the public's perception that underinvestment in education is a chronic problem. Even if education is a pure private good, the market mechanism may not lead to the optimal investment in education. The primary reason for this market failure is asymmetric information in capital markets. If capital markets are complete, each new generation can borrow the funds required to accumulate the optimal private level of human capital. Unfortunately, capital markets are not complete and asymmetric information can lead to adverse selection and a 'market for lemons' problem (Akerlof, 1970). This market failure is at the heart of the public's understanding of the higher education access problem.

Lenders are unable to distinguish between good and bad credit risks. They cannot tell the difference between low and high quality students, nor can they determine which students are able, or intend, to repay education loans. As a result, the interest rates charged on those loans are priced as a weighted average of the risk of loaning to a poor credit risk and of loaning to a good credit risk. For the poor credit risk, the interest rate charged is less than the interest rate that would be charged if the borrower's loan was fully priced according to the true risk he represents, and for the good credit risk the interest rate charged is higher than the interest rate that would be charged if his loan was priced according to the true risk. The good credit risk is paying too much for education loans and the poor credit risk is paying too little for education loans. As the proportion of bad credit risks rises, the penalty imposed on the remaining good credit risks increases. These incentives create an adverse selection effect in the market for education loans. The proportion of bad credit risks rises as good credit risks withdraw from the market until the market is populated only by bad credit risks. In the end, some Pareto optimal transactions do not take place. This is a credit market failure due to asymmetric information. Without government backed loans or other public intervention, private investment in education will be too low and the accumulation of human capital will be suboptimal.

These problems become more acute as the distribution of income becomes more inequitable. Fluctuations in the distribution of income are a necessary part of the market mechanism. When real wages rise for individuals with skills that are in high demand, this inevitably results in a change in the distribution of income towards these individuals and away from others. The fluctuations send signals to workers about the reallocation of their efforts towards replacing obsolete human capital. Unfortunately, the workers on the losing end of this process face ever higher hurdles as the income distribution becomes more skewed as the trend over the past three decades shows.

Education and the accumulation of human capital have important public good characteristics. Economic growth will be faster if investment in education is higher, and the quality of life will be better if a larger proportion of the population is educated. More educated people make better private choices and many of these private choices have external effects on their communities. They take better care of their health, are less likely to abuse drugs and alcohol, and are less likely to engage in criminal behavior. Better private decisions lead to lower social costs in all of these areas.

There are other reasons why underinvestment in education persists in the absence of public intervention. By definition, young people lack the experience and the education to appreciate how important education will be to their own future. They are increasingly likely to take this short term view if they are the children of parents who made a similar choice and who have little appreciation for the long-run benefits of education. When considering the current opportunity cost associated with education, they give the future benefits too little weight in evaluating the costs and benefits of investing more in education today and they are frequently unaware of the option value of a college degree. Therefore, it is essential that these students get the right advice and that they heed that advice.

The intergenerational social contract is the natural solution to persistent underinvestment in human capital. The contract recognizes the potential capital market failure and the public good character of education. The contract began in earnest with the creation of public schools and the adoption of the universal right to primary and secondary education. The contract must adapt to new circumstances and it must evolve to reflect new realities.

1.6   PROSPERITY AND THE SOCIAL CONTRACT

Unraveling the mystery surrounding sustained economic growth is an important task for the economics profession and for the civilized world in general. Solving the economic growth mystery will create significant social dividends, since its resolution addresses the root cause of most of the world's pressing social problems. The emerging consensus is that the complex relationship between culture, the income distribution, and human capital plays a central role in economic growth (Harrison and Huntington, 2000; Romer, 1994). In order to appreciate what is at stake with respect to higher education, it is worth exploring what we know about economic growth and the role of human capital in that process.

In the 1980s growth theory took a new path. The empirical shortcomings associated with neoclassical growth theory led to the new endogenous growth theory. Paul Romer states that endogenous growth theory

> distinguishes itself from neoclassical growth by emphasizing that economic growth is an endogenous outcome of an economic system, not the result of forces that impinge from outside. For this reason, the theoretical work does not invoke exogenous technological change to explain why income per capita has increased by an order of magnitude since the industrial revolution. The empirical work does not settle for measuring a growth accounting residual that grows at different rates in different countries. It tries instead to uncover the private and public sector choices that cause

the rate of growth of the residual to vary across countries. (1994, 3)

The unexplained 'accounting residual' is what some call the measure of our collective ignorance about economic growth. The link between education, new knowledge, technology, and the capital stock is a vital part of understanding the 'accounting residual'. What is clear is that the linkage involves complex spillovers and public good features, and that education is at the center of the process.

In the conventional neoclassical growth model, as exemplified by the Solow growth model (1956), the production function can be represented by the Cobb–Douglas function

$$Y = A(t)K^{\beta_1} H^{\beta_2} L^{\beta_3},$$

where $A(t)$ represents the technology coefficient, K is the capital stock, H is the human capital stock, and L is the labor stock. Since $A(t)$ is a function of time only, it is exogenously given to the model. Neoclassical growth theory suggests that convergence of real incomes across countries should take place over time. Diminishing marginal returns imply that the marginal productivity of capital should be higher in countries where the capital stock is low and that the marginal productivity of human capital is higher in those countries where the stock of human capital is low.

Empirically, we should observe convergence of growth rates across countries, migration of capital from high capital stock countries to low capital stock countries, and migration of human capital from high human capital stock countries to low human capital stock countries. The data reveal something entirely different. Convergence has not occurred and in many instances divergence appears to be the trend. Even though capital is highly mobile, the movement of capital from countries with high capital stocks to countries with low capital stocks is small at best and the flow of immigrants with high human capital is in the opposite direction from that which the theory predicts.[6] These resource flows suggest that the arbitrage opportunities are the opposite of what the theory predicts. The flow of capital, both physical and human capital, from countries with low capital stocks into countries with high capital stocks suggests increasing returns to capital in the high capital stock countries. Similarly, Kremer presents evidence that, contrary to the conclusions drawn from the neoclassical model, growth rates over time have been increasing (1993).

The conflicts observed between theory and evidence in the neoclassical growth model suggest the technology factor (A) cannot be a simple exogenous function of time. A must be the endogenous product of cultural and economic forces. If so, then, the output of say the jth firm in the economy can be expressed as

$$Y_j = A(K, H, L) K_j^{\beta_1} H_j^{\beta_2} L_j^{\beta_3},$$

where the un-subscripted stocks (K, H, and L) represent spillover or externality effects on productivity from society's accumulation of these factors. Combining the endogenous technology factor with imperfect competition leads to rewards for private research and development.

In a seminal article, Galor and Zeira demonstrate that long-run macroeconomic growth is sensitive to the initial conditions associated with the distribution of income and wealth (1993). Their study is motivated by the persistent empirical evidence that links equity in the distribution of income with higher economic growth. The vehicle by which the distribution of income impacts secular growth rates is the link between credit market imperfections and 'indivisibilities in investment in human capital' to the accumulation of human capital, which make the growth path to which the economy converges sensitive to the initial distribution of income (1993, 35). The initial distribution of income and wealth coupled with imperfect credit markets leads to dynastic effects where underinvestment in human capital is transmitted from one generation to the next in perpetuity. The authors note:

> It is shown in the paper that the economic dynamics of dynasties depend on initial wealth. There are rich dynasties, in which all generations invest in human capital, work as skilled [labor] and leave a large bequest. There are poor dynasties, in which people inherit less, work as unskilled (labor), and leave less to their children. Hence the initial distribution of wealth determines how big these two groups of dynasties are, and therefore what is the long-run equilibrium in the economy. (1993, 36)

The Galor/Zeira model provides a theoretical foundation for the lack of convergence observed in the international growth rates and it explains dynasties of structurally unemployed families within individual economies. In conclusion, they argue 'we can represent our results as describing the importance of having a large middle class for the purpose of economic growth' (1993, 51).

In a subsequent paper, De Gregorio presents theoretical and empirical evidence that borrowing constraints reduce the accumulation of human capital and lead to a lower growth rate (1996). He considers two different samples for the empirical analysis, a sample of OECD countries and another sample composed of developing countries. In each sample, he finds that borrowing constraints lead to lower levels of investment in human capital and slower growth rates (1996, 51). Similar empirical results are reported by Perotti who also explores the channels through which the income distribution influences growth (1996). Perotti's evidence supports the conclusion that the income distribution impacts growth through credit constraints and the accumulation of human capital.

The foregoing theoretical and empirical evidence regarding the factors that drive economic growth makes it clear why access to higher education for students from low income families is a critical national issue. The secular replacement of need based aid with merit based aid has disturbing implications for long-run economic growth. The trend could not occur at a worse moment. Technology is rapidly widening the gap between the real wages paid to high skilled labor and to low skilled labor precisely at the time when the composition of the college age student body is shifting from middle class children to low income children who are not as well prepared for college and cannot afford to pay for college. Simultaneously, college costs are rising at rates that exceed all other sectors of the economy.

The widening gap between the real wages paid to skilled versus unskilled labor is a market signal. The market is raising the relative return to high skilled labor. If there are no barriers to economic mobility, workers will respond by investing in their human capital and acquiring the appropriate job skills. Education is the vehicle by which workers are transported from low skills to high skills. If that vehicle is not available to low and middle income workers, the middle class will be hollowed out by technical progress and social and economic mobility breaks down. Imperfect credit markets prevent access to education. Without public policy intervention, this process leads to dynasties of low income workers. Any factor or agent that contributes to higher real education costs also contributes to reduced social mobility and all of the problems associated therewith.

At the end of World War II about 5 percent of adults over the age of 25 had a college education. Today, over 25 percent of adults over the age of 25 have college educations. The rising proportion of college-bound students was not uniformly distributed across all groups within our society, however. As Table 1.7 reveals, the proportion of minority groups over 25 years of age attending four or more years of college has risen but it still lags well behind the proportion of whites who attend college. Indeed, the proportion of minorities who attended college in 2000 was about half the proportion of whites who attended college in 2000. Further increases in the proportions for all groups will carry significant social costs, since the students next in line come disproportionately from the economically disadvantaged in all categories.

As new students come increasingly from economically disadvantaged families, their lack of academic preparation suggests the marginal cost of educating these students will be higher than in the past. On the other hand, the social costs associated with not continuing to raise the proportion of the population attending college may be higher than ever. As the gulf between those with and without an advanced education widens, social costs will undoubtedly rise with it. Increasing relative poverty and declining social mobility must lead to higher crime rates, more domestic violence, more child abuse, more drug and alcohol abuse, and a less healthy population. The potential social costs are too important to be ignored.

Table 1.7   Proportion of population 25 and over with four or more years of college, 1910–2001

Year	Total	White	non–Hispanic	Hispanic
1910	2.7			
1920	3.3			
1930	3.9			
1940	4.6	4.9	1.3	
1950	6.2	6.6	2.2	
1960	7.7	8.1	3.5	
1970	11.0	11.6	6.1	
1980	17.0	18.4	7.9	7.6
1990	21.3	23.1	11.3	9.2
2000	25.6	28.1	16.6	10.6
2001	26.1	28.6	16.1	11.2

Source: NCES, Digest of Education Statistics, 2002, Table 8.

1.7   KNOWLEDGE, TECHNOLOGY, AND THE RISING ANTE

There is a very important link between technical progress, structural unemployment, and education. At any point in time the state of knowledge is reflected by the technology employed in the economy. In turn, the technology determines the optimal set of labor skills required for cost minimization. If the mix of labor skills required by the technology does not match the labor skills mix supplied by the labor force, structural or mismatched unemployment is created. The more rapid the technical change and the more inflexible is the labor supply's response, the greater is the rate of growth in structural unemployment. Therefore, during periods of rapid technical change greater demands are placed on the educational system to train new workers with current skills and to retrain existing workers with obsolete skills. If the educational system fails in this effort, for whatever reason, the ranks of the permanently unemployed and the under-employed will increase. The real incomes of this group will fall relative to those with marketable skills, and the distribution of income will widen. The longer this process endures, the greater is the risk that a class of permanently disadvantaged individuals will be created. The wider the income gulf between the structurally unemployed and the middle class, the less economic mobility society will observe. The exponential growth rate in new technology places exponentially growing demands on the education system to perform at higher levels. If the education system cannot keep pace, the rate of technological advance must slow down or go overseas.

Throughout history increasing knowledge leads to increasing technology and to a rising education requirement in the labor force. The initial labor requirements following the industrial revolution were minimal. As the technology improved, primary education became the labor norm, followed by secondary education during the first half of the 20th century. World War II led to an unprecedented increase in technology, and education requirements proceeded at pace. Fortunately, the social contract in the United States adapted to the new reality. A significant reason for this adaptation was public concern about the economy after the soldiers returned from World War II. It was not known at the time whether or not the economy would slip back into depression as the economy stepped down from a war footing. Fortunately, the savings forced by rationing and the depletion in the stock of consumer durables prevented such a problem.

The GI Bill following World War II had the dual advantage of temporarily keeping millions of former soldiers back from the labor market and substantially increasing the nation's investment in higher education (Stanley, 2003). It was one of the most successful government programs ever. Prior to the war, higher education was available only to the wealthy, which was not a problem then because the prevailing technology required only a secondary education. The post-war technology was another matter. The human capital required by the new technology was rising in a reinforcing loop: the rising investment in human capital created new knowledge, the new knowledge led to the creation and adoption of new technology, and the new technology raised the education level required. The reinforcing loop sustained a remarkable post-war progress in the United States. That progress is the foundation for the country's international standing as the sole remaining super power.

The circular process between knowledge, technology, and the level of education required to attain a middle class living standard has continued. Today it is no longer true that an undergraduate degree is the ticket to a middle class livelihood. Graduate degrees and a lifetime of continuing education are rapidly becoming the norm.

Technology has no national loyalties. The imperative to produce better products at lower cost will drive production to wherever it can find the optimal combination of resources for the task at hand. If the proper quantity and quality of labor does not exist in the US, production will migrate to wherever the necessary resources are found. As the production goes, so go the jobs.

America's comparative advantage is in the quality of its labor supply, the depth of its capital stock, and the rate of technical progress. Furthermore, America's college and university system has been a magnet for the best and the brightest from the rest of the world. We have undoubtedly benefited from the rest of the world's 'brain drain'.

1.8   CONCLUSIONS

Long-run economic prosperity depends on the formation of human capital. The initial distribution of income and wealth determine the rate at which human capital is accumulated. Unfortunately, credit market imperfections can prevent the optimal private investment in human capital from taking place. Human capital also has external or spillover effects on macroeconomic growth. Therefore, without public policy intervention the economy would experience chronic underinvestment in human capital and economic growth would be slower than is optimal. The foregoing is the essential economic argument for public subsidies that promote 'access' to education.

The education social contract is the solution to what otherwise would be chronic underinvestment in human capital. There are three parties to the social contract: the adult generation, the younger generation, and the education establishment. The contract provides that as long as education quality is maintained and the costs are reasonable, the adult generation will subsidize the education of the younger generation with the understanding that the younger generation will pass it forward to the next generation. The key to the preservation of the contract is the burden imposed on the younger generation when the time comes for them to pass it on to the next generation. The burden must be reasonable with respect to the benefits the adult generation received in its youth when its education was subsidized by others. The adult generation cannot be expected to honor the social contract if quality declines or the costs are unreasonable. Since the education establishment is responsible for quality and cost, it is the primary steward of the social contract. The independence granted to the education establishment through academic freedom places an additional obligation to act in the public interest. The preservation of the social contract depends on the actions taken by the education establishment.

The objective evidence suggests the social contract is in danger. The economic burden imposed on students and their families, as measured by net tuition, has risen considerably faster than any other price indicator in the economy. In the case of public higher education institutions, part of the rise in net tuition is explained by a relative decline in external support, specifically state and local government support; however, the real external support per student has remained relatively constant. The rest of the increase in net tuition at public institutions can be attributed to increases in cost per student that are beyond what a reasonable person might expect. In private higher education, real external support has increased so the additional burden is due to cost increases.

The primary cost drivers are thought to be labor costs, administrative costs, technology, 'mission creep', and government regulation. There is some evidence that higher education institutions are providing new services demanded by students, their families, and society and the cost of these new services is bundled with the cost of providing traditional educational services. The result is that cost per student and net tuition rise faster than one might expect. Similarly, there are unfunded government mandates that raise costs faster than one might expect. These are services and costs imposed on higher education by students and the public, so higher education should not be blamed for these cost increases. Also, public higher education should not be blamed for that part of the increase in net tuition that is due to declining external support.

Real faculty salaries at private institutions have increased, while real faculty salaries at public institutions have declined. Real administrator salaries grew substantially during the period under consideration. Administrator salaries grew much faster than faculty salaries. Growing real salaries are not a problem as long as the growth in salaries equals the growth in productivity. Under those conditions the impact on cost per student is neutral. Every indicator suggests productivity fell in all labor categories rather significantly during the period. The combination of rising salaries and declining productivity has an accelerating impact on cost per student.

Some may argue that the decline in productivity is actually an indication of a rise in quality, since more faculty and staff per student would seem to suggest students are getting a better education and more services. However, there is nothing in the quality indicators (GRE scores, average time to completion of degree, or science instruction) that would suggest a material improvement in quality. Others may argue that a decline in college preparation will require an increase in the number of faculty and staff per student in order to attain the same academic outcome. There is some support for this argument, although the decline in the quality of entering students is not enough to explain the apparent decline in productivity.

In the end, an objective observer would conclude that higher education has been relatively ineffective at controlling costs and that in the national interest things need to change. The task ahead is to gain enough understanding of the economics of higher education to devise public policies that will put the proper incentives for change into play.

NOTES

1. Clearly this is a debatable point, since it very much depends on what was purchased by those government expenditures. If they were used to produce more social capital, then they increase the wealth bequeathed to future generations. If they were used to expand entitlements, they are a burden on future generations.

2. See Stanley Fish (2004) and Michael Berube (1998). Stanley Fish recommends an aggressive confrontation with all those who may criticize higher education and Michael Berube claims that wasting public resources is actually good for higher education.

3. See Bronner (1998), Honan (1994), and Mabry (1999) for examples.

4. The service-sector Consumer Price Index is obtained from the Bureau of Economic Analysis.

5. See Steve Stecklow (1995) and *The Chronicle of Higher Education*, February 6, 2004, A23 as examples.

6. See Lucas (1988).

2. Foundations

The university's characteristic state may be summarized by the words of the lady who said, 'I have enough money to last me the rest of my life, unless I buy something.'

Hanna Gray   (1930 –)

2.1   THE COMMERCIAL FIRM AND ACADEMIC INSTITUTIONS

Although colleges and universities are unlike commercial firms in several important respects (Winston, 1997, 1999), they are each subject to similar economic influences (Coase, 1937; Alchian and Demsetz, 1972). Some of the important differences are their objectives, their pricing policies, their production technologies, their governance structure and, most particularly, their long-term relationships with clients. Building on earlier work, Clotfelter identifies 'four distinctive features' that separate the university from the commercial firm (1996, 23–29):

1. the university's commitment to excellence rather than profit;
2. the independence of action enjoyed by faculty;
3. the university's shared governance structure; and
4. the 'ephemeral' nature of the services provided by higher education.

Another striking difference between commercial firms and higher education is their respective pricing policies (Winston, 1999). Since the average student receives a subsidy and the institution follows a balanced budget policy, the average student's net price is less than the average cost of providing an education. Such an arrangement is not possible among commercial firms since setting price below average cost leads to bankruptcy.

While these differences exist and are important, they are somewhat misleading. The representative academic institution does not provide student subsidies from its own pocket. It contracts with a third party benefactor who is willing to supply the subsidy. If the institution fails to find a benefactor, it cannot continue operations in the long-run or it must charge the average student a price that is at least as high as its long-run average cost. Without benefactors

42

the institution either shuts down or chooses pricing policies that are similar to commercial firms. Therefore, the most important similarity between firms and academic institutions is that long-run survival depends on covering cash outflows with cash inflows. The difference is that the traditional firm supports all of its cash inflows with revenues generated from its customers, whereas the representative academic institution obtains its cash inflows from students and third party benefactors. Neither institution is relieved of the responsibility of at least balancing its cash flows. For the representative higher education institution, acquiring academic subsidies is an essential activity, an activity that is indispensable to maintaining its current status or to enhancing its academic standing. Within the economic theory of higher education, the market mechanism by which academic subsidies are allocated is not fully understood. At the margin, this activity is critical to the institution's eventual position in the quality hierarchy.

Some members of the higher education community vigorously resist the suggestion that higher education has any similarity to commercial firms (Winston, 1999). Part of this resistance is ideological and the rest of the resistance is due to an imperfect understanding of the modern theory of the firm. It is true that the firm in the competitive model bears little resemblance to the typical higher education institution; interestingly, the perfectly competitive firm bears little resemblance to almost all commercial firms.

In the competitive model, firms and consumers confront each other at arm's length in a commodity market where efficiency is well served by each agent pursuing her own individual interest. The firm's homogeneous product is produced and delivered to the consumer for her private use. Their connection in the market may be transitory, or it may last for an extended period through repeat purchases. Buyers and sellers understand the motivations of the other party and they are aware it is their responsibility to protect their own interests.

The relationship between a student and her college/university is not transitory and it is not an arm's length relationship. Most members of the academe, outside the economics profession, probably have the competitive model in mind when they reject the suggestion that firms and higher education institutions have common characteristics. In fact, they are right. The firm that produces a commodity product, with perfect foresight, in a perfectly competitive market bears little resemblance to a college or a university.

However, the competitive firm bears little resemblance to any economic enterprise we may encounter. The competitive firm and industry are not expected to resemble reality. The competitive model serves both a normative and a positive role. It is the efficient standard by which all other market structures are evaluated, since the results that follow from pure competition are Pareto optimal. It is an analytical device used to measure the social cost of imperfect market structures. This is pure competition's normative role. In this sense, it is fair to say that the perfectly competitive firm bears little resemblance to any enterprise, profit maximizing or not. The competitive model is intended to be descriptive only in the 'as if' sense. The positive role played by the competitive model is that many firms and industries behave as if they are perfectly competitive.

Rothschild and White (1995) model higher education as if it were a competitive industry. They find the competitive profit maximizing model has too many results that are inconsistent with observed behavior in higher education. The implication is that higher education institutions do not behave as if they are competitive profit maximizing firms. It would be premature to conclude from this that the theory of the firm as a whole has little to offer in our quest to understand higher education. After all, oligopolies and monopolies do not behave as if they are perfectly competitive firms either.

The range of unusual topics successfully addressed by economists is extensive: sports, crime, art, sex, family life, risky behavior, and game shows. The winner of the John Bates Clark Medal in 2004, Steven Levitt, has made a name for himself by applying economic analysis to an astonishing variety of topics, from the danger posed by drinking drivers to corruption in Sumo wrestling. Given the exotic nature of many of these topics, it seems improbable that formal models of rational behavior cannot yield important results in the analysis of higher education.

The similarities between commercial firms and higher education institutions increase significantly when one introduces uncertainty, asymmetric information, and the presence of experience goods. For both firms and higher education institutions, reputations resolve contracting problems when the environment is uncertain, when there is an unequal distribution of information among agents, and when quality cannot be determined prior to purchase. Education is an experience good. Students can determine the value of the service only after its purchase, and the amount of time that must pass before value can be determined is substantial. Furthermore, once the student graduates the relationship is irreversible, for all intents and purposes. The student's and the institution's interests are bound by the institution's academic reputation, and this common interest lasts for the alumnus' lifetime.

Long-term relationships based on reputations also exist among commercial firms and their customers. In health care, nursing homes, the legal profession, and child care, consumers have multi-period relationships with service providers where trust is a critical part of the relationship (Winston, 1992). The services supplied by these industries are also experience goods. In health care, and occasionally in the law, the decision to purchase the service can be irreversible. For example, choosing one form of cancer treatment instead of another frequently forecloses alternative options in a situation where there is great uncertainty about the outcome, and the patient must trust the judgment of the physician.

When reputations matter, one of the most significant differences between firms and higher education institutions is the irreversible nature of the relationship between the institution and its alumni. Successful alumni are irreplaceable. Other assets, such as physical plant, can be replaced. At every point in time, the institution's reputation depends on the success of its alumni and its options are fixed by the irreversible enrollment decisions of the past. One very important function of honorary degrees is to expand an otherwise fixed list of successful 'alumni'. As a consequence, every entering class is an irreversible long-term investment, since some proportion of that class will become alumni, and students not enrolled cannot become alumni (Martin, 2000). The admission decisions we take today determine the composition of tomorrow's alumni portfolio and each current administration is facilitated – or constrained – by all prior enrollment management decisions.[1] It is clear that student recruiting has critical long-run implications for the institution's quality reputation.

Each year, the institution has the opportunity to invest in a new group of students who are potential alumni. All successful alumni contribute to the institution's quality reputation through their deeds and through their financial donations to the institution. In the short run, the institution's investment opportunity is constrained by its physical space, financial resources, and quality reputation. The cohort of prospective students depends on the institution's quality reputation. It is from this cohort that the institution must recruit students and convert those recruited students into alumni. Institutions with very high quality reputations can recruit students from anywhere in the world and generally have queues of students waiting for each available slot. Institutions with low quality reputations find their prospective student lists are geographically restricted, there are few candidates for each slot, and there are multiple competitors for the students the institution is trying to recruit. As an institution moves up the quality ladder, each student in its prospective student cohort has fewer opportunities that are close substitutes. The decline in the number of substitutes suggests the enrollment demand curve becomes more inelastic with respect to price as quality reputation increases.

Higher education institutions do not behave as if they are profit maximizing firms, a proposition most of us are ready to accept. However, the foregoing also suggests that many economic characteristics found in higher education are shared by firms in imperfect market structures. Their objective functions are not the same, but this does not mean that the behavior we observe in higher education does not have a rational foundation. The commercial firm is known to be an evolving organism that responds to the environment it encounters. Should we conclude that higher education institutions are not also a product of their economic environment? The survivor principle suggests that higher education institutions' behavior has some survivor value, even if we currently have an imperfect understanding of their objectives. Hence, the institutional characteristics we observe must have some optimal properties.

Given that higher education institutions are rational actors, it is worth the time to explore the basic forces responsible for the evolution of the modern firm, since those forces are likely to be at work on the modern higher education institution as well. Technology, transactions cost, and asset ownership have all shaped the modern commercial firm. These forces must also have an impact on higher education institutions.

2.2   ORIGINS OF THE FIRM AND THE COLLEGE

In theory, all transactions can be completed by independent agents contracting across markets. Entrepreneurs, workers, landlords, and capitalists can contract with other agents without forming institutions that internalize contracting on a more or less permanent basis. Governing boards, administrators, faculty, and students could also contract through the market mechanism in order to provide educational services. This might be a 'virtual university' in today's nomenclature. In other words, there is no theoretical imperative for either firms or higher education institutions to exist. Clearly, they do exist; so, that implies they solve problems that cannot be resolved by the market mechanism.

Origins of the Firm

The theory of the origin of the firm is a rich and exciting literature (Coase, 1937; Alchian and Demsetz, 1972; Grossman and Hart, 1986; Hart and Moore, 1990). Starting with the proposition that all transactions can be accommodated by the market mechanism, we ask why some transactions are internalized within institutions and others are left to the market mechanism. From the firm's perspective this is the classic 'make or buy' decision, which may be the most studied question in the theory of the firm (Holmstrom and Milgrom, 1994, 972). This question is at the heart of vertical and horizontal integration, as well as conglomerate mergers. Similarly, 'outsourcing', 'downsizing', 'core competency', and 're-engineering' are all motivated by this issue.

Transactions costs

Ronald Coase (1937) provided a vital insight when he noted that transactions[2] are not costless. Agents must search for other agents with complementary intentions, they must negotiate contracts with each other, and they must monitor contract compliance after the contract is signed. Market contracting involves transactions cost. Transactions costs are also incurred when economic activity is conducted within the institution. Optimization by the institution requires that it minimize the total cost of transactions. This clearly holds for the profit maximizing firm and it must also hold for any higher education institution guided by rational behavior.

Transactions costs are minimized when the marginal cost of internal transactions equals the marginal cost of external transactions. This optimal condition establishes the 'border of the firm', the dividing line between internal and external transactions. It follows readily that anything that impacts the marginal cost of transactions must change the border of the firm. Hence, changes in technology, information, monitoring, enforcement, or resources will change the optimal border of the firm. Therefore, the commercial firm is a living and evolving entity. The firm's optimal border in 1950 is unlikely to be the optimal border in 2004. While Coase's transaction cost analysis helps us understand the boundary of the firm, it provides little insight as to what goes on inside that boundary. The firm still appears to be a 'black box' from the outside.

Technology

A more complete picture of the internal structure of the firm is provided by Alchian and Demsetz (1972). The keys to understanding the internal structure are technology and the monitoring issues that arise from that technology. Alchian and Demsetz argue that technology played a critical role in the evolution of the modern commercial firm. Prior to the industrial revolution, 'cottage industries' were the dominant organization for economic production. Individual workers produced their own output within the confines of their own cottages. Individual weavers wove cloth on hand-powered looms and they sold their output to buyers who then resold the product to others. Market prices were perfectly capable of rewarding the weavers' productivity, since their individual output was readily observable.

The industrial revolution gave rise to the factory system and the demise of cottage industries. Water power, steam power, and fossil fuel power led to the centralization of production where greater energy could be applied to the production process. Production was transformed from individual to team production and inseparable team production created serious monitoring problems.

Let cottage industry production technology be represented by the strongly separable production technology where the output of the ith worker is

$$x_i = f(w_i),$$

w_i is the ith worker and $f(w_i)$ is the production technology. If there are n workers using the same technology, then total output is

$$x = \sum_{1}^{n} f(w_i), \tag{2.1}$$

Clearly the marginal product of the individual worker is easily measured in the strongly separable production technology associated with cottage industries.

Alternatively, team production implies an inseparable production technology where total output is defined by

$$x = F(w_1, w_2, ...w_n). \tag{2.2}$$

A necessary condition for team technology to replace cottage technology is that it must lead to a production surplus, given the same resource utilization. In other words,

$$F(w_1, w_2, ...w_n) \geq x = \sum_{1}^{n} f(w_i), \tag{2.3}$$

Reorganizing workers in a factory system creates a potential surplus that induces entrepreneurs and workers to adopt the new technology.

The new technology creates a serious monitoring problem, however. The marginal product of individual workers now depends on the effort expended and the skill applied by other workers. Total output is larger, but individual contributions are harder to measure. Inseparable team production leads to an incentive for individual workers to shirk. The free rider problem created requires that worker efforts be monitored. However, the problem of who monitors the monitor steps to the forefront. The solution to this problem is to allow the monitor to be the residual claimant. If the monitor is the residual claimant, she has an incentive to maximize the surplus created by awarding wages according to productivity within the team. Therefore, the internal structure of the profit maximizing firm can be explained as an optimal solution to the monitoring problems inherent in team production. The market mechanism can set the rewards for the team's output, but it cannot efficiently allocate that reward to individual team members.

Again, we note that production technology is not static, so any change in production technology that creates a larger surplus and allows some team members' productivity to be measured independently of other team members may lead to the outsourcing of the activities performed by those team members. The inverse also holds; any new technology that increases the potential surplus and brings new workers into the team will expand the border of the institution. Technology is an important determinant of the border of the institution.

Asset ownership

Grossman and Hart (1986) and Hart and Moore (1990) argue that the firm's identity is determined by the ownership of assets, since it is the ownership of assets that confers the residual claim. Furthermore, it is the ownership of assets that confers the right to 'selectively fire the workers of the firm' as opposed to having to collectively 'fire' agents in a market transaction (Hart and Moore, 1990, 1120). Hart and Moore also conclude that efficiency is improved by giving asset ownership to indispensable agents and that complementary assets should be jointly owned (1990, 1123–4). The results are also sensitive to how important agents are in the generation of surplus; if their services can be readily obtained on the spot market, they are less important to the generation of surplus. Owning an asset gives rise to incentives to conserve and invest in that asset.

The distribution of asset ownership in the production process is an important aspect of the origin and structure of any enterprise (Alchian and Demsetz, 1972, 792; Holmstrom and Milgrom, 1994). For example, this issue refers to who owns the tools used in production versus who uses the tools in production. Owners have a stronger incentive to conserve assets than do users who are not owners.[3] Holmstrom and Milgrom identify the three primary incentive instruments as pay, asset ownership, and job design (1994, 972). Bureaucratic institutions are characterized by fixed pay, the fact that monitors own all the assets, and that monitors design the jobs. In decentralized institutions pay tends to vary with performance, some assets are owned by workers, and workers have some control over job design. Asset ownership conveys benefits in the form of influence, greater returns, and independence.

All together now!

Considering the three instrumental effects on the origin of the firm (transaction costs, technology, and asset ownership), a general picture of the classic firm arises. Alchian and Demsetz conclude that

> The essence of the classical firm is identified here as a contractual structure with: 1) joint input production; 2) several input owners; 3) one party who is common to all the contracts of the joint inputs; 4) who has rights to renegotiate any input's contract independently of contracts with other input owners; 5) who holds the residual claim; and 6) who has the right to sell his central contractual residual status. (1972, 794)

Coase's argument reveals that the classic firm is the least cost solution to the transactions problem and Grossman, Hart, and Moore suggest that claims to residuals are determined by asset ownership as well as the monitoring incentive suggested by Alchian and Demsetz.

Organized capital markets lower the cost of raising capital by allowing risk-averse investors to diversify the risk of holding assets. Unfortunately, this leads to the separation of ownership and control in the modern firm, which weakens the monitoring of those who control the firm and can give rise to serious principal/agent problems. Recent corporate scandals are evidence of a continuing principal/agent problem among publicly held firms. In theory, an efficient market for the control of publicly held firms should minimize the agency problems. Imperfections in the market for senior managers, political interference, and legal obstacles in the market for control tend to make the agency problem worse. 'Corporate raiders' and arbitragers are perceived to be an unsavory lot by the public, who have an imprecise understanding, at best, of their role in market efficiency. This frequently gets in the way of their natural function, which is to clean up the corporate environment. They are the vultures of the corporate ecosystem.

Origin and Structure of Higher Education Institutions

Differences and similarities between commercial firms and higher education institutions now stand in bold relief. They are both characterized by joint input production, they employ several input owners, one party is the central contractor, and they both must minimize transaction costs. The differences are that higher education institutions do not have the right to renegotiate all of the input contracts (tenure), do not hold the residual claim (charitable status), cannot sell the right to the residual claim, many assets are owned collectively, and there is no market for control of higher education institutions. Given that transaction costs, inseparable production technology, monitoring issues, and asset ownership are factors that influence the evolution of higher education institutions, why has the solution to these problems taken a different path in higher education?

Existence

Productivity within any organization depends on how well that organization meters production and allocates rewards (Alchian and Demsetz, 1972, 779). Therefore, it is logical to assume the path taken by higher education institutions leads to higher efficiency than would be the case if it adopted the same incentive structure as the commercial firm, given the characteristics of academic production and distribution. Understanding why higher education institutions exist is straightforward, they minimize transaction costs and team production leads to a higher output than strongly separable academic production.

Additional reasons for the existence of higher education institutions may have to do with signaling in labor markets. Students could contract directly with professors for individual courses and by so doing, create their own academic curriculum. The student's purpose is to invest in human capital and then to sell the services provided by that human capital to others. The problem with individual contracting is asymmetric information with respect to the student and with respect to any buyer of the services offered by the student. By definition, the student is uninformed and cannot know before the fact what her curriculum needs might be. Similarly, the buyer of her services cannot observe the quality of her curriculum experience prior to her being hired.

It is well known that education is considered a signal in the labor market; it is assumed to be a measure of the quantity and the quality of human capital attained by a worker. A successful quality signal must be costly in terms of resources and effort; otherwise the signal is easily mimicked by lower quality workers. If it is more difficult for less gifted/energetic students to matriculate, the signal provides a basis for a separating equilibrium. The signal must serve to sort high quality workers from low quality workers. This requires a second party who is an independent monitor to set standards for matriculation, and that is the institution's role in the signaling process. This includes a signal that reflects both acquired and native human capital. If students construct their own curriculum and contract individually with faculty, where they have the capacity to 'fire' the faculty, effort minimization will lead to a lower quality result and a poor signal. In addition, the transactions cost of individual contracting will be higher.

Central contracting by colleges and universities also exists because of technology. The technology responsible for the demise of cottage industry in higher education was the curriculum. Once the value of an integrated course of study was discovered, the 'cottage system' for higher education was replaced by schools, colleges, and, eventually, universities. The invention of curricula also created an opportunity to reduce transaction costs by hiring administrators to exploit economies of scale and scope in recruiting, monitoring, and educating students. Being relieved of the responsibility for searching for students, faculty members increase their productivity by specializing in academic pursuits.

Moving from individual contracting to central contracting is a necessary condition for the existence of institutional reputations with infinite lives. This changes the economics of reputation and the problems faced by potential benefactors. Under individual contracting between students and faculty, potential benefactors must either support individual students or endow individual professors. The transactions costs associated with supporting individual students will be high, while endowments of individual professors are limited by the finite lifetimes of those professors. The formation of an institution with an infinite lifetime solves both of these problems. In addition, the problem of quality cheating before the end of the time period is reduced, and benefactors can contribute permanent endowments that result in some form of immortality for the donor.

No residual claimant

Technology drives the internal structure of higher education institutions in a manner similar to the commercial firm. The invention of outcome driven curricula imposes a quasi-team production technology on higher education that has different monitoring problems from the commercial firm. Individual classroom instruction is strongly separable among faculty, as is scholarly output. Faculty members work as teams only when they design and oversee curriculum. The classic three legs of the stool upon which faculty evaluation rests are teaching, scholarship, and service. The only team effort is service, and it is almost always last in the list of criteria by which faculty excellence is measured. Individual scholarship is easily metered and rewarded. Individual teaching productivity can also be measured, but it is subject to more measurement error and is costly to monitor by a central contractor. The relative ease with which scholarly output can be measured tends to skew the reward system towards that indicator of faculty productivity. If scholarly output and teaching quality are strongly complementary, then scholarly output serves as a latent indicator of both types of productivity. If they are competitive, then teaching suffers.

The least cost solution to the teaching monitoring problem is for students to monitor teaching under the supervision of the central contractor. Similarly, tenure review subjects each faculty member to a period of intense monitoring by students, other faculty, and the central contractor before permanent employment status is granted. Tenure serves to sort faculty according to those who need continuous monitoring and those who are self-monitored. Tenure proceedings are supposed to select the self-monitored faculty members. Alchian and Demsetz observe that in the professions, 'watching a man's activities is not a good clue to what he is actually thinking or doing with his mind' (1972, 786). Hence, central monitoring of faculty teaching activity is inefficient. The monitoring role played by the central contractors (the administration and the governing board) is weakened by the nature of academic technology and this is part of the explanation as to why the central contractor does not have a claim to the residual like the commercial firm.

The absence of a residual claimant in higher education can also be explained by the distribution of asset ownership. The single most valuable asset held by the institution is its quality reputation. The quality reputation determines the institution's position in the hierarchy of institutions, and that position determines the quality of the students it is able to recruit and the endowment it is able to draw. There may be some capital asset value associated with location,[4] but physical plant is easily replaced if destroyed and institutions have an easier time raising funds for physical plant than they do other assets. The institution's quality reputation is a composite product of the faculty's academic reputation, alumni reputations, student reputations, and administrator reputations. These reputations are complementary[5] in the production of the institution's reputation, so it follows naturally from Hart and Moore (1990) that the institution's reputation should be owned collectively by all of the primary stakeholders and that there should be no single residual claimant.

The most important and indispensable asset used to produce and distribute knowledge is the faculty member's human capital. In the absence of slavery, only the faculty member can own that asset. This ownership confers independence and in some cases significant mobility (Coleman, 1973). As reported by Holmstrom and Milgrom (1994, 989), the extent of supervision, tools employed, and latitude enjoyed by faculty members comes close to satisfying the IRS' 'Independent Contractor Checklist.' The faculty's human capital is subject to obsolescence. The independence, asset ownership, and freedom of job design serve to give faculty the incentive to avoid obsolescence. Since the incentive instruments (pay, asset ownership, and job design) are complementary (Holmstom and Milgrom, 1994), command is highly decentralized in higher education while it tends to be considerably more centralized in the commercial firm.

Reciprocal monitoring in governance

The reciprocal governance structure observed in higher education is the optimal response to the absence of a residual claimant. If the central contractors (the administration and the governing board) are not the residual claimants, then the monitoring of the central contractors' effort is an issue. It might be argued that the governing board should be the sole monitor of the administration. However, governing boards are an inefficient monitor because of their lack of proximity to administrators. Faculty members are well placed to observe the day-to-day actions of administrators, just as students are in the same position with respect to faculty. If administrators had the right to alter the faculty membership or renegotiate contracts with faculty, the faculty's ability to monitor administrators would be seriously undermined. Hence, an interlocking system of reciprocal monitoring evolved in higher education, the purpose of which is to reduce shirking by the institution's primary agents (faculty, administrators, board members, and students).

One significant monitoring issue remains: who monitors the governing board? In a non-profit institution, governing boards are monitored by the public through the legal system and government agencies. Even if the institution is a private non-profit institution, it is a quasi-public institution whose tax exempt status depends on prescribed behavior. Alumni associations also monitor the governing board. It is unlikely that public scrutiny and alumni monitoring will be sufficient to prevent agency abuses. The market for control among commercial firms is a powerful external force that is wholly absent in higher education. The amount of agency abuse among commercial firms suggests that agency problems may be as, or more, significant in higher education (Alchian and Demsetz, 1972, 790). I argue that the quality hierarchy in higher education is the market's solution to unresolved agency problems in higher education. It may be an imperfect solution, but it came about as a mechanism to reduce quality cheating among higher education institutions.

Tenure

Academic tenure is a contentious public issue. It has become more contentious as the public has suffered from corporate restructuring, downsizing, and re-engineering. The rapid rise in the cost of higher education has also done little to improve the public's humor on this issue. Despite the current hostility towards academic tenure, it is worth noting, as do McPherson and Schapiro, that tenure has demonstrated survivor value and, therefore, must have some efficiency benefits (1999b, 97).

The historical and sociological justification for tenure is that it is necessary in order to preserve academic freedom. It is argued that those outside the academe will not tolerate the pursuit of controversial questions and tenure is necessary to protect scholars from their wrath. Others argue that academic freedom can only be protected by democratic traditions and a national constitution that protects free speech. McPherson and Schapiro note that during the normal course of faculty activities, they are asked to evaluate students, other scholars, and public policy and if they do not have tenure they would be subject to undue influences that threaten their objectivity (1999b, 94).

The more interesting economic justifications for tenure are an efficiency wage to encourage productivity in an environment where monitoring is difficult (Schwartz, 1988) and asymmetric information between faculty and administrators that forces administrators to delegate critical personnel decisions to faculty (Carmichael, 1988). The difference between the capitalized value of the lifetime contract and the capitalized value of the same salary subject to unemployment risk is a wealth transfer to the faculty member which is an implicit efficiency wage. In general, the higher the average wage offered by the institution, the higher will be the implicit efficiency component of the wage due to tenure. High efficiency wages attract high performance scholars and teachers who are more productive than their less gifted or motivated colleagues.

A related wage argument comes from the unique role played by endowments in higher education (see Chapter 4). Given the skills possessed by most faculty members, they can earn higher incomes in the for-profit sector or in the professions. The lower wage paid by higher education is a screening device. Only people whose natural scholarship and desire to teach exceed their money motivation will select such a career. However, even these motivated individuals will not select a career that offers them both low and risky pay. The combination of tenure and a substantial endowment insures the faculty member against income risk. The same insurance is provided in public higher education through the combination of tenure and the fact that the institution is a government agency.

Asymmetric information regarding curriculum, academic preparation, and scholarship leads administrators to delegate important personnel decisions to faculty. However, this creates a monitoring problem. Faculty may hesitate to hire and to promote the best possible candidates, since these people are potential competitors for their positions on the faculty. Tenure insures faculty against this threat.

McPherson and Shapiro argue that 'It is useful to think of academic tenure as a set of constraints on the discretion of managers (the 'administration') over various aspects of the academic enterprise' (1999b, 92). The aspects of the enterprise to which McPherson and Shapiro are referring are who is hired to teach and research, what subjects will be taught and researched, and how teaching and research will be conducted. This is a limited domain of responsibility within the institution and as such, it is not quite the same as what I have suggested in the foregoing passages, although it is certainly within the spirit of what I am arguing. I agree that tenure imposes a 'set of constraints on the discretion of managers'. However, I argue that the set of constraints includes not only the academic personnel and curriculum issues, but also the monitoring of rent-seeking behavior by other agents in the institution. Indeed, I think most of the efficiency gains that lead to tenure's survival can be attributed to the constraint on managerial rent-seeking associated with faculty monitoring.

Nothing in the foregoing should be construed to conclude that faculties are not given to their own rent-seeking behavior. Faculties are notorious for their hesitancy in monitoring each other's rent-seeking behavior and for their tendency to treat department budgets as a wages fund to be allocated on the basis of the spoils system. Administrator, student, and board member monitoring of faculty are all an integral part of the governance structure in higher education that exists in order to compensate for the absence of a market for control of the institution.

Summary

Higher education institutions exist because they minimize transactions costs, because of inseparable team production, and because asymmetric information requires that an independent third party must measure and certify the quantity and quality of human capital if education is going to be a successful signal in the labor market. Curriculum technology requires a limited form of team production in higher education, which weakens the monitoring role normally played by the central contractors. There is no residual claimant in higher education because of the common ownership of the principal asset and the weak monitoring role played by the central contractors. The absence of a residual claimant requires reciprocal monitoring among faculty, students, administrators, and governing boards. Competition along the quality hierarchy serves the same role as the market for control of commercial firms. It limits the natural agency problems that arise in higher education.

The similarities and the differences between traditional firms and higher education institutions create a constant tension between those who see colleges and universities as fundamentally different from commercial firms and those who see the two as being essentially the same. Unfortunately, the disagreement within the academe prevents serious efforts to improve productivity when the real cost of higher education is rising faster than real incomes (Chapter 1). The cost/income trend makes it very difficult to maintain access to higher education, and access is increasingly important for long-run economic growth. During a period when knowledge opportunities abound, the prospects for those who cannot gain access to higher education are not good. This problem is compounded by the shift away from need based financial aid towards merit based financial aid. A consensus within the higher education community is required, and the consensus must recognize that productivity improvement and cost control are important social objectives.[6]

The foregoing helps us understand the confusion and consternation expressed by the public and some board members when they encounter traditions, practices, and procedures on our campuses. The threat is that many outsiders believe productivity (hence, lower costs) can be improved by making higher education's governance structure more closely resemble the commercial firm. The converse may be true. Anything that weakens the reciprocal monitoring structure is likely to lead to more agency problems and higher costs. Indeed, the secular rise in overhead costs in higher education may be the consequence of the declining role that faculty play in institutional governance. Hence, when faculty obstruct the students' role in monitoring teaching productivity, this lowers the quantity of effort applied to teaching and lowers teaching quality. Therefore, board members should press for stronger student and alumni monitoring of teaching. Similarly, if the faculty's role in monitoring administrator behavior is weakened, we expect more rent-seeking behavior by administrators at the expense of both academic output and quality. The historical rise in administrative costs and the recent explosion in top academic executive salaries (see Chapter 1) suggest the existence of agency problems in the administrative ranks. Collusive behavior by faculty and administrators also leads to higher cost and lower productivity (Ortmann and Squire, 2000).

A final caveat is appropriate for this section: the interlocking governance structure characteristic of higher education means that when things go wrong at an individual institution, they can go wrong for a variety of reasons, so a single prescription for improving all of higher education will fail. Sometimes the problem comes from faculty, other times it comes from administrators, and at still other times it may be due to the board, students, or the alumni.

2.3   OBJECTIVE FUNCTIONS FOR HIGHER EDUCATION

Estelle James argues that the representative institution seeks to maximize academic prestige (1990, 81). While this suggestion is intuitively appealing, the proper metric for prestige is not immediately obvious. It is important to note, however, that maximizing academic prestige shifts the emphasis to the institution's long-run objective, since prestige is constant in the short run. If the institution's ultimate objective is to maximize academic prestige, then its short-run behavior must be incentive compatible with that objective. Therefore, if long-run academic prestige and the institution's human capital output are positively correlated, then maximizing short-run academic output is incentive compatible with maximizing academic prestige. What is required is a specific connection between academic output in the short run and long-run academic prestige. For all of the analysis that follows, I assume that quality reputation and academic prestige are equivalent expressions.

Alumni and Prestige

The creation of institutional quality begins with the recruitment of quality students. Grossman describes the dynamic relationship between good students, good alumni, the endowment, and the institution's academic prestige as follows:

> Colleges are eager to attract students who have exceptional academic, artistic, or athletic talent not because most faculty prefer to teach students who are smart and interesting, but also because the academic, artistic, and athletic achievements of talented students enhance the reputation of a college and the value of its degrees. This effect pleases alumni, who are the main benefactors of private colleges, and also makes a college more attractive to other prospective students. In this regard, colleges are like any business for whom 'quality' customers enhance the reputation of the product and attract other customers. (1995, 519)

While discussing the motivation of the Overlap institutions, Frances Ferguson Esposito and Louis Esposito indicate this group's objective was:

> to maximize the quality of the institutions' student bodies. Each college wanted to maximize the ratio of 'very best' students in the country to their total students, i.e., to maximize the average SAT score and the high-school class rank of its first-year class. Successful fulfillment of this goal would increase both revenues and prestige for the institution. Having a greater number of the 'best' students meant more successful graduates, which translated into increased revenues through increased alumni contributions, a larger endowment and greater prestige (over the long run). (1995, 443–4)

In a similar context, Cook and Frank remark that:

> Top students are attracted to the schools with the best reputations, the most prestige, and the greatest past success in matriculating good students. Schools further down in the academic hierarchy continue to attract a limited number of top students because of compensating advantages such as location, low tuition, or family tradition. But a remarkably high and growing proportion of top students end up in a small number of elite schools. (1993, 121)

The mechanism postulated by Cook and Frank is a dynamic reputation effect. They cite survey results that suggest students and their parents evaluate university quality on the basis of the accomplishments of the students who attend the institution (1993, 129). The more successful an institution is in attracting good students through time, the easier it is for them to attract good students, since the accomplishments of alumni feed back to attract more good students. It is this dynamic reputation effect that leads to the tournament style result. In order for any institution to move up the quality hierarchy, it must attract a larger proportion of good students. Similarly, holding on to the status quo requires that the institution must continue to attract the same proportion of good students. None of this can be accomplished without subsidies.

Subsidies and Prestige

Consider the market for academic subsidies. The benefactors who supply these subsidies are private contributors – either individuals or institutions – and the governments that direct tax revenues earmarked for higher education. Students and their families are the recipients of academic subsidies. If benefactors and students contract directly, students can in turn contract independently with higher education institutions. In this case, the student's subsidies would be attached to the student and go wherever the student goes. While some subsidies are attached to the student, most scholarships are conditional on the student remaining at a particular institution.

This suggests that obstacles to direct contracting exist between benefactors and students. Some of these obstacles are:

1. the quantity of human capital produced, given a specific student and a specific subsidy, depends on the institution the student attends, since the human capital is the joint product of the student, the institution, and all of the other students attending the institution;
2. the amount of the subsidy to award to each student requires considerable experience with student evaluation;
3. monitoring the student's progress requires proximity to the student; and
4. increasing returns to scale exist in the administration of academic subsidies.

Therefore, the optimal solution for benefactors is to outsource the administration of academic subsidies to the least cost provider of these services – the individual higher education institutions.

Many of the skills associated with the production of human capital are the same as the skills required to administer subsidies and to monitor the students' progress. Hence, academic institutions as a group are the least cost providers of administrative services for these subsidies. The administration of subsidies and the production of human capital offer considerable economies of scope. As an illustration, suppose an individual benefactor wishes to contribute the income from $1 million each year to deserving students. The direct administration of this annual subsidy will be very expensive for an individual benefactor. Alternatively, if the benefactor contributes the $1 million to an institution's endowment and leaves the administration of the endowment to the institution this requires only one decision.

The problem, of course, is: how does the benefactor choose which institution will receive the endowment? Each potential private benefactor is most familiar with their own alma mater and this first-hand knowledge is the most reliable estimate of that institution's marginal social value as a producer of human capital. This knowledge comes from their experience and the experience of their classmates. For benefactors who are not graduates of the institution, the rate and the amount that alumni contribute to the institution's endowment is a reasonable proxy signal for the marginal social value of human capital produced by the institution in the past. Therefore, alumni contributions are the institution's most valuable signal with respect to the marginal social value of its human capital output. Furthermore, this signal is observable by other private and public benefactors who are not alumni. It follows that the cumulative value of the endowment is a good measure of the institution's historic social contribution and in that sense it is an indicator of the institution's quality reputation.

In summary, the production of new knowledge and the distribution of existing knowledge require subsidies in order to achieve the social optimal quantities. An individual institution's long-run share of academic output depends on its control of academic subsidies. In order to maximize its quality reputation, the institution must maximize its control of academic subsidies. Quality reputation rises as the institution's control of academic subsidies increases, and the institution's control of academic subsidies increases as its historic production of new knowledge and/or distribution of existing knowledge increases.

Because education is an experience good and the value received is observed only after a considerable lag, the marginal social return to incremental academic output also occurs after a considerable lag. Holding one's position in the quality hierarchy requires that the institution maintain its control of academic subsidies relative to the institutions below and above it in the hierarchy. Moving up the ladder requires increasing the institution's control of academic subsidies relative to institutions below and above it in the hierarchy. Since subsidy control depends on prior production and distribution of knowledge, the institution must produce and distribute knowledge beyond what is expected from its current quality reputation for extended periods of time in order to achieve a material increase in its long-run control of academic subsidies. This explains why significant upward movement in the quality hierarchy is rare.

Alternatively, an institution can consume its quality reputation by not maximizing the production and distribution of knowledge during the production period (technical inefficiency) or not maximizing quality in the short run. The production and cost model in Chapter 3 and the quality maximization model in Chapter 5 suggest that institutions that consume their quality reputations demonstrate x–inefficiency (Leibenstein, 1965). Secular declines in the quality hierarchy are more probable than is a secular rise in the hierarchy.

Experimenting with Objective Functions

While Hopkins and Massy's (1981) formalization of an objective function for the typical higher education institution is not the first attempt at such a construction (Newhouse, 1970), it is the most complete attempt, since it considers both static and dynamic versions of the model. They propose a 'value function' with multiple arguments that is maximized subject to a budget constraint (1981, 73–130). Clearly, the mathematics of this objective function is the same as in traditional utility theory and some of the same issues arise as in utility theory. The value function represents 'the consensus of the values of the key decision makers, although this bypasses the question of whether such a consensus actually exists or, if so, how it is formed' (1981, 74). This passage recognizes the existence of numerous diverse stakeholders in higher education and that the interests of those stakeholders are not always perfectly aligned. The value function is a social welfare function that may or may not exist. Furthermore, it is not known whether the value function is cardinal or ordinal. Putting these issues aside, I present the basic static model in the following passages.

Let the institution's value function be

$$V = V(x_1, x_2, ..., x_n),$$

where the x_i are the outcomes that generate value. We might adopt an activity analysis approach (Lancaster, 1966), and assume a production function that transforms choice variables into outcomes. Or, we can interpret the value function as the combined value and production function and interpret the x_i as choice variables. In the interest of brevity, I will follow the latter approach rather than the former. If $R(x)$ is the revenue function and $C(x)$ is the cost function, the institution's objective function is

$$\max \overline{V} = V(x_1, x_2, ..., x_n) + \qquad (2.4)$$
$$\lambda[R(x_1, x_2, ..., x_n) - C(x_1, x_2, ..., x_n)].$$

The first order conditions for this objective function are

$$\overline{V}_i = V_i + \lambda[R_i - C_i] = 0 \, \forall \, i = 1, 2, ..., n \qquad (2.5)$$
$$\overline{V}_\lambda = R - C = 0.$$

The Lagrange constraint parameter, λ, is the marginal value of a one dollar increase in revenue and/or the marginal value of a one dollar reduction in cost. Hence, λ is positive. If value is monotonically increasing in all choice variables, the marginal revenue product of the choice variable is less than the marginal resource cost of the choice variable. The second order conditions will be satisfied if the value function is strictly quasi-concave, the revenue function is concave, and the cost function is convex.

At this level of generality, comparative statics effects will be characterized by income and substitution effects and the interpretation of individual choice variables will be difficult. For example, assume that $n=2$, x_1 is enrollment, and x_2 is average student quality; that is, institutional value depends on enrollment and average student quality, which is not an unreasonable interpretation of this objective function. It is also reasonable to assume that revenue is increasing in both enrollment and average student quality, while the marginal cost of enrollment and quality are positive. Without imposing further structure on the revenue function, the cost function, and/or the value function, very little emerges as a testable hypothesis from this formulation.

A similar level of generality in the theory of the commercial firm yields the same kind of result; very few testable hypotheses. For example, there are multiple stakeholders in the commercial firm: labor, management, and the owners. The commercial firm could also be modeled in a fashion similar to Hopkins and Massy's approach, a value function subject to a non-negativity constraint on profit. Since the owners are the residual claimants, we employ our knowledge of the governance structure to articulate a more specific objective function, an objective function that yields more testable results. Still we might represent diverse owners with a value function. Instead, we implicitly assume that the utility of all owners is monotonically increasing in profit, which relieves us of the problem of considering a welfare function for owners that may or may not exist. Little generality is lost by this assumption and considerable insight is gained.

In any event, the Hopkins and Massy approach to modeling the representative institution is the generic form for all subsequent modeling of higher education institutions, including the intergenerational model contained in Chapter 5. In that model, the institution is assumed to maximize quality (the value function) subject to a budget constraint. Alternative approaches are also possible. For example, Ehrenberg and Sherman (1984) assume the institution maximizes an institutional value function whose arguments are quality from different types of students subject to a budget constraint. Among other important results, they find that scholarships increase as student quality increases, increase as the elasticity of the probability the student will enroll increases, and decline as the probability the student will enroll increases.

Hopkins and Massy's 'value function' could be interpreted as prestige or reputation, which is maximized subject to a budget constraint. This approach has two problems, however. First, a metric for prestige does not exist, so the generic problems that exist with the value function also hold for a prestige function. Second, maximizing prestige per se suggests that the benefits of this objective are more psychological than economic, when in fact institutions pursue prestige because higher prestige means control over more economic resources and better students. In other words, long-run prestige maximization maximizes the institution's control over the economic resources derived from students, endowment, and grants. In turn, maximizing academic output (new knowledge and human capital) during the production period and maximizing quality in the short run maximizes prestige in the long run.

Enrollment maximization may also be considered an appropriate objective function (Tiffany and Ankrom, 1998). In this case, an enrollment demand function is the value function where the choice variables are tuition, T, average student subsidies, s, and average student quality, q. Then, the objective function is

$$\max \bar{e} = e(T,s,q) + \lambda[R(T,s,q) - C(T,s,q)]. \tag{2.6}$$

Reasonable assumptions are that enrollment is declining in T, increasing in s, and declining in q. Given

$$R(T,s,q) \equiv (T-s)e(T,s,q),$$

the first order conditions for this objective function lead to a contradiction if one assumes an interior solution for T, s, and q. A corner solution for q does not lead to a contradiction, which suggests that institutions that maximize enrollment choose minimum quality and choose minimum efficient scale in enrollment. Unexploited returns to scale are common in higher education (see Chapter 3) and the emphasis placed on quality in higher education suggests that the objective function in (2.6) is not the proper specification.

Another more promising variant of the Hopkins and Massy formulation is the assumption that the institution seeks to maximize human capital output subject to a budget constraint (see Chapter 3). Indeed, the peer production technology considered by Rothschild and White (1995), among others, can be employed to derive the institution's cost function and the scholarship allocation results found in both Rothschild and White (1995) and Ehrenberg and Sherman (1984).

Rothschild and White note that institutions cannot charge tuition according to the human capital accumulated by each student, so they charge tuition according to the observable number of students enrolled and then reimburse the students for their marginal productivity through scholarships. Neither the student nor the institution knows the marginal value of the education obtained by the student immediately upon graduation. Indeed it may be decades before the student can evaluate the value of her education and the institution observes that value indirectly, if at all. These characteristics reflect the difficulties associated with the assessment of 'outcomes' in all of higher education. The efficient distribution of academic subsidies across institutions and individual students must reflect the marginal social value produced by each institution. Furthermore, there are considerable transaction costs associated with the annual evaluation and allocation of academic subsidies. An individual student, who is to be the recipient of a subsidy, must be identified and the quantity of subsidy allocated to that student determined. In addition, the student's progress must be monitored.

2.4   PRINCIPAL/AGENT ISSUES

Gordon Winston observes that asymmetric information makes trust a necessary condition in order to avoid a market failure (1992), otherwise the 'lemon effect' may prevent mutually beneficial transactions (Akerlof, 1970). Professor Winston argues that growing public hostility towards higher education is due to 'the growth of hard, aggressive, rational behavior' on the part of higher education institutions (1992, 24). While the CEO of a commercial firm might find that comment curious, there is an element of truth in what Professor Winston is telling us, but perhaps not in the way it first appears. The problem is not with rational behavior in higher education, there may actually be too little of that; it is with significant agency problems in higher education (Ferris, 1992a, 1992b; Johnes, 1999). Public hostility towards higher education is due to unresolved agency problems in higher education. It is not because we are misunderstood; it is because self-regulation has not controlled the agency problem.

Cost as an Indicator of Agency Problems

Consider the average cost of education reported by decile from the least to the most elite institutions; the average cost rises exponentially from the fourth decile to the first decile (Winston, 1999, 19). The average cost is almost three times as high in the first decile as it is in the fourth decile. However, the quality of the students in the first decile is substantially higher than in the fourth decile and peer production technology (Rothschild and White, 1995) would suggest that, other things being equal, production costs should be lower in the first decile than in the fourth decile. Also, Charles Clotfelter reports that 'undergraduate courses in one social science department at Harvard University had an average size of 242 in 1991–92, compared with an average size of only 24 students in that same department at Carleton College' (1999, 5). This scale difference should imply that average cost is lower at Harvard than at Carleton. Hence, the average cost differences suggest the presence of significant rents at the top tier institutions.

Furthermore, the endowments of the elite institutions grew at astounding rates during most of the 1990s, while their tuitions net of average scholarships continued to grow faster than the rate of inflation (Clotfelter, 1996, 4–5). Their wealth was growing very rapidly while they were asking their students to pay more for the services they provide. Recalling these events, Ehrenberg observes:

> The public became increasingly outraged that the payout rates at these institutions were so low relative to their endowment values at a time when many of the institutions were raising their tuition levels by substantially more than the rate of inflation. This anger 'encouraged' the trustees of these institutions to change their spending policies, and many announced a substantial increase in their endowment payouts. Although some announced that the increase would permit them to hire more faculty and provide better research support for them, most asserted that a major reason

for the increased payout was to enable the institutions to substantially improve their financial aid programs. (2000, 43)

This has not escaped the public's attention, because it closely resembles the spirited pursuit of individual self-interest rather than the behavior of a charity with a commitment to a social objective.

A clearly articulated objective function for the representative higher education institution is what is missing from this calculus. Without that objective function and the theorems that follow, we cannot separate rent maximizing behavior from rational institutional behavior and without this separation the control of agency costs is more difficult. Finally, if agency cost is not controlled, higher education will lose the public's trust and it would be reasonable to expect significant public regulation once the trust is lost. Therefore, higher education's interest would be better served if we move vigorously to address the agency problems known to exist on our campuses.

Accounting and Economic Budgets

Hansmann describes universities as 'donative-commercial nonprofits' which emphasizes the importance of the source of the university's positive cash flows (1981). Some of the cash inflows are donated and some come from customers, as is the case for commercial firms. If higher education institutions intend to produce human capital beyond the amount that would be produced as a result of private benefits alone, they must subsidize the student's acquisition of human capital. Academic subsidies are indispensable to the production of human capital at levels that reflect both private and public benefits. However, cash outflows must be covered in the long run; so, universities must raise 'donations' to balance their cash flows.

Hansmann also notes that universities are subject to a 'non-distribution constraint' (1981), which means there is no legal requirement that universities distribute any surplus to their 'stakeholders'. The non-profit status and the non-distribution constraint do not prevent the institution from earning a surplus in real terms; they do, however, prevent the institution from reporting a surplus in its accounting budget. Higher education institutions balance their accounting budget, which can be done by lowering the payout ratio and letting the surplus accumulate as an increase in the endowment, or they can increase the accounting expenditures by paying rents to the agents who control the institution. Indeed, any combination of the foregoing will result in a balanced accounting budget. The institution can hide a chronic real deficit by raising its endowment payout rate until the accounting budget is balanced (Martin, 2001a). As is true for any enterprise that has positive cash flows, the controlling agents can extract rents from these cash flows (Grossman, 1995, 522).

In short, higher education institutions are subject to principal/agent problems, perhaps more so than is the case for commercial firms. The secular rise in administrative cost may be evidence of this principal/agent problem (Leslie and Rhoades, 1995; Clotfelter, 1996; Ortmann and Squire, 2000). The absence of a market for control means there is no natural limit on agency cost, other than the social conscience of the agents. Furthermore, the media are conditioned to expect agency problems in commercial firms, but are normally not looking for agency problems in higher education. The usual suspects in this case are faculty, administrators, and governing boards. One might expect independent rent-seeking behavior by faculty or administrators and one might expect collusion between faculty and administrators. The reciprocal monitoring between faculty and administrators foreseen in the governance structure may not take place.

Faculty members collect rents by shirking their scholarship, teaching, and/ or service responsibilities. Time not spent attending to these duties can be used to consume leisure, consult, or manage their own business. Similarly, administrators may encourage faculty to shirk their service responsibilities since this includes their role as monitors. A disengaged faculty is a compliant faculty. The service roles normally reserved for faculty are filled with staff members whose contract is controlled by the administrator, precluding any possibility that staff members would serve as monitors.

Since incentives matter, faculty members continue behavior that is rewarded and discontinue behavior that is not rewarded. If the reward structure values scholarship, but does not value teaching or service, the rational faculty member will disengage from service and minimize his or her teaching effort. Over time, this creates a national/international market for scholars, since scholarly output is readily capitalized as an individual reputation for scholarship. It is not an accident that there is no national market for teachers. A necessary condition for a national market for excellent teachers is the existence of individual reputations for teaching quality. If teaching is not monitored, it is impossible to build individual reputations for quality teaching at anything other than the local level.

Quality Competition and Agency Cost

Since colleges and universities have produced academic output at subsidized prices for extended periods, it is clear that some mechanism has limited the potential principal/agent problem. If the problems are unchecked, the confiscation of rents by the controlling agents would prevent institutions from acting as the least cost administrators of academic subsidies. One of the maintained hypotheses in this book is that the maximization of quality reputation and the quality hierarchy is the mechanism that helps control the principal/agent problems inherent in higher education.

Suppose the higher education market was horizontal rather than hierarchical. If quality reputations and academic productivity are uniform among institutions, then each institution sends an identical quality signal. In a competitive stationary state equilibrium, academic productivity would be uniform, the marginal social value of any donation to an individual institution would be the same, and competition in the subsidy market would result in uniform endowments across institutions. Since education is an experience good and the length of the lag required before quality is revealed is long, agency problems would make this equilibrium unstable. Quality cheating would destabilize the equilibrium.

The hierarchical quality structure is driven by significant differences in academic subsidies. Connecting this fact with the traditional pricing practice of subsidizing the average student, it suggests that any institution's position in the hierarchy is dependent on its continued ability to attract academic subsidies. A contraction in the flow of donations means lower relative subsidies for the average student and a decline in the quality hierarchy. In order to continue to attract subsidies commensurate with its position in the quality hierarchy, the institution must signal an alumni quality level equivalent to its competition. Failure to do so would mean a decline in subsidies in the following time periods. Similarly, if an institution wishes to ascend the quality ladder, it must signal alumni quality beyond its current status. This establishes a dynamic upward pull on quality reputation that reduces the expropriation of rents by the controlling agents. Competition for academic reputation at least lowers the cost of the principal/agent problem latent in all non-profit higher education, and anything that reduces quality competition also reduces the constraints on the principal/agent problems.

While quality competition may limit the principal/agent problem, the evidence suggests that it has not eliminated the problem. For the past two decades, the rate of increase in tuition has exceeded the rate of inflation and the proportion of each higher education dollar spent on administrative functions has increased steadily (Leslie and Rhoades, 1995; Mabry, 1999; National Commission, 1998). Therefore, administrative expenditures have not only increased at a rate faster than inflation, but they are taking a larger share of total expenditures each year. Of each dollar spent on higher education each year, less is going to quality competition.

Ortmann and Squire call the rising administrative share of total cost the 'administrative lattice' and they report that other authors credit information technology, government regulation, student demand for amenities, and mission creep as the primary causes of the administrative lattice (2000, 378). It is doubtful that information technology is a primary driver of higher administrative costs, since this technology has been responsible for a burst of service sector productivity in the past decade. It is quite probable that higher education has been x–inefficient in its employment of information technology. Getz, Siegfried, and Anderson present evidence that higher education is extraordinarily slow to adopt innovations and this tendency also has its roots in principal/agent issues (1997).

Ortmann and Squire, among others, believe that principal/agent problems are most likely to be the root cause of rising administrative costs in higher education. In a game-theoretic model they demonstrate that the combination of 'administrative lattice' and the 'academic ratchet' are major drivers of rising administrative costs (2000, 381). The 'academic ratchet' refers to the tendency of faculty to shirk their shared governance responsibilities in favor of scholarship, personal income opportunities, or leisure. This shirking comes at the expense of teaching, advising, counseling, and other shared governance tasks. Since administrator salaries are positively related to the size of the budget they manage, they have an incentive to fill this gap with administrative staff. The principal in the Ortmann and Squire model is the 'overseer', who in practice is the board of trustees. In the overseer/administrator game the administrator knows which budget is the optimal budget with respect to the institution's objective (to maximize quality reputation). The overseer does not know which budget is the optimal budget and his only choice is to 'either accept or reject the Administrator's recommendation' (2000, 385). Since administrators and faculty have an incentive to overstate the budget, administrators recommend expenditure levels beyond the optimal budget. The overseer's objective is to maximize quality reputation and quality is expensive, so the overseer chooses to accept the administrator's budget recommendation.

Getz, Siegfried, and Anderson provide an empirical analysis of the rate at which 30 innovations were adopted by 238 colleges and universities (1997). The innovations were distributed across all activities within the institutions. Overall they find that innovation takes three times longer in higher education than it does in the commercial firm and, oddly, private higher education institutions are slower to adopt innovations than are public institutions (1997, 611). Surprisingly, the slowest rate of adoption occurs among financial innovations. The authors remark that this is unexpected 'in view of the fact that some of these innovations can be adopted administratively, without the need for time-consuming consensus building' (1997, 617). They also note that institutions in the South and in rural locations have the slowest rate of adoption. They conclude that: 'Those who view higher education as poorly managed may find modest substantiation here' (1997, 628). These results offer empirical support for the conclusions drawn from the Ortmann and Squire game-theoretic model (2000). Innovations are routinely labor saving, so any delay in the adoption of innovations will increase both the 'administrative lattice' and the 'academic ratchet'.

2.5 OVERVIEW

Sophisticated models of the firm lead to important implications for higher education institutions. When the environment is uncertain, when information is asymmetric, and when quality cannot be determined prior to purchase, reputations matter in the theory of the firm and in higher education. Academic institutions produce new knowledge through research and distribute existing knowledge through the education of students. Society subsidizes academic institutions because knowledge has public good properties and because we believe in equality of opportunity. The human capital that is the product of the educational process is produced with the student-input technology that helps explain scholarship allocations. However, human capital maximization alone is insufficient to explain academic behavior. In the long run, academic institutions seek to maximize prestige. Prestige maximization is achieved by maximizing expected alumni quality in the short run. The social reward for efficiency in the maximization of alumni quality is an increase in academic subsidies. These rewards are received with a lag because the measurement of alumni quality is observed with a lag. The unresolved principal/agent issues in higher education also threaten access to higher education.

NOTES

1. If the institution allocates most of its resources to recruiting students and few resources to career services, this indicates the administration is thinking in the short term and not the long term.
2. Many of these transaction costs arise because contracts are not complete. A complete contract is a legal agreement that details the responsibilities of all parties under every conceivable state of nature. Since the conceivable states of nature are infinite, complete contracts are impossible. Incomplete contracts address the monitoring and enforcement problems found in all contracting contingent incentive structures.
3. The expression 'beaten like a rented mule' captures the spirit of this observation, as does 'no one washes a rented car'. The owner of the mule has an incentive to maintain the mule's productivity over its lifetime, while a lessee wishes to extract as much output from the mule as possible during the course of the lease agreement.
4. On the other hand, there may be some location liabilities even among the most prestigious institutions in the country. The University of Chicago and the University of Pennsylvania are cases in point.
5. The complementarity is demonstrated by all of the national ranking systems and the peer production technology, where rank increases as the quality of the students, faculty, and administration increases.
6. Berube argues that 'inefficiency is good for higher education', when he asserts that quality and inefficiency are the same thing (1998, B4). He concludes that the 'corporate model', which seeks to raise productivity and lower cost, must necessarily reduce quality when applied to higher education. The assertion is Luddite in nature and at odds with a clear and unequivocal history of rising product/service quality in the for–profit sector.

3. Production and cost

The customer is the most important part of the production line.

W. Edwards Deming   (1900 – 1993)

3.1   COST MINIMIZATION IN HIGHER EDUCATION

Bowen (1980) argues that higher education governance abhors any daylight between revenues and expenditures such that expenditures rise immediately to whatever revenues may exist. It is important to note that the reverse is not true. Expenditures do not automatically fall whenever revenues fall. In fact, expenditure levels are notoriously sticky on the downside in higher education. Ehrenberg likens this process to the fabled cookie monster, where

> administrators are like cookie monsters searching for cookies. They seek out all the resources that they can get their hands on and then devour them. They put these resources to use funding activities that the institution feels are important and that will make some aspect of its operations better. (2000, 11)

This culture leads some authors to speculate that higher education institutions may not minimize cost (Newhouse, 1970, 71; Brinkman, 1989; Clotfelter, Ehrenberg, Getz, and Siegfried, 1991, 343; Ehrenberg, 2000).

If higher education institutions do not minimize cost, the implications for higher education policy and the study of higher education are profound. Without cost minimization, the regularity conditions that describe cost minimization do not hold and the institution's cost function does not exist. All attempts to estimate cost, returns to scale, or the production function are therefore fatally flawed. Fortunately, there is a way out and I will not have to abandon this chapter!

It is important to recall that accounting costs and economic costs are not the same thing. The behavior correctly catalogued by Professors Bowen and Ehrenberg refers to accounting cost. In higher education the accounting budget is frequently balanced while the economic budget is in surplus. The difference between the two is agency rent.[1] This rent is extracted from the institution through accounting expenditures that are in excess of economic costs. The agents responsible for the extraction of those rents are faculty, administrators, and board members. This potential agency rent is the same thing as Williamson's (1975) budgetary 'slack', which is defined by Getz and Siegfried as the 'expenditures over and above what is necessary to attract and retain the necessary resources to accomplish an assigned task' (1991, 344). One might also call this behavior 'perk maximization'.

I hasten to add that these rents are not captured without the creation of some social value. They frequently do not represent the taking of personal income or raw greed, such as embezzlement. They represent the allocation of accounting expenditures towards activities that significantly benefit one or more group of agents beyond what would be the least cost provision of those services. For example, young scholars are motivated to climb the academic ladder to more prestigious institutions because they know the reward for this effort is not only higher salary, but lower teaching loads, better students, more research support, and, maybe above all else, greater status in their chosen profession. Conceptually, there is no difference between these superstar rents for academics and the rents earned by celebrated actors, athletes, or musicians. However, the rents are an important inducement to the creation of new knowledge, from which society derives considerable benefit. In that sense they represent a real wage paid to scholars for the production of new knowledge and new wealth from that knowledge.

The agents are maximizing potential rents (or potential perks) that equal the difference between accounting cost and economic cost (see Chapter 5). Economic cost minimization is a necessary condition for the maximization of potential rents. Therefore, academic cost functions exist, even in the presence of behavior that appears to be expenditure maximization, and the empirical attempts to estimate them constitute time well spent. However, perk maximization does complicate the empirical estimation of economic cost functions.

3.2   ACADEMIC OUTPUT

Higher education institutions produce and distribute knowledge (Hare and Wyatt, 1992). New knowledge is produced by research. Human capital is produced when knowledge is successfully distributed to students and to the public through the institution's service activities. Research universities produce new knowledge and distribute existing knowledge, while liberal arts colleges specialize in the distribution of existing knowledge. For all that follows, academic output refers to the creation of new knowledge and/or the distribution of existing knowledge. Equivalently, higher education institutions are engaged in academic output when they conduct research or when they produce human capital.

Knowledge has both private good and public good characteristics. Private consumption benefits those who acquire knowledge and the private consumption of knowledge also benefits the public. The public good character of knowledge is one of several reasons why academic output is subsidized by every advanced society. Beyond the public good property, knowledge is subsidized for equity reasons, for paternalistic motivations, and because students have liquidity constraints (Trostel, 1996, 3–5). Our sense of equity suggests that every young person should have an equal opportunity to succeed, which leads us to subsidize access to higher education. This is the primary social objective behind need based aid. Since education is an experience good, some argue that uneducated young people do not appreciate the significance of education and, left to their own deliberations, they invest too little time and too little financial resource in education and the acquisition of knowledge. This explains the role of parents in their child's education choice (Winston, 1996, 7).

The existence of asymmetric information and adverse selection in capital markets leads to liquidity constraints that prevent students from borrowing against their future income in order to finance education (Martin and Smyth, 1991). With perfect foresight, lenders are willing to make education loans to students. When information is asymmetric, lenders cannot separate good student borrowers from bad student borrowers and as interest rates rise good student borrowers are rationed out of the market and bad student borrowers are not rationed out of the market.[2] A bad borrower is a student who intends to default on the loan or one who cannot manage his personal finances well enough to repay the loan. The adverse selection effect from higher interest rates causes lenders to ration credit to student borrowers and the credit rationing creates liquidity constraints for students. The liquidity constraints explain the existence of subsidized student loans. Finally, the evidence clearly indicates that long-run economic growth is positively correlated with the production and distribution of knowledge (Docquier and Michel, 1999; Zhang, 1996). It is for these reasons that society is willing to subsidize academic output.

Broadly defined, human capital is any labor characteristic that has positive market value (Becker, 1975; Schultz, 1961). Therefore, human capital has a variety of characteristics. Some obvious characteristics are physical, verbal, analytical, and technical skills. It may be less obvious that social skills also have market value. Being broadly read, having good conversation skills, and being respectful of the opinions of others can be very important in leadership and management positions. Tolerance, whether of alternative cultures or alternative interests, is a characteristic that has asset value in the global market; therefore, it can also be considered human capital. As a consequence, diverse student bodies and diverse faculties contribute to the individual student's accumulation of human capital. Liberal arts colleges are particularly well suited to exploit these externality effects, due to small class sizes, a residential orientation, and suburban or rural locations. The small college structure maximizes the opportunity for student to student and student to faculty interaction.

The college and the student jointly produce the human capital purchased by the student (Rothschild and White, 1995; Winston, 1996, 1997). The student is an indispensable resource (input) in the production of her own human capital. Furthermore, the student frequently has an external effect (for better or for worse) on the human capital accumulated by other students. Each student may take a direct role in the production of her own purchased output, she may indirectly influence the output accumulated by others, or she may have both effects on output. The unusual connection between customers (students) who receive the firm's output and are simultaneously joint producers of that output also occurs in the for-profit sector. Rothschild and White find that, in addition to higher education, these characteristics are observed at spectator sports events, in the health care industry, and in the legal profession (1995, 574). The production externalities observed in education are also found in peer effects and in the theory of clubs (Winston and Zimmerman, 2004; Zimmer and Toma, 2000; Bartolome, 1996; Brueckner and Lee, 1989).

The externality effect of other customers is illustrated by entertainment events.[3] Spectator sports events consist of the game played by the athletes and the crowd's reaction to that game. If other fans are listless and undemonstrative, one could just as well view the televised version of the event. Hence, other fans contribute to the overall experience. While ticket prices vary by seat location, they do not vary by individual fan in accord with the fan's contribution to the event. In this respect the pricing of sports events and the pricing of higher education are different.

The customer as input role is also observed in health care and the legal profession. Health outcomes frequently depend on the contributions patients make towards their own health in combination with the services provided by health care professionals. With the exception of infectious disease, the indirect contributions of other patients to the individual patient's outcome are minimal. The same can be said for legal outcomes. Again, medical and legal fees are not based on the client's contribution to output.

Rothschild and White's paper on pricing in higher education contains a formal model of the customer-input technology (1995). The authors assume customers contribute directly and indirectly to the institution's output of human capital in a joint production technology with constant returns to scale. As is the tradition in the evaluation of market structures, Rothschild and White derive the social optimal allocation of students across the human capital suppliers first (1995, 578–9). This allocation is based on the maximization of social welfare. The solution to the social optimal problem reveals that the marginal rate of substitution between students of a given type and the educational inputs is equal across all institutions, and the production of each type of human capital at each institution is carried to the point where its marginal cost is unity. These results suggest students are matched with institutions such that the social cost of producing human capital output is minimized and optimal human capital output by each institution occurs where the marginal cost equals the marginal social value.

Following the identification of the social optimal allocation, Rothschild and White derive the perfectly competitive allocation and compare that allocation with the social optimal allocation (1995, 579–82). The competitive price allocation is consistent with the social optimal allocation. The interesting part is in the nature of the competitive prices. The authors note that the pricing results may seem 'strange at first glance'; however, they are attributable to the unusual role played by tuition (1995, 580). The competitive firms cannot charge directly for the human capital acquired by each student, so tuition is charged on the basis of the observable number of students attending the institution, then the institution reimburses the student for their contribution as an input, based on their individual marginal productivity. Each student receives a price discount that reflects her individual contribution to output. Since students are also inputs, the higher quality students are the more productive inputs. 'In the more traditional framework, they receive (larger) scholarships' (1995, 581). While students may not pay the same price, even for the same level of human capital, the price differences do not constitute price discrimination, since the cost of supplying human capital to different students is not the same. The results are consistent with a zero profit, efficient equilibrium.

Rothschild and White are well aware that colleges and universities are not profit maximizing institutions. Their intent is to derive the theoretical results that follow if these institutions maximize profit and then to compare the results with observed college and university behavior. If the theory corresponds with observed behavior, then it might be argued that colleges and universities behave as if they are profit maximizing firms. The authors compare their model's results with observed behavior and find strong similarity between their pricing hypothesis and the widespread tuition discounting and financial aid practices of most institutions. However, they find 'we do not know whether these scholarships represented different net tuition levels for students of differing types (productivity) or a more conventional form of price discrimination by universities among students of the same type' (1995, 582). Their point in this instance is that the scholarship distributions we see in practice may reflect productivity differences, simple price discrimination, or both.

Beyond the basic similarities between their pricing theory and typical practice, there are some important inconsistencies between the Rothschild and White model and what one observes in higher education. The differences between the Rothschild and White theory and institutional practice are:

1.   The tuition charged by high-quality institutions versus lower-quality

institutions does not reflect their human capital differences;
2. Tuition does not vary significantly within institutions for different disciplines; and
3. Tuition does not vary significantly across institutions according to their respective technologies (say, for example, teaching versus research institutions).

In conclusion, Rothschild and White find that 'much of universities' behavior is at odds with our predictions of a competitive equilibrium by profit–seeking institutions' (1995, 583). The scientific implication is that something is amiss with the theory. The first culprit that Rothschild and White identify is the profit maximization assumption, where they note 'it is difficult to state what universities are trying to maximize or even who is doing the maximizing' (1995, 583).

In the production cycle the institution's short-run task is to maximize human capital for each class enrolled. Once students are enrolled, it is assumed the institution produces human capital with the Rothschild and White student-input production technology. Given that the institution will make optimal production decisions in the production cycle, the institution seeks to recruit the highest quality student cohort possible in the annual enrollment cycle (see Chapter 5). The institution's ability to recruit high quality students is constrained by its academic reputation and by its current control of academic subsidies. Subject to the scholarship budget constraint, the institution allocates scholarships in order to maximize expected alumni quality. I assume that these optimal decisions are taken in each enrollment cycle.

3.3 THE PRODUCTION CYCLE

The academic production cycle covers the enrollment period for the typical student, from initial enrollment to graduation. The educational activities occurring during this period produce human capital, and the production cycle generates the total cost function. The production model employed here is a variant of the peer production model explored by Rothschild and White (1995), among others, where human capital externalities peculiar to each student are present.

Adding value is a growing public concern for all education (Meyer, 1997; Cawley, Heckman, and Vytlacil, 1999) and that concern comes from the historical emphasis placed on inputs as a performance measure in education. The emphasis on inputs follows naturally from the fact that education results are notoriously subjective and because the lags between cause and effect in education can be as long as a generation. The emphasis on expenditures per student and student quality indicators, such as SAT exams, high school class standing, and grade point averages, all measure the quantity or quality of inputs rather than the value that is generated by the institution.

In the production model that follows, I consider both value added maximization and simple human capital maximization during the production cycle. This analysis yields some interesting insights regarding this issue. The most important insight is that value added maximization and total human capital maximization are equivalent in the sense that they lead to the same allocation of resources. The differences between the two show up in the types of students recruited by the institution, which has implications for the mix between pure need based aid and pure merit aid.

Some argue that elite institutions primarily recruit very gifted students from extraordinarily well connected families and that the frequently observed successes of their alumni are primarily due to the initial quality of the students and their family connections. In other words, the institutions add little value for the prices they charge. Their students will succeed whether they attend the elite colleges or not. This is a populist and uncharitable argument from which it is very difficult for these institutions to defend themselves. It is hard to see how the distribution of very bright and very wealthy students could be any different. Unless we change the core principles upon which our society rests, prices must ration slots at the very best institutions. Perhaps we should all be grateful to those institutions for not filling their student ranks with the most moronic children of the very wealthy simply because they have the ability to pay the highest price!

By contrast, Berea College is an example of an institution that seeks to maximize value added. Berea provides a full scholarship to every student it admits and it requires all enrolled students to work on campus. Furthermore, there is a family income cap on admissions. If the student's family income is higher than the cap, the student cannot apply for admission. This practice guarantees that all scholarships are need based scholarships. The elite institutions serve the children of the wealthiest families in the country, while Berea is primarily serving the children of low income families.

Institutions that maximize value added seek to substantially increase the odds that their students will succeed, and their contributions are thought to reflect their charges more accurately. Supposedly, these are the institutions that 'transform people's lives' (Pope, 2000). The difference between value added maximization and human capital maximization is a subtle but important distinction, since efficiency would require that institutions be compensated for the value they add.

The model reveals that optimal resource allocation during the production cycle is the same for either objective function. The intuition is clear: once students are enrolled, the optimal solution is to maximize their accumulation of human capital. The institution's objective – value added or total human capital maximization – will be reflected by the type of students the institution recruits. The secular decline in need based financial aid relative to merit based financial aid suggests that institutions are shifting away from value added maximization and towards simple prestige maximization.

Maximization

Let the strictly quasi-concave value added production function for the *i*th student be

$$v^i = v^i(y^i, h^j) \text{ for } i \neq j, \tag{3.1}$$

where y^i is the composite education input. Assume the *i*th enrolled student's entry level human capital is s^i and assume there are *m* different entry levels for human capital, such that

$$S_m > S_{m-1} > S_{m-2} > \dots S_1. \tag{3.2}$$

Hence, the enrolled student with the lowest initial human capital is s_1 and the enrolled student with the highest initial human capital is s_m. Therefore, the *i*th student's total human capital is

$$h^i = v^i(y^i, h^j) + s^i_m, \tag{3.3}$$

and total human capital is

$$H = \sum_{i=1}^{e} h^i(y^i, h^j), \tag{3.4}$$

where *e* is the total number of enrolled students.

The peer or externality effect of the *j*th student on the human capital accumulated by the *i*th student is measured by the sign of the derivative $\partial h^i / \partial h^j \equiv h^i_j \equiv v^i_j$ and the sign of the cross derivative $\partial^2 h^i / \partial y^i \partial h^j \equiv h^i_{yj} \equiv v^i_{yj}$. If both of these derivatives are positive, the *j*th student has a positive external effect directly on the *i*th student's human capital and indirectly through the marginal product of the composite academic input. The signs of these derivatives can be positive, zero, or negative. The impact of a positive peer externality on the marginal productivity of the composite academic input is illustrated in Figure 3.1.

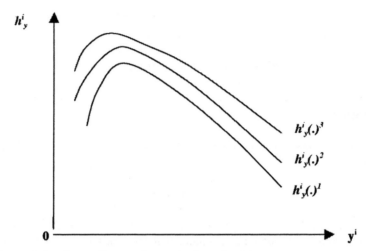

Figure 3.1   Peer effects and marginal productivity

Let the price of the composite education input be p. The cost constraint is

$$C = p\sum_1^e y^i, \tag{3.5}$$

and the production cycle objective function is

$$\max \overline{H} = \sum_1^e h^i(y^i, h^i) + \lambda[C - p\sum_1^e y^i]. \tag{3.6}$$

The first order conditions for this objective function are

$$\overline{H}_i = [1 + \sum_{j\neq i} h_i^{\,j}]h_y^i - \lambda p = 0\,\forall i \tag{3.7}$$

$$\overline{H}_\lambda = C - p\sum_1^e y^i = 0,$$

where $h_i^{\,j} \equiv \partial h^j/\partial h^i$ and $h_y^i \equiv \partial h^i/\partial y^i$. The marginal cost of human capital is $MC = \lambda^{-1} > 0$. Strictly quasi-concave human capital production functions ensure that the second order conditions are satisfied.

Total value added is

$$V = \sum_{i=1}^e v^i(y^i, h^j) \tag{3.8}$$
$$= H - S,$$

since $H=V+S$ from (3.3) and (3.4). Given the cost constraint in (3.5), the value added objective function is

$$\max \overline{V} = H - S + \beta[C - p\sum_{1}^{e}y^{i}]. \tag{3.9}$$

Since the human capital entry levels are parameters, the objective function in (3.9) can be rewritten as

$$\max [\overline{V} - S] = H + \beta[C - p\sum_{1}^{e}y^{i}],$$

which is identical to the human capital maximization objective function in (3.6). Therefore, the solutions that maximize (3.6) also maximize (3.9). The maximization of value added and total human capital are identical except for the constant initial condition S.

The following proposition follows immediately.

Proposition 3.1) Maximizing total human capital or maximizing value added lead to the same optimal solution.

The intuition behind this result is clear. Once students are enrolled, the optimal solution is to maximize total human capital. The production decisions taken by the institution are the same in either case. I suspect this conclusion will resonate with most faculty members. My intention is to do the best I can for each student the College provides me with, regardless of their initial preparation. I may not be happy about unprepared students, but I would not abandon those students.

The implication for student recruiting during the annual enrollment cycle (see Chapter 5) is more interesting. Given that human capital and value added are both maximized during the production cycle, then H can be maximized during the annual enrollment cycle by maximizing S. The higher the enrolled students' initial human capital, the greater will be the institution's total output of human capital.

Alternatively, maximizing value added during the annual enrollment cycle does not necessarily mean minimizing S, even though $V=H-S$. The reason is that students who have very low initial human capital may also have very low ceilings on the human capital they are able to accumulate during the production cycle. Despite their very best efforts, the probability they will survive the production cycle is lower. In other words, the student's potential maximum human capital (the natural limit on her ability to acquire human capital) is very likely to be an increasing function of her initial human capital. Hence, maximizing S during the annual enrollment cycle increases the potential ceiling on H, while minimizing S lowers that ceiling and also lowers potential value added.

From the foregoing, we have

Proposition 3.2) The institution that maximizes total human capital, irrespective of value added, maximizes the initial human capital of the students it enrolls during the annual enrollment cycle. The institution that maximizes value added selects individual students on the basis of the disparity between their human capital potential and their initial human capital subject to a minimum initial human capital.

These results should be reflected by the mix between pure merit based aid and the need based aid selected by the institution. Therefore, institutions whose long-run objective is to maximize total human capital place a greater emphasis on pure merit based aid (higher initial human capital), while institutions that are maximizing value added place greater emphasis on need based aid (higher potential value added).

The secular decline in need based aid suggests that higher education institutions in general are turning away from value added maximization and towards human capital maximization. This trend could indicate a growing principal/agent problem. It is also very important to notice the counter-intuitive role that income based price discrimination plays in this issue. Pricing without considering income (pure merit based pricing) leads to human capital maximization, while price discrimination based on income (need blind admissions, followed by price discrimination) is consistent with value added maximization. Undoubtedly, the trend away from need based aid has also been facilitated by the national rankings of institutions that place so much emphasis on the quality of the student inputs enrolled at the institution.

The Allocation of the Composite Input

Consider the situation where there are no peer production effects; that is, $h_i^j = 0 \forall i$ and j. In this event, the composite education input is employed in the production of human capital for each student such that their marginal products are the same and are all equal to λp. Since $1/\lambda$ is the marginal cost of human capital and can be interpreted as the 'shadow price' of human capital, the necessary conditions yield

$$mch_y^i = p \ \forall i,$$

in the absence of any peer production effects. This can be interpreted as a classic cost minimization condition.

Alternatively, assume there are three types of students: students with positive peer production externalities, zero peer production externalities, and negative peer production externalities. Let the positive peer production externality students be type r, the zero peer production externality students be type o, and let the negative peer production externality students be type n. From the first order conditions in (3.7),   (3.10)

$$h^i_y - \lambda p = -h^i_y \sum_{j\neq i}^{e} h^j_i.$$

Therefore, for all type r students, the composite educational input is employed such that its marginal product is less than the marginal product of the type o students, and for all type n students, the composite educational input is employed such that its marginal product is greater than the marginal product of the type o students. Or,

Proposition 3.3) Maximizing human capital output in the presence of peer production externalities leads the institution to allocate education inputs more intensively to students with positive externalities and less intensively to students with negative externalities.

At the margin, more human capital is produced by allocating fewer inputs to students with negative externalities and more inputs to students with positive externalities.

The foregoing analysis assumes student externality effects cannot be altered by the application of specialized education inputs. If tutoring and counseling can increase the externality effect of individual students, then negative externality students could become at least peer neutral and the positive externality student effects can be enhanced. Then, all of the marginal products are less than λp and the intensity of the use of education inputs varies with the productivity of the individual student.

Evaluating Returns to Scale

Let the optimal solutions to the first order conditions in (3.7) be $\hat{y}^i (C, e, p)$. Then, optimal human capital output is

$$H = H(C, e, p). \qquad (3.11)$$

Dividing both sides of (3.11) by enrollment, we have the average human capital per student,

$$h = h(C, e, p). \qquad (3.12)$$

Equation (3.12) can be implicitly solved for the cost function which is a function of h, e, and p. Hence, the total cost function is

$$C^T \equiv eC(e, p, h),$$

where $C(e, p, h)$ is average total cost per enrolled student. The only unobservable variable in this cost function is average human capital per student. The institution's perceived quality must be an increasing function of the average human capital produced per student and average human capital per student is a natural proxy for quality reputation, q'. Therefore, I substitute q' for h and the long-run cost function used in the quality maximization model is

$$C^T \equiv eC(e, p, q'), \tag{3.13}$$

where q' is assumed to be identically equal to h. The foregoing specification is consistent with the empirical evidence that average cost per student rises as the institution's quality reputation rises. Hence, I assume that higher quality reputations signal higher human capital output per student.

The total cost function in (3.13) demonstrates an important ambiguity in higher education cost functions: the institution's real output is human capital but enrollment is the only observable variable, so returns to scale are tricky to estimate. Identifying minimum efficient scale is correspondingly difficult.

Total human capital in (3.4) is $H=he$ and a proportional change in human capital output is

$$dH/H = [dh/h + de/e] = k,$$

where k is a constant for the purpose of evaluating returns to scale in human capital output. Since H equals the product of h times e, scaling H up means equal proportional changes in h and e; that is, $dh/h = de/e$. The average cost of human capital production is equal to total cost in (3.13) divided by H; then, total differentiation of the average cost of total human capital with respect to h and e yields

$$d[C^T/H] = \{eC_e + C[\eta_{Ch} - 1]\}(de/eh), \tag{3.14}$$

given equal proportional changes in h and e. The term η_{Ch} is the elasticity of the average cost per student with respect to human capital per student.

The sign of the differential in (3.14) depends on the sign of the first term in brackets on the right-hand side, since e and h are positive and de is positive. Furthermore, minimum efficient scale in the production of human capital is identified by the point at which the differential is equal to zero. If it is negative, the institution is experiencing increasing returns to scale and if it is positive the institution is experiencing decreasing returns to scale. Similarly, returns to scale in terms of enrollment are measured by the sign of C_e, since this is the slope of the average cost per student function. Remember empirical returns to scale with respect to enrollment are measurable, but empirical returns to scale with respect to human capital are not measurable.

The next proposition follows from equation (3.14),

Proposition 3.4) If the average cost per student is elastic with respect to human capital per student ($\eta_{Ch} > 1$), minimum efficient scale with respect to human capital output occurs at a lower enrollment level than does minimum efficient scale with respect to enrollment and if the average cost per student is inelastic with respect to human capital per student ($\eta_{Ch} < 1$), minimum efficient scale with respect to human capital output occurs at a higher enrollment level than does minimum efficient scale with respect to enrollment.

By default, the two measures yield the same minimum efficient scale if average cost is unit elastic. The significance of this result is that empirical measures of returns to scale based on enrollment will overestimate true returns to scale if average cost per student is elastic with respect to human capital per student and it will underestimate true returns to scale if average cost is inelastic with respect to human capital per student.

3.4 EMPIRICAL ANALYSES OF HIGHER EDUCATION COSTS

There is a brisk and longstanding empirical literature on the estimation of education cost functions and the measurement of economies of scale and scope in education. Notable examples of this literature are Cohn, Rhine, and Santos (1989), Brinkman (1990), Johnes (1997), and Koshal and Koshal (1995) (2000). While the empirical work is extensive, it does not speak with one voice.

There are multiple reasons why the empirical evidence is hard to decipher. All of these reasons contribute to serious omitted variable problems in the estimation of education cost functions and important omitted variables lead to biased parameter estimates. Since the specifications of the estimated equations differ across studies, the significance of the omitted variable problem varies from one study to the next, as do the signs and significance levels of included variables. The instability in parameter estimates leads to instability in the estimate of economies of scale and scope.

The first and perhaps most serious reason for omitted variable problems in the empirical estimation of education cost functions is illustrated by the production and cost theory in the previous section: the real education output is unobservable. Education produces human capital and human capital is unobservable. The only observable variable is enrollment, or the number of graduates. We cannot observe the human capital per student or per graduate, so empirical estimates of cost based on just enrollment/graduates and the price of inputs suffer from a serious omitted variable problem. A second best solution to this problem is to use proxies for the unobservable human capital per student. In this spirit, Koshal and Koshal (2000) use average SAT scores and student faculty ratios as proxies for human capital output per student. Both of these proxies are input measures.

The second omitted variable problem comes from the fact that higher education institutions produce multiple products, which suggests that their cost functions are actually multi-product cost functions (Cohn and Cooper, 2004). The three primary outputs are thought to be teaching, research, and service (Cohn and Cooper, 2004). Measurement errors abound with both research and service. The analog from human capital production to new knowledge from research is counting scholarly output by counting publications or grant money. Counting publications suffers from the same problem as counting students in lieu of measuring human capital output; we do not know how much new knowledge is created with each publication.

The third omitted variable problem arises in cross section estimation of cost functions. Getz and Siegfried (1991, 345–8) note that cross sectional analysis assumes each institution produces a homogeneous output and that they are each in long-run equilibrium. In fact, individual institutions may be experiencing planned or unplanned reductions or increases in enrollment. Getz and Siegfried note[4] that 'failure to control for the rate of change in enrollment will lead to understatements of cost during periods of enrollment growth and overstatements during periods of decline, which may generate false evidence of scale economies' (1991, 345).

The production and cost theory in the previous section suggests yet another potential source of omitted variable problems. There is a further wedge between accounting cost and economic cost which is composed of agency rents. One would not expect these rents to be constant across institutions, so cross sectional estimates of cost and scale economies may be biased if the researcher does not control for differences in agency rents. If potential rents are a uniform increasing function of academic rank, academic rank may be an appropriate proxy for agency rents.

Although the empirical results are not conclusive, they are more likely to suggest the existence of economies of scale and scope rather than diseconomies. In fact, Cohn and Cooper conclude that these economies exist for higher education institutions (2004). Similarly, Koshal and Koshal (2000) find evidence that suggests that economies of scale and scope exist in liberal arts colleges. The implicit 'minimum efficient scale' measured by these studies is in terms of enrollment. Furthermore, Koshal and Koshal find that scale economies at liberal arts colleges are not exhausted over multiples of average enrollment levels (2000, 216–17). In contrast, Getz and Siegfried conclude that scale economies at liberal arts colleges are exhausted at around 1100 students (1991, 354–6). There are some potential omitted variable problems with Getz and Siegfried's model, since the only explanatory variables are enrollment and enrollment squared.

As with Koshal and Koshal's study, those researchers who find evidence of economies of scale tend to report results that suggest the scale economies extend beyond their sample experience. The implication is that most higher education institutions do not exploit all available returns to scale. This evidence can be reinterpreted with respect to Proposition 3.4) in the previous section. That proposition suggests that if the average cost per student is elastic with respect to human capital output, the minimum efficient scale for human capital output will occur at an enrollment level that is less than the enrollment level at which the average cost per student reaches its minimum. In other words, empirical measures of economies of scale based on enrollment will tend to overestimate true economies of scale in terms of human capital output. Therefore, it is possible that higher education institutions are exploiting all of the relevant economies of scale in human capital production. In that case, their output of human capital may be taking place at the least average cost.

The foregoing result depends on whether or not the average cost per enrolled student is elastic or inelastic with respect to average human capital output per student. Since human capital output is not observable, an empirical estimate of this elasticity will not be straightforward. I will confess, however, that my priors suggest to me that the average cost is elastic with respect to human capital output per student. My reasoning in this case is based on the labor intensive nature of human capital production. By analogy, consider the manner in which PhD students are trained. The amount of human capital per student produced in PhD programs is clearly higher than the amount of human capital per student produced in undergraduate programs and the cost per student in PhD programs is demonstrably higher than it is per undergraduate student. The cost is higher for several reasons: the amount of capital equipment per PhD student; the very small class sizes that characterize PhD programs; and the intensive faculty-student relationship required to prepare a PhD student. This suggests that average cost per student is elastic with respect to human capital output per student.

3.5   SUMMARY

Due to the ambiguous nature of the governance structure encountered in higher education, it has been suggested that colleges and universities do not minimize cost. This presents a serious dilemma for the empirical study and analysis of higher education cost. If costs are not minimized, cost functions do not exist and any statistical relationship between output and cost may be fortuitous at best.

If the institution has an objective other than expenditure maximization, cost minimization is a necessary condition for rational behavior. The existence of a cost function appears to be a problem if the diverse agents who affect resource allocation seek to maximize expenditures in the areas that benefit them. I suggest that even this circumstance does not endanger the existence of the cost function, although it does complicate the empirical estimation of that cost function. The reason for this conclusion is that rent maximizing agents are also acting rationally and a necessary condition for maximizing rents is minimizing economic costs. Potential rents are equal to the difference between revenues and economic costs. If agents are rent maximizers and they extract rents through such things as higher perks, accounting revenues will appear to equal accounting cost while revenues and economic costs are in surplus. The difference is equal to agency rent. Therefore, rational behavior by the institution or its agents suggests that economic costs will be minimized and the economic cost function will exist.

Higher education institutions produce and distribute knowledge. New knowledge is produced through research, and existing knowledge is distributed through teaching and service. The distribution of knowledge creates human capital. The technologies employed to produce research, to teach, and to provide public services are different, although there may be important economies of scope in these three activities. The production and cost model contained in this chapter considers the maximization of human capital production using the peer production technology.

The secular decline in need based financial aid and the secular rise in merit based financial aid suggest that higher education institutions may be placing less emphasis on adding educational value and more emphasis on enrolling students who will become the most influential alumni. The difference can be modeled by value added maximization and total human capital maximization during the production cycle. The production model reveals that value added maximization and total human capital maximization lead to the same resource allocation. The intuition is clear. Once a student is enrolled, the optimal strategy is to maximize the human capital she acquires while she is at the institution. The differences between value added maximization and total human capital maximization appear in the types of students the institution recruits. In

Chapter 5 it is assumed that institutions maximize student quality during the annual enrollment cycle. Student quality may be interpreted as the most gifted students (meritorious), as students with the greatest potential for improvement (value added), or any combination of these two types of students.

The efficient allocation of resources used to produce human capital implies that higher education institutions employ education inputs more intensively with students who have positive external effects on other students and employ education inputs less intensively with students who have negative external effects. In this sense, students with positive externalities are complementary to education inputs, while those students who have negative externalities are competitive with education inputs.

The institution's cost function depends on enrollment, input prices, and average human capital per student. While enrollment is observable, human capital per student is not observable. Since average cost per student is positively correlated with the institution's quality reputation, I assume that quality reputation is a proxy for average human capital output per student. The institution's quality reputation at any point in time signals its relative position in the ranks of human capital output per student.

Minimum efficient scale is defined in terms of human capital output, whereas enrollment is the most readily available measure of output. The model suggests that minimum efficient scale with respect to human capital output occurs at a lower enrollment level than the minimum efficient scale suggested by enrollment alone, if the average cost of enrollment is elastic with respect to human capital per student. Since the empirical evidence suggests that scale economies (in terms of enrollment) persist well beyond average enrollment levels for most institutions, the foregoing result suggests that they may be closer to minimum efficient scale with respect to human capital production than previously thought.

NOTES

1. Cohn and Geske (1990) remind us that it is always important to remember the differences between accounting cost and economic cost when considering technology estimation through cost functions. Cohn and Cooper (2004) further note that economic costs are more inclusive than accounting costs, since economic costs include all opportunity costs. However, when agency rents are being booked as accounting costs the opposite is true. Other things being equal, accounting costs are more inclusive than economic costs when agency rents are extracted as accounting costs.

2. In this sense, higher interest rates adversely select from the pool of potential borrowers. As interest rates rise, the default rate rises and expected profits decline.

3. One might call this the 'Studio 54 effect'. During the height of this New York nightclub's popularity, the owner personally oversaw the admission of patrons with the intent of 'casting' each night as an entertainment event. The apparent purpose was to maximize the positive

externalities. In other words, the customer mix was important in determining the quality of the output.

4.   Getz and Siegfried attribute this discovery to Brinkman (1990).

4. The charity market

Do good by stealth, and blush to find it fame.

Alexander Pope   (1688 – 1744)
Epilogue to the Satires

4.1   ENDOWMENTS AND VOLUNTARY SUPPORT

Endowments are perhaps the most distinctive financial characteristic of charitable institutions. In higher education these endowments are frequently several times as large as the organization's annual expenditures (Fisman and Hubbard, 2003, 227–9). As reported by Ehrenberg (2000, 43) and by Hansmann (1990, 36), the accumulation of endowments at times appears 'excessive' to the public. Such large reserves of liquid assets held by institutions, rather than individuals, are rare in other sectors of the economy. If a corporation accumulated an equivalent share of its total assets in this liquid form, it would make itself a prime acquisition candidate. Hence, the existence of a market for control limits the accumulation of liquid assets among commercial firms.

Formally, the term endowment refers to the restricted part of the institution's portfolio of financial assets. The restrictions imposed by the original donors require the institution to hold these assets in perpetuity (Ehrenberg, 2000, 35). Hansmann notes that the courts typically do not condone perpetual restrictions since they tend to freeze resources in inefficient applications, but charitable endowments are an exception to that legal precedent (1990). The unrestricted part is the 'quasi-endowment' because the institution treats them as if they are restricted (Hansmann, 1990, 8). In an emergency, the institution can use all of the earnings (normal income and capital gains) from the restricted endowment and all of the earnings plus the asset itself from the quasi-endowment. In all that follows, 'endowment' refers to both the restricted and unrestricted parts of the portfolio.

The flow of new contributions to higher education is measured by voluntary support, which is composed of contributions from alumni, non-alumni individuals, corporations, foundations, religious organizations, and other organizations. The largest component of voluntary support comes from individuals, either alumni or non-alumni. These two groups accounted for 53 percent of the total annual voluntary support in 1997 and 48 percent in 2002 (Kaplan, 2003,

2). Since this period covers the correction in equities markets and the dollar amount of individual contributions actually rose by a substantial percentage, the loyalty expressed by individuals to higher education is impressive. The constant dollar voluntary support per student for all of higher education from 1981 through 2001 is plotted in Figure 4.1. These data reveal that the annual support per student more than doubled over this period and grew at a compound growth rate of approximately 1.6 percent. During this same period, voluntary support as a proportion of institutional expenditures rose from 6.3 percent in 1981 to 8.1 percent in 2001. The annual flow of voluntary support may be directed to either covering operating expenses or building the endowment. In 2002, 52 percent of voluntary support was used for current operations and the rest went for capital purposes.

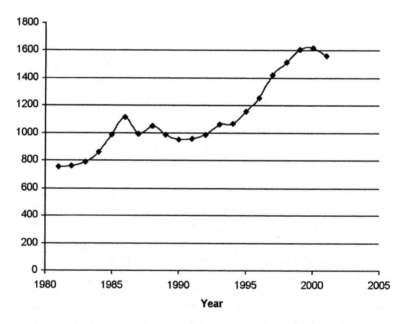

Source: Kaplan, Ann E., *2002 Voluntary Support of Education*, Council for Aid to Education, 2003, 4.

Figure 4.1   Constant dollar voluntary support per student: 1981 – 2001

Historically, administrators and their governing boards have been conservative with regard to how hard they 'work' the endowment both in terms of the payout rate and the risk they accept in their portfolios. Ehrenberg reports that the average payout rate in higher education is between 4 and 4.5 percent (2000,

37). Hansmann notes that the rates adopted are generally less than the real rate of return on the portfolios, which causes the real value of endowments to rise regardless of new voluntary support (1990, 10–11). Prior to the 1970s, the risk position in most endowment portfolios was very low. It was not uncommon to find portfolios primarily composed of bonds. That has changed steadily over the last three decades.

Table 4.1 contains the weighted average asset allocations in endowments for higher education institutions in 1999 and 2003. Despite the significant correction in the equities market during that period, the largest component in the asset allocation is still in equities. Together, equities, fixed income securities, and cash account for over 87 percent of the average endowment. While this is not as conservative a portfolio profile as in earlier periods, it is still conservative by today's standards.

Table 4.1   Higher education endowment asset allocation: 1999 and 2003

Asset Class	1999 (%)	2003 (%)
Equity	64.3	57.1
Fixed Income	23.6	25.9
Alternative	5.3	8.2
Real Estate	2.0	2.8
Cash	4.0	4.0
Natural Resources	0.2	0.4
Other	0.5	1.6

Source: TIAA–CREF, 2003 NACUBO Endowment Study, Washington, DC: National Association of College and University Business Officers, 2004, 9.

A more nuanced understanding of portfolio allocations in higher education endowments can be obtained by looking at the weighted average asset allocations by size of the endowment (see Table 4.2). The major differences in asset allocations appear to take place between endowments that are less than $500 million and those that are over $500 million. The endowments over $500 million make greater use of hedge funds, private equity, and venture capital than do the smaller endowments. In 2003 the endowments with more than $1 billion allocated over 28 percent of their assets to hedge funds, private capital, and venture capital, while those endowments between $50 and $100 million kept over 90 percent of their assets in equities, fixed income securities, and cash.

Spending rates have been relatively stable over the past ten years. Not only do they appear relatively stable over time but they also seem to be rather uniform across institutions by size of endowment. Table 4.3 contains spending rates by size of endowment for 1994, 1999, and 2003. The spending rates appear to have drifted up slightly for all endowment sizes over the period from 1994 to 2003. The only other regularity of note in these data is that spending rates for smaller endowments appear to be slightly higher than spending rates for larger endowments. Since the larger endowments typically have more aggressive asset allocations and they are spending less for current operations, the riskier portfolios appear to be designed to grow their endowments more rapidly.

Table 4.2   Endowment asset allocations by size of endowment: 2003

Asset Class	Size of Endowment ($ billions)			
	> $1.0 (%)	0.501–1.0 (%)	0.101–0.5 (%)	0.051–0.100 (%)
Equity	44.8	54.4	56.5	58.7
Fixed Income	18.6	18.2	23.5	27.2
Real Estate	4.2	4.2	2.9	2.8
Cash	1.8	1.4	2.7	4.9
Hedge Funds	19.9	13.4	8.3	4.3
Private Equity	5.2	4.2	2.2	0.6
Venture Cap	3.0	2.7	1.3	0.3
Nat. Resources	1.9	1.1	0.8	0.1
Other	0.7	0.4	1.8	1.1

Source: TIAA–CREF, 2003 NACUBO Endowment Study, Washington, DC: National Association of College and University Business Officers, 2004, 8.

Endowments that are several times as large as annual expenditures are a common financial feature of higher education institutions. The annual voluntary support that feeds both current operations and the endowment has continued to grow in real terms even during the recent bubble in the equity market. Over time the asset allocations within the endowments have become less conservative. The larger the endowment, the less conservative is the asset allocation. Spending rates have remained relatively stable, but appear to be trending up slightly. Institutions with smaller endowments tend to have higher spending rates.

Table 4.3   Spending rates by size of endowment: 1994–2003

| Size of Endowment | Year | | |
(\$ billions)	1994 (%)	1999 (%)	2003 (%)
> 1.000	4.9	4.1	5.3
0.501–1.000	4.8	4.4	5.4
0.101–0.500	4.9	4.5	5.2
0.051–0.100	5.1	4.9	5.3

Source: TIAA–CREF, 2003 NACUBO Endowment Study, Washington, DC: National Association of College and University Business Officers, 2004, 14.

4.2   WHY IS TOO MUCH ENDOWMENT NEVER ENOUGH?

The manner in which endowments are solicited and managed suggests the intent is to accumulate ever larger endowments; the accumulation of endowment is not something dictated by donors or forced on the institutions by outsiders. Therefore, some important economic forces must be at work in the drive to accumulate endowment.

Random Shocks and Variable Cash Flows

Henry Hansmann considers why universities have endowments (1990). He notes that the desire to 'preserve intergenerational equity' is the most frequently cited reason for the accumulation of endowments in higher education.[1] He also argues that intergenerational equity is the least compelling economic reason to accumulate an endowment (1990, 14–16). First, if history is any indicator, future generations will be wealthier than the current generation, so it would be more logical to transfer wealth from future generations to the current generation by borrowing now and using future tuition to pay back today's loans. Second, real wealth will be higher in the future if we invest more heavily today in the creation of new knowledge and in the distribution of existing knowledge. Third, if future endowment gifts are predictable, then they 'should be included in any intertemporal budget plan' (1990, 16). This would be particularly appropriate if higher expenditures today increase the probability of future donations. Finally, the good works to which today's expenditures can be put are less risky than the ends to which the endowment might be directed in an uncertain future. For instance, higher expenditures today can improve intra-generational equity by increasing access to higher education now. Greater access today clearly means higher wealth in the future. So, the intergenerational equity argument really works best in reverse. Hansmann considers and discards other arguments, such as 'lumpy funding' and tax incentives, for building endowments (1990).

Hansmann's most compelling argument for the existence of endowments is the case he makes for liquidity and security (1990, 21–29). This theme is advanced in a more recent article by Fisman and Hubbard, where they explore the precautionary savings motive for holding endowments:

> In a for-profit organization, shareholders act as the residual bearers of risk. Because non-profits, by definition, have no residual claimants, there must be some other means of absorbing shocks that exist in a world of uncertain donations and uncertain needs for program expenditures. One possibility would be simply to allow for shocks to revenue streams to be passed on to program expenditures, thus effectively making the recipients of an organization's services bear the burden. However, a desire for 'production smoothing' naturally leads to a search for an alternative buffer. Thus non-profit organizations will hold precautionary savings in the form of endowment fund balances, to protect against adverse revenue shocks. (2003, 217–18)

Every enterprise, whether a commercial firm or a non-profit organization, must balance its cash flows and every enterprise is subject to random shocks to those cash flows. Commercial firms have access to both debt and equity markets to cushion shocks to their cash flows. Since the cost of diversification for the commercial firm's owners is approximately zero, they are well positioned to absorb such shocks. Indeed, equity markets are so efficient at diversification they eliminate all firm-specific risk, so owners are not rewarded for bearing firm-specific risk. Shareholders are rewarded for bearing systematic or macro-economic risk, which is the only type of risk that cannot be avoided through diversification.

In contrast, there are no residual claimants in higher education and these institutions have access only to debt. The 'equity' held by non-profit stakeholders is not diversified. The most important higher education asset is reputation. This is an intangible asset and it is not easily collateralized. Most importantly, reputation has no residual asset value in liquidation. If the institution goes bankrupt, the asset value represented by reputation is lost. Hansmann remarks 'since great age is a scarce attribute among educational institutions, it can become a source of social cachet; old colleges and universities have an advantage in becoming exclusive ones' (1990, 28). Weisbrod and Dominguez use age as a proxy for quality reputation (1986, 87). The next most significant asset held in common by the institution's stakeholders is the campus and its buildings. Therefore, institutions without an endowment are holding an undiversified portfolio composed of real estate at a single location and a valuable, but intangible, asset. As a result, higher education institutions have great value at considerable risk.

The representative institution is vulnerable to both institution-specific and systematic risk. Systematic risk is best exemplified by events such as the Great Depression, which are characterized by extended periods of economic or political uncertainty coupled with a high probability of a dramatic reduction in financial asset values. The problem with endowments during these periods is that their ability to cushion such shocks is frequently reduced by the event itself. Hence, the institution must plan for capital losses when the endowment is needed most, which implies the planned endowment will appear excessive during normal times. Given the typical institution's expected life, it can anticipate multiple macroeconomic events on a scale with the Great Depression. Any one of those events could be fatal to the institution without an endowment to cushion the shock.

Institution-specific shocks may occur more frequently. Any scandal that seriously damages the institution's reputation will take years of effort and expense to repair. Such a scandal may disrupt annual giving, forcing the institution to rely heavily on its endowment, and the institution may find it difficult to hold its position in the academic hierarchy during such an event.

Higher education institutions are particularly susceptible to cash flow shocks since they have high fixed costs and a governance structure that cannot respond quickly to changing circumstances. Short-run operating leverage is symmetric. When enrollment rises, the institution enjoys a considerable boost in its net cash flows, and when enrollment drops, the institution's losses mount quickly. The two largest components of this fixed cost are physical plant and faculty, although one can argue that most institutions consider their staff a fixed cost as well.

Like the owners of commercial firms, stakeholders in higher education cannot avoid systematic or macroeconomic risk. However, by combining reputation, tradition, and location with a large and liquid portfolio of diversified financial assets they can create portfolio insurance against institution-specific risk and if the endowment is large enough this insurance will cushion the impact of systematic risk.

Consider how this works for faculty in academic labor markets. Wages paid in higher education for professional skills are lower than comparable wages in the for-profit sector or the professions. The lower wage is a self-selection device. If scholarship and teaching are the candidate's primary motivation, he is more likely to choose an academic career. Those who are most willing to sacrifice income for these reasons are self-motivated and require less monitoring. The asset value of tenure is a function of bankruptcy risk, since the institution defaults on tenure through bankruptcy. As the endowment increases, the institution is less likely to go bankrupt and the asset value of tenure increases. Higher education institutions offer low initial wages and a valuable tenure asset to faculty who succeed. Furthermore, the tenure asset is an important recruiting tool for senior scholars in the race for academic prestige. Hansmann identifies this as a potential agency problem, since faculty and administrators may invest too heavily in their own job security (1990, 36).

Hansmann also argues that higher education institutions accumulate endowments because they insulate the institution from 'outside demands' (1990, 29–32). The independence offered by endowments has an upside and a downside. The endowment protects the institution from raw political and ideological agendas; but it may also make it less responsive to students, alumni, and the public interest. For example, the larger the endowment, the less likely the institution will be subject to predation from a single wealthy donor with an agenda. Alternatively, being unresponsive to the needs of students and alumni may be in the short-run interest of those who control the institution, but it will not be in the institution's long-run interest. In other words, with independence comes an agency problem.

Since endowments are easily measured and denominated in terms that are familiar to trustees, they spend more time and energy on this issue. Competition with one's peers is the preferred form of competition; so, trustees measure their success as trustees relative to the fundraising success at their competitor's institutions. Hence, capital campaigns behave like arms races and can lead to 'conspicuous endowments'. The most appropriate motto may be 'too much endowment is never enough'. As a result, trustees are unlikely to be concerned about the principal/agent problems that attend endowments.

Fisman and Hubbard compare the principal/agent issues that surround endowments with the principal/agent issue associated with discretionary cash flows in the commercial firm (2003, 220). Jensen argues that discretionary funds create opportunities for agency rent-seeking through the consumption of excessive perks, pursuit of pet projects, inflated salaries, or outright theft (1986). The solution according to Jensen is high debt loads, since debt service minimizes discretionary cash flow. Fisman and Hubbard cite two recent examples[2] of substantial 'expropriation of endowments' by officials at different charities (2003, 220). The precautionary saving motive explored above makes it impossible to leverage academic institutions to the point that discretionary cash flows are eliminated. Precautionary saving serves a real economic purpose in higher education and the agency problems it creates are an unpleasant side effect of that purpose. In any event, it is important to recognize the problem exists and to explore how its adverse impacts might be minimized.

Oversight of Charities

According to Fisman and Hubbard, there are three oversight groups who can contribute to a solution: the government, the media, and the donors (2003, 221–3). For the reasons identified below, I argue there is a fourth group who provides a valuable oversight role: the charitable foundations that make grants to institutions. Beyond the limited oversight provided by the IRS, most regulation of charities is carried out by state governments and that regulation varies substantially from one state to the next. The level of government scrutiny pales in comparison to the oversight offered by the SEC and the Justice Department with respect to commercial firms. Even with that level of government oversight, agency problems occur frequently in commercial firms. Khanna and Sandler find evidence in UK charities that government grants have a significant 'crowding-in' effect on private contributions to charities (2000). They attribute this result to the seed money effect of these grants and to the signal sent by government grants. Potential donors view the government grant as evidence the government will be monitoring the charity more closely (2000, 1555).

Government regulation of charities through the Internal Revenue Service has the most potential for curbing agency problems. The charity's tax-exempt status is a two-fold benefit to the institution. First, the tax-exempt status represents a certification that the charity meets minimal conditions as a charity and secondly, contributions to the institution are tax deductible. Withdrawal of tax-exempt status would be an unequivocal signal that something was wrong. A report by the General Accounting Office (GAO) entitled *Tax-Exempt Organizations: Improvements Possible in Public, IRS, and State Oversight of Charities* published on April 30, 2002 considered the accuracy of the information reported by charities in IRS form 990, the adequacy of IRS oversight, and IRS data sharing with state regulatory authorities. The GAO report found that charities regularly misrepresent their actual fundraising costs in form 990 by shifting costs from fundraising expenses to the provision of services in order to make themselves appear more efficient, and that the IRS has no evidence to substantiate the data reported by charities. The report also found that the IRS had no strategy for the oversight of non-profit organizations, its enforcement staff in the tax-exempt division is declining, the number of form 990 filings is increasing, and the data flow between the IRS and the state enforcement agencies was inadequate.

Most of the abuses discovered in the non-profit area are revealed by the media through investigative reporting. Media oversight is also an imperfect solution, since the discovery of abuses requires sophisticated legal and financial skills that are not common among journalists and because the media may hesitate to reveal misconduct because of the damage done to the valuable services charities provide. Exposing the greedy CEO of a publicly held commercial firm is one thing, but exposing the head of a charity that performs vital public services is another. This hesitation probably explains how the pedophilia problem in the Catholic Church could have escaped public attention for so long.

Since the board of trustees has the legal responsibility for oversight, it is not surprising that most of the burden falls on their shoulders. Their ability to exercise oversight depends on the institution's governance structure. Major donors normally assume responsibilities as board members, where they represent themselves and other donors. The important characteristics of board structure are the size of the board and the composition of the membership. Large boards can make oversight more difficult for the same reason that large committees are less efficient than smaller working groups. On the other hand, institutions prefer larger boards since they create more opportunities for fundraising. The non-distribution constraint and the absence of a single residual claimant lead to multiple stakeholders, and each of these stakeholder groups has some monitoring responsibilities (see Chapter 2). Normally, board composition/attendance consists of administrators, donors, and alumni, leaving students, parents, and faculty as the unrepresented stakeholders.

The oversight role played by foundations remains largely unexplored. Lise Vesterlund reports a conversation between John Stossel and Ted Turner, where Mr. Turner states:

> Giving a lot of money away is almost as difficult and complicated as making it. You have to hire people to do it. They've got to analyze things real carefully. (2003, 632)

These comments reflect asymmetric information between donors and charities. Donors cannot readily observe the quality of the public goods provided and acquiring information about quality is costly. The asymmetry is persistent, since donors do not consume the public goods provided by the charity. In the market for academic subsidies the foundation's role is similar to the role played by investment bankers in the for-profit sector. The investment banker's reputation acts as a performance bond when they underwrite a new issue and investors look to those reputations as an indicator of the quality of the new offering. If a major foundation makes a substantial grant to an institution, this conveys a signal to potential donors. Since foundations are in the 'market' on a daily basis evaluating where to invest resources, they are the most skilled evaluators of academic quality. If they are willing to invest in a given institution, this is an important quality signal.

Precautionary Savings

Fisman and Hubbard set out to test the precautionary saving hypothesis in charitable industries using data from 1987 to 1996 (2003, 223–31). The dependent variable in most of their analysis is 'endowment intensity', which is measured as endowment divided by annual expenses. This variable is a good measure of the institution's reserve financial capacity, since it represents the number of years the institution could continue in operation if all current revenues disappear. They create a second variable equal to annual donations divided by annual revenues and call this variable 'donation intensity'. The donation intensity variable measures how dependent the charity is on annual donations to fund annual operations. There are four sources of revenue available to most charities: annual donations, government grants, endowment income, and client driven revenues.[3] Since the institution has considerable discretion with respect to endowment income, it is the most stable of the four revenue sources in the short run. Annual donations and government grants may be the most volatile revenue sources, followed by client driven revenues.

The data consists of 4546 organizations in 23 separate charitable industries. The median endowment intensity and donation intensity for higher education reported by Fisman and Hubbard are 2.41 and 0.196, respectively (2003, 227). The representative higher education institution has sufficient endowment to continue its current operations for a little over 2.4 years and it relies on annual donations to provide approximately 20 percent of its revenues. Of equal interest is the 'fat' in the tails of the distribution. The bottom 10 percent of the higher education institutions have a median endowment intensity of 0.91, while the top 10 percent have an endowment intensity of 7.46 (2003, 229). Hence, endowment intensity in higher education is highly skewed towards the elite institutions. Since the mortality rate is highest among the institutions in the lowest tier of the hierarchy and we rarely, if ever, observe a bankruptcy among the top tier institutions, the minimum endowment intensity consistent with risk-free default must be greater than one and considerably less than 7.5. That does not mean, however, that an endowment intensity of 7.5 is excessive, since default security is not the only legitimate motive for accumulating endowments. The precautionary motive for accumulating endowment also includes the funds necessary to maintain the institution's reputation relative to its closest competitors and the funds required to do that must increase as you move up the hierarchy.

The relationship between endowments, the academic hierarchy, and the institution's reputation is like a ratchet. Once the institution gains a position in the hierarchy, it has a limited window within which it can anchor itself in that position. Each position in the hierarchy is contestable and the threat is from the institutions immediately below. The institutions in the ranks above may exchange places without disturbing the ranks of the institutions below them. Similarly, an exchange of positions between two institutions does not affect the ranks above the two institutions. The barriers to entering the rank immediately above are driven by the relative size of one's endowment. The larger the differential between your endowment and the endowment of the institution in the following rank, the less likely you are to be 'bumped' from that rank. If the institution below you receives an 'institution transforming gift', your rank is in danger, so the best strategy is to accumulate endowment as rapidly as possible to protect your rank and to put the institution within striking distance of the next highest rank. It is a classic arms race with the peer institutions, where power is measured by endowment.

In order to explore the determinants of endowment intensity, Fisman and Hubbard estimate the median endowment intensities for the 23 charity sectors using controls for revenue volatility, labor intensity, and access to credit markets (2003, 225–30). Revenue volatility is measured by the standard deviation of revenues during the period from 1987 to 1996. Labor intensity is measured by labor expenses divided by total expenses and credit market access is measured by a zero/one dummy variable, which is equal to one if the institution borrowed money during the period. The results suggest that endowment intensity is positively correlated with revenue volatility and negatively correlated with labor intensity. The credit market variable was not significant. These results are consistent with the precautionary saving motive for endowment accumulation, if one considers labor a variable cost. In higher education, one should not consider academic labor a variable cost in the short run.

Ehrenberg and Smith investigate 'the sources and uses of annual giving at selective' institutions (2003). Annual giving to colleges and universities is used to support current operations, building and equipment, debt service, and additions to the endowment. It totaled approximately $19.5 billion in 2000 (2003, 223). Their data consists of annual observations covering the 31-year period from 1969–70 to 1998–99 for 30 selective research universities and 30 selective liberal arts colleges. On average, the share of total annual donations coming from alumni is almost twice as high for liberal arts colleges as it is for universities, while donations from foundations and corporations are higher for universities than liberal arts colleges (2003, 225). Universities use over half of their annual donations to support current operations, while liberal arts colleges use over 40 percent of their donations for buildings and equipment (2003, 225). Universities use over 30 percent of their annual donations to enhance their endowments, while liberal arts colleges use about 15 percent of their annual donations to enhance their endowments (2003, 225). The most interesting empirical results from Ehrenberg and Smith's model are:

> Richer institutions ... receive higher levels of giving from all sources (success

breeds success), save for corporate giving to the colleges (2003, 229)

and with respect to the uses of annual giving and the wealth of the institution

the marginal effect is greatest for both the colleges and universities for giving to further build the endowment. (2003, 232)

Hence, the wealthier institutions as measured by endowment per student receive higher donations from almost all sources and are more likely to use those donations to grow their endowments.

Assuming diminishing marginal productivity for annual donations in terms of current academic output, the marginal productivity of a dollar donated to a wealthy institution will be less than a dollar donated to an endowment poor institution. The fact that marginal dollars are more likely to wind up in the endowment at wealthy institutions would seem to contradict this conclusion. In any event, these results are at odds with what we would expect from economic theory, which suggests that the incentive for potential donors to free ride should be higher if other donors have already contributed to the public good. Lise Vesterlund rationalizes these results in a signaling model of fundraising, where it is demonstrated that the contributions of others are interpreted as a quality signal (2003).

4.3 CHARITY, WARM GLOW, COLD PRICKLE, AND SIGNALS

Pure altruism in the private provision of public goods assumes the donor's utility function depends only on the quantity of the public good produced and the quantity of private goods consumed by the donor. Nash equilibrium in this case is characterized by limited contributions to the public good by only the very rich and by the crowding out of privately produced public goods by government produced public goods (Glazer and Konrad, 1996, 1019). The empirical and experimental evidence suggests something entirely different, however. Glazer and Konrad report that a super majority of Americans regularly contribute to charities and that public crowding out is modest at best (1996, 1019). During the 1980s tax rates and government grants were both cut and the expectation among many observers was that private contributions would decline precipitously; in fact private contributions continued to rise throughout the decade (Andreoni, 1998, 1187). In another article, Andreoni notes that these contradictions between theory and empirical evidence are a persistent economic puzzle (1995, 1).

Other anomalies are routinely observed in college and university capital campaigns. As identified by Andreoni, the characteristics of capital campaigns that seem at odds with the pure altruism model of charity donations are

> that capital campaigns rely heavily on 'seed grants' and large 'leadership gifts' that are publicly announced before the general fund drive begins. In fact, a well-known rule of thumb for capital campaigns is that one third of the goal must be raised in a 'quiet phase' before the public fund drive is launched. One might guess that such leadership gifts would only encourage free riding among later givers, whereas fundraisers surely believe that they encourage gifts. By contrast, continuing campaigns (annual campaigns) turn directly to general fund-raising, without relying on the leadership phase. (1998, 1187)

Theory suggests the announcements should induce subsequent donors to donate less. In a sequential model of the private provision of public goods, Varian demonstrates that at worst announcements reduce subsequent donations and at best the fundraiser should be indifferent to announcements (1994).

The empirical evidence is clear, however; announcements have the reverse effect, they tend to increase cumulative donations rather than reduce them. This conclusion is supported by Khanna and Sandler's study of UK charities where they find that government grants cause significant crowding-in of private donations (2000). It is also supported by List and Lucking-Reiley's experimental results for a university capital campaign to provide a threshold public good (2002).

The conflict between theory and evidence suggests that something is amiss with the pure altruism model. The first attempt to address these anomalies was through the impure altruism model, where it is assumed that the donor's utility is also a function of the amount donated towards the private provision of the public good.[4] Hence, the pure altruism model assumes the ith donor's utility function is

$$u^i = u^i(x, G),$$

where x is a vector of private goods and G is the public good; while the impure altruism model assumes the ith donor's utility function is

$$u^i = u^i(x, g, G),$$

where g is the amount donated to the production of the public good by the ith donor. The altruism is said to be impure because the donor receives personal utility benefits from contributing. This is the 'warm glow' formulation of charitable giving.

The 'cold prickle' effect comes from the utility foregone by free riding on the charitable gifts of others. Andreoni presents experimental evidence that suggests the results depend on how the game is framed and that the warm glow utility and the cold prickle utility are not symmetric (1995). In other words, if the game is framed as the production of a positive externality the results lead to significantly higher donor participation rates that are consistent with other empirical observations. Alternatively, if the game is framed as a contribution to the avoidance of an equivalent negative externality, the results are more consistent with what one would observe in the pure altruism Nash equilibrium. Hence, the evidence does not appear to be entirely consistent with the impure altruism model either.

Glazer and Konrad provide a third motive for charitable giving that is consistent with the empirical evidence (1996). They model charitable giving as a signaling game where charity demonstrates wealth. The desire or motive to demonstrate wealth has long standing in economic analysis. It was subject to biting scrutiny in 1899 by Thorstein Veblen in *The Theory of the Leisure Class*, where he argued that conspicuous consumption, conspicuous leisure, and conspicuous waste are all manifestations of the desire to demonstrate wealth (1973). Glazer and Konrad argue that conspicuous behavior is an inefficient wealth signal for a variety of reasons: it has negative social connotations; the behavior is not readily observed by many people[5] or by those who matter to the donor who wishes to demonstrate wealth; and conspicuous behavior can easily be mimicked by people who are not truly wealthy (1996, 1019–20).

On the other hand, charity is approved by society; is verified by an independent party so it is difficult to mimic; can be targeted to impress the right peer group; and crowding out of donations by lower income people who do not experience a warm glow from donations raises the average income level of those who donate, which enhances the wealth signal. Glazer and Konrad report empirical evidence that strongly suggests that signaling wealth through charity is a dominant motive for many donors (1996, 1020–21). First, despite the admonition by Pope at the beginning of this chapter, the number of anonymous donors is quite small. They constitute less than 5 percent in most cases. If recognition was not the motive for charity, the proportion of anonymous donors would be higher.[6] Second, charities routinely classify donations by such classifications as 'silver', 'gold', or 'platinum' gifts, where each level is defined over a range of gift values. In most cases, the average gift in each classification is approximately equal to the lower bound for that classification; that is, most donors contribute the minimum required to qualify for each classification. These results are not consistent with the pure and impure altruism theory of charity.

Signaling as a motive for charity does not depend on the increased provision of the public good, since the public good need not enter the donor's utility function[7] in order to induce the donor to contribute. The donor's utility function under pure signaling is

$$u^i = u^i(x, s),$$

where s is the signal purchased by the donor. Note the signal is a private good. While our discussion of signaling in this section is motivated by desires to demonstrate wealth, that may not be the only personal attribute that donors wish to demonstrate by their donation. For example, the desire to be noticed by a specific group or to be associated with that group can convey status to the donor, and that status can generate positive utility for the donor. Or, donors may wish to signal public concern even when they do not derive personal benefits from the public good. These motivations are given formal attention by Harbaugh (1998). Clearly, the donor may have mixed motives for the donation. He may be an impure altruist who derives utility from the production of the public good and utility from the signal. However, it is clear the signaling donor cannot be described as a pure altruist.

Of equal interest is what signaling theory suggests for the behavior of institutions who receive donations from benefactors who seek to reveal their wealth or increase their status. The pure signaling donor will donate, whether that donation results in an increase in the public good or not. However, the institution must be able to attract the attention of the audience that donors intend to signal and market competition for these donations among competing institutions will lead the institutions to produce the public goods preferred by the audience preferred by the optimal donor set. Successful charities have long lists of respected benefactors, benefactors who will be aware of gifts given by any donor desiring to signal wealth or enhance their status. Given that different audiences convey different status, there will be different charitable niches for different institutions.

Finally, there is the well known tolerance among donors for institutions that have high fundraising costs. If donors are exclusively interested in the provision of public goods or they derive a warm glow from donations, they should prefer institutions with low fundraising costs. Alternatively, if a significant proportion of those fundraising costs arise because the institution publicizes the gifts and those who give, then the signaling donor is more likely to tolerate high fundraising cost.

Since signaling poverty has little social value, the foregoing suggests that fundraising costs per dollar raised should be an increasing function of average donor income. Benefactors who contribute to higher education institutions at the bottom of the academic hierarchy are interested in the provision of public goods and/or the warm glow from giving; hence, they expect the receiving institutions to minimize their fundraising costs. Alternatively, benefactors who contribute to institutions at the top of the hierarchy expect institutions to facilitate their desire to signal wealth and status. The results reported by Tuckman and Chang are consistent with these conclusions (1998). They consider data drawn from 12746 IRS Form 990s from 1988. The observations cover charities in 26 different charitable sectors. In each case, the average fundraising expenditure as a percentage of total revenues is higher than the median fundraising expenditure as a percentage of total revenues. This suggests that charities that raise the most money spend larger percentages to raise those funds. To the extent that average donor income is higher for the most successful charities, the fact that the average percentages exceed the median percentages suggests expenditure proportions rise with average donor income. In the case of education institutions, Tuckman and Chang report that the average percentage is 14.8 percent and the median percentage is 10.8 percent (1998, 217).

The anomalies produced by capital campaign announcements, seed money, and leadership gifts can be explained in a pure altruism model when there are non-convexities in the production of the public good. Andreoni considers a pure altruism capital campaign model with three phases: the preparation phase, the nucleus phase, and the public campaign (1998, 1188–90). The most important strategic assumption is that donations must reach a threshold level, say D, before any public good can be produced.

> Unless there is a single large benefactor who is willing to guarantee this minimum quality, an equilibrium will spring up at zero contributions, even though another equilibrium exists at an interior point. Until the charity is sure to reach the threshold, no one has an incentive to give, meaning, of course, that without certain efforts the threshold may never be exceeded. (1998, 1189–90)

These results are most applicable to capital campaigns that are targeted to produce a specific real asset, such as a new sports complex, or to launch an entirely new charity. They are less applicable to continuing capital campaigns where the goal is to expand existing output or to raise the quality of that output. In these later cases, the marginal productivity of the initial dollar donated is positive, whereas the marginal productivity of the initial dollar donated is zero in the non-convex case. Andreoni argues that similar results can be obtained if there are non-convexities in donor preferences such that the campaign cannot 'succeed' unless a threshold contribution level is attained (1998, 1211).

The capital campaign anomalies can also be resolved in a signaling model. Asymmetric information regarding the quality of the services provided by the institution and the cost of acquiring quality information suggest that a leadership donation by a prominent donor or donors reveals information about the institution's quality. In a sequential fundraising game, Lise Vesterlund proves that equilibrium with announcements is optimal and that the asymmetric information leads to higher contributions to high quality charities than would occur if quality were common knowledge (2003, 650–51). The announcements serve as a separating signal between high quality institutions and low quality institutions. The high quality institutions will prefer to announce and the low quality institutions will prefer not to announce. The donation distribution effect away from low quality institutions towards high quality institutions occurs because the absence of announcements from low quality institutions raises the cost of donating to those institutions relative to the cost of donating to high quality institutions.

4.4   FUNDRAISING OBJECTIVE FUNCTIONS

From a social perspective, it matters whether the objective of charitable fundraising is revenue maximization or net revenue maximization. Charities that maximize revenues during fundraising display an indifference to the cost of fundraising, while charities that are maximizing net revenue also minimize the cost of fundraising. Minimizing the cost of fundraising is consistent with a charity whose ultimate purpose is the production of public goods, while revenue maximization is evidence of an agency problem. Tuckman and Chang note that the

> *Philanthropy Journal* reported in its October 20, 1997, issue that professional fundraising solicitors raised nearly $50 million in 1996 for non-profits in North Carolina. These solicitors kept $34 million for themselves to cover fees and costs. (1998, 211)

Such results cannot be in the public interest and they highlight the agency problem that exists with all fundraising. Professional fundraisers, whether they are employed within the charity or are outside contractors, know they will be evaluated on the basis of how much money they raise and that fundraising costs are a constraint on how much they can raise in any given campaign. It is not uncommon for fundraisers to remind their critics that it takes money to raise money.

Susan Rose-Ackerman considers the impact of lump-sum government grants on charities managed by administrators with 'strong philosophical or professional commitments' (1987, 810). She finds that these grants make the institution less accountable to private donors and they reduce the institution's fundraising activities. The administrator's utility function and the donor's donation function both depend on the quantity and the quality of the services provided. For each quantity and quality combination, the institution maximizes total donations less solicitation costs. The optimal solution from the net revenue maximization is employed in the second stage where the administrator's utility function is maximized subject to the net revenue constraint and the cost of producing the services provided. She concludes that her results can 'explain why the current interest in expanding the revenue base of non–profit organizations coincides with a drop in their public support, and it also suggests that a corresponding shift in service mix will occur' (1987, 820).

Although Rose-Ackerman is writing in 1987 her findings seem appropriate today with respect to public higher education which has 'progressed' from state supported institutions to state located institutions as their public support has declined. The state institutions are relying more heavily on private resources each year and there do appear to be some noticeable changes in their mission as private donors increase their influence. As private money comes to dominate decision making at public institutions, one can expect the administrator's philosophical and professional commitments will come into closer alignment with the philosophical and professional commitments of the donors. This may or may not be in the public interest.

The purpose of fundraising in the non-profit sector is to provide additional resources to support the private provision of public goods. It follows naturally that the objective function for fundraising is to maximize the surplus created by total donations less fundraising costs. The following model is a variation on Rose-Ackerman's charity model (1987). Assume donors are purchasing wealth or status signals and the individual donors donate more as the quality of the signal increases. Hence, the *i*th donor's donation function is

$$D(S^i, i) \geq 0.$$

where S^i is the quality of the signal and $\partial D/\partial S^i \equiv D_s > 0$. Assume there are diminishing returns to the quality of the signal, such that $\partial^2 D/\partial S^i \partial S^i \equiv D_{ss} < 0$.

Let the quality of the signal be the product of the institution's quality reputation, q^r, and the 'demonstration expense' incurred by the institution on behalf of the *i*th donor, s^i. The demonstration expense represents the financial effort made by the institution to recognize the contributions made by individual donors. These expenditures consist of such activities as listing donors' names in the annual development report, featuring the donor prominently in college publications, or special charity events honoring a single donor. Thus, the quality of the *i*th donor's signal is

$$S^i \equiv s^i q^r.$$

This formulation assumes the institution's demonstration expense and quality reputation are complementary in the signal production.

Suppose each donor's donation function can be rank ordered according to the size of their donation given a common demonstration expense $D(sq^r, i) \geq D(sq^r, j) \forall i$ and j. If the institution spends the same amount for donor demonstration on each donor, the expected donations are known. Assume the number of potential donors is N, the number of solicited donors is n, no donor contributes unless the donor is solicited, and that the cost per solicitation is c. Given these assumptions, the fundraising objective function is

$$\max R(s^i, n) = \sum_0^n D(s^i q^r, i) - cn - \sum_0^n s^i. \tag{4.1}$$

The first order conditions for this objective function are

$$R_s = D_s(s^i q^r, i)q^r - 1 = 0 \forall\, i \tag{4.2}$$
$$R_n = D_s(s^n q^r, n) - c - s^n = 0.$$

Diminishing marginal returns with respect to the signal in the donation functions ensure that the second order conditions will be satisfied.

The interpretation of these first order conditions is straightforward. The solicitations are rank ordered according to donations, and the marginal solicitation occurs where the donation equals the marginal solicitation cost plus the demonstration expense. Demonstration expenditures across donors are allocated such that the marginal dollar spent on demonstration for each donor yields $1/q^r$ dollars in donations. Demonstration expenditures are allocated across donors such that the marginal productivity of the last dollar spent in terms of increased donations is the same across all donors.

Donors who give more are rewarded with higher demonstration expenditures. Given

$$D(sq^r, i) > D(sq^r, j) \,\forall s,$$

then

$$\int_0^s D_s(zq^r, i)dz > \int_0^s D_s(zq^r, j)dz \,\forall s.$$

Therefore,

$$D_s(sq^r, i) > D_s(sq^r, j) \,\forall s.$$

Then, from (4.2) it follows that

$$D_s(s^i q^r, i) = D_s(s^j q^r, j), \tag{4.3}$$

at the optimum. Equation (4.3) suggests that the demonstration expense for the jth donor must be less than the demonstration expense for the ith donor.

Therefore,

Proposition 4.1) Demonstration expenses per donor are an increasing function of the donor's contribution.

The marginal donation functions per unit of signal are plotted in Figure 4.2.

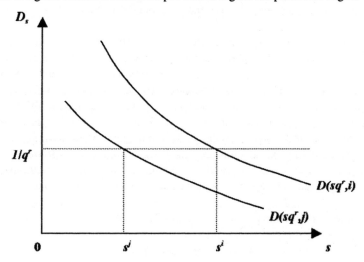

Figure 4.2   Marginal donation productivity by donor

Substituting the optimal solutions into the objective function, the indirect net revenue function is

$$R(c, q'),\qquad(4.4)$$

and total differentiation of the net revenue function with respect to the institution's quality reputation and with respect to the cost of solicitation yields

$$dR/dq' = \sum_{0}^{n} D_s(s^i q', i)s^i > 0$$

and

$$dR/dc = -n < 0.$$

Therefore, we have the following proposition:

Proposition 4.2) Net charitable revenues are an increasing function of the institution's quality reputation and a decreasing function of solicitation costs.

The indirect net revenue function in (4.4) establishes the link between the institution's quality reputation and its control of academic subsidies. As the institution's quality reputation rises, its net charitable revenues rise with it. This net revenue function is employed in the intergenerational reputation model in Chapter 5.

The empirical evidence with respect to fundraising objective functions is ambiguous. Khanna and Sandler present evidence from UK charities that suggest they are net revenue maximizers, while some of the charitable sectors appear to raise funds short of net revenue maximization (2000, 1545). In an earlier study, Posnett and Sandler report similar results that suggest UK charities are net revenue maximizers and note that Weisbrod and Dominguez (1986) found that US charities tend to be revenue maximizers. Posnett and Sandler find that UK charities 'raise funds until the marginal influence of fund-raising on donations is one' while Weisbrod and Dominguez find that US fundraising is 'carried to the point where its marginal influence on donations is zero' (1989, 88).

The objective function for revenue maximization is

$$\max R^m(s^i, n) = \sum_0^n D(s^i q^r, i)$$

and the first order conditions are

$$R^m_s = D_s(s^i q^r, i)q^r = 0 \, \forall i$$
$$R^m_n = D_s(s^n q^r, n) = 0.$$

The first order conditions for net revenue maximization in equation (4.2) can be re-written as

$$D_s(s^i q^r, i) = 1/q^r \, \forall i.$$

Since the institution's quality reputation is a real valued index that is monotonically increasing in reputation, the marginal influence of fundraising on donations will also be approximately equal to zero if the institution is maximizing net revenues. Therefore,

Proposition 4.3) High quality charities carry fundraising activities to the point where the marginal influence on donations is approximately zero regardless of whether their objective is to maximize revenues or net revenues.

The foregoing proposition suggests that it is difficult to empirically separate revenue maximization from net revenue maximization. It will require careful controls for differences in quality. The question is important because revenue maximization is indifferent to the cost of fundraising, while net revenue maximization also requires the minimization of the cost of fundraising.

4.5 CONTRACTING AND ACADEMIC SUBSIDIES

The theory of charity suggests that benefactors contribute for at least three reasons: they wish to increase the provision of public goods, they derive utility from the act of giving, and/or they wish to signal wealth or status. In higher education, the ultimate recipients of this charity are the students. Theoretically, there is no reason why benefactors and students cannot contract directly. While this happens occasionally, it is the exception rather than the rule. Most benefactors contract with intermediaries who act as their agents in the distribution and administration of academic subsidies. The agents are typically either foundations or higher education institutions.

It is useful to consider why benefactors rarely contract directly with students. First, by contracting with institutions the donor can direct the contribution to the targeted audience if he is signaling or to the most efficient provider of the public good if he is motivated by the provision of public goods. The donor loses control if he contracts directly with individual students. If he is interested in signaling or in the efficient provision of public goods, the subsidy may ultimately go to an institution that is neither a good signal nor an efficient provider of public goods.

Rather than give the student the option of where she attends college, the donor ties the student to a specific institution. In this case, it is less costly to hire the institution as his agent and forgo contracting with individual students. Therefore, the second reason why donors do not contract directly with students is that the transaction costs are higher than contracting with an agent who administers the subsidy. The institution can take advantage of returns to scale in the administration of subsidies by contracting with multiple donors. These economies of scale are unavailable to individual donors. Furthermore, higher education institutions can take advantage of important economies of scope as well. The higher education institution must recruit students, and considerable economies of scope are available if it can simultaneously match students with donors.

The third reason why donors rarely contract directly with students is because individual contracting leads to higher monitoring costs. Once a student receives a subsidy, there are moral hazard problems that can only be resolved by monitoring each student's academic progress. For an individual donor the monitoring costs for multiple students at multiple institutions will be high. In addition, the donor may not possess the skills required to monitor academic progress. On the other hand, higher education institutions must monitor students' progress in order to maintain academic standards, so the marginal cost of monitoring for the purpose of efficiently using subsidies is approximately zero.

Finally, donors and students face similar problems with the services provided by higher education institutions. Neither donors nor students know what they are purchasing before the student enrolls. Higher education is an experience good with long lags before the quality of the experience is revealed. Assuming the wealthy donor's choice with respect to charitable contributions reflects the same preferences he expresses with respect to private consumption goods, the wealthy donor's choice of which institution he chooses to support signals high quality education to prospective students. This signal is of particular value to students if the donor is an alumnus, since it confirms that the donor's personal experience was a high quality experience. Similarly, the institution's ability to recruit high quality students signals high quality education to prospective donors. The interaction between these two reinforcing signals over extended periods of time builds both the reputation for quality and the means to achieve that quality, adding further credence to the institution's claim that it is a high quality producer.

There is a downside to these arrangements, however. The student's oversight role with respect to the current quality of services rendered is weakened because she does not control the compensation flowing to the institution. Under these circumstances, it is easier for the institution to engage in short-run quality cheating and agency rent maximization. If the charitable support is as mobile as the student, then she can withhold compensation if there is a quality of service issue. When the charitable support is tied to the institution, the institution can simply replace an unhappy student with a more pliable student customer. The current trend towards financial aid that is attached to the student rather than the institution should help to improve the quality of instruction. This is essentially the same argument as made by those who advocate school vouchers for primary and secondary schools.

NOTES

1. For a recent example of this justification for endowments see the endowment study prepared by TIAA–CREF for NACUBO (2004).
2. The cases they report are Alleghany Health Education in 2000 where $52 million was diverted and The Bishop Estate in 1997 where part of a $10 billion endowment was diverted.

3.   Some charities are pure charities rather than donative commercial non-profits and do not have any client driven revenues.
4.   See Glazer and Konrad for a more complete list of this literature (1996, 1019).
5.   Unless the behavior is truly outrageous, in which case it may defeat the purpose intended.
6.   A prominent exception to this trend is the $50 million dollar anonymous gift recently pledged to Middlebury College (*The Chronicle of Higher Education*, May 7, 2004). The gift is the largest in the college's history. There was an additional $10 million dollar anonymous gift that was used to match part of the first gift.
7.   If the public good does enter the donor's utility function and/or the donor derives a warm glow from giving, the donor has multiple motives for charity.

5. An enterprise model

CASSIO Reputation, reputation, reputation! O, I have lost my reputation! I
have lost the immortal part of myself, and what remains is bestial.

Othello Act 2, Scene 3
William Shakespeare (1564 – 1616)

5.1 MOTIVATING REPUTATION

This chapter contains a formal model of the representative institution, where
the institution's long-run objective is to maximize quality reputation. Since the
institution's quality reputation depends on the accomplishments of its graduates, the incentive compatible short-run objective is to maximize expected
alumni quality. Optimal[1] pricing, capacity, and quality choices are derived
from the model. The institution can affect alumni success through the quality
of the students it recruits, the quality of their academic experience, and the
career support the alumni receive after graduation.

As the number of successful alumni increases, the institution attracts greater
endowment through the market for control of academic subsidies. The market
for academic subsidies consists of benefactors and higher education institutions. Since education is a quasi-public good and benefactors wish to signal
wealth or status, benefactors are willing to supply subsidies to students. There
are important economies of distribution and monitoring that lead benefactors
to employ institutions as agents who control the endowments that generate annual subsidies. Larger endowments enable the institution to attract better students in a reinforcing loop. In the long run, the institution's quality reputation
is determined by the quantity of academic subsidy the institution controls.

The results obtained from the formal model have specific policy implications for the institution. The model also yields explicit multiple definitions of
capacity, long-run/short-run financial equilibrium, and investment in academic
reputation. The graphical representation of long-run stationary state equilibrium yields the strategic analysis of pricing and enrollment policies.

5.2 PLANNING PERIODS

Assume there are three planning periods: the annual enrollment cycle, the short run, and the long run. Following traditional theory, the long run is the period of time required to change all of the inputs, including academic reputation. The services provided by higher education are experience goods, where the quality of the experience is not revealed for as long as a generation. Therefore, the long run in higher education is intergenerational.

In the short run, at least one factor is fixed. Clearly, academic reputation is fixed in the short run as is traditional plant capacity. It may also be argued that overlapping tenure contracts imply that staffing is at least a quasi-fixed input in the short run. Hence, the institution makes its pricing and enrollment decisions in the face of high fixed costs in the short run. During the annual enrollment cycle, physical plant, staff, and permanent enrollment are constant.

In the analysis that follows, we consider these planning periods in order. The purpose of the annual enrollment cycle model is to derive the institution's quality adjusted expected enrollment demand function. The expected enrollment demand function is dependent on tuition/fees, the average scholarship budget, student quality, and the institution's academic reputation. This demand function is employed in the short-run and long-run models where the institution chooses the decision variables appropriate to the planning period.

The Annual Enrollment Cycle: Selecting Student Quality

The annual student recruiting cycle is subject to binding[2] financial, enrollment, and reputation constraints. All recruiting takes place during this cycle and is subject to these constraints. The institution allocates scholarships (tuition discounts) among the pool of admitted students in order to enroll the best possible class. The number of admitted students depends on the institution's tuition and fees schedule, T, and the institution's quality reputation, q^r.
Let

a be the number of admitted students,
p^i be the probability the ith student will enroll,
s^i be the scholarship/discount offered to the ith student, and
q^i be the quality metric for the ith student.

Then,

$$a = a(T, q^r), \qquad (5.1)$$

where $\partial a/\partial T \equiv a_T < 0$ and $\partial a/\partial q^r \equiv a_r > 0$. Similarly the probability that the ith student will enroll is

$$p^i = p^i(T, s^i, q^i, q^r). \tag{5.2}$$

The probability that an individual student will enroll is increasing in the discount offered to the student and in the institution's quality reputation

$$\partial p^i/\partial s^i \equiv p^i_s > 0 \text{ and } \partial p^i/\partial q^r \equiv p^i_r > 0.$$

The enrollment probability is decreasing in tuition and fees and in the quality of the ith student:

$$\partial p^i/\partial T \equiv p^i_T < 0 \text{ and } \partial p^i/\partial q^i \equiv p^i_q < 0.$$

The demographic distribution of gifted students and the fact that they are heavily recruited implies the probability that the ith student will enroll declines as the quality of that student increases.

It follows immediately that expected enrollment is

$$\bar{e} = \sum_1^{a(T, q^r)} p^i(T, s^i, q^i, q^r), \tag{5.3}$$

and expected total quality is

$$Q = \sum_1^{a(.)} p^i (.)q^i. \tag{5.4}$$

Similarly, the expected total budget for scholarships (tuition discounts) is

$$\bar{S} = \sum_1^{a(.)} p^i (.)s^i. \tag{5.5}$$

Equations (5.3), (5.4), and (5.5) provide the foundation for the institution's enrollment cycle objective function.

Maximizing Total Quality

If s is the average scholarship (tuition discount) and e is enrollment, then a total scholarship budget is implied by

$$S \equiv se. \tag{5.6}$$

Every pair in the s, e space implies a scholarship budget. Given T, q^r, an enrollment target, e, and the scholarship budget in (5.6), the institution maximizes total quality by allocating the scholarship budget across the pool of admitted students. Formally, the objective function for the enrollment cycle is

$$\max \overline{Q} = \sum_1^{a(.)} p^i(.)q^i + \beta[S - \sum_1^{a(.)} p^i(.)s^i] +$$

$$\lambda[e - \sum_1^{a(.)} p^i(.)]. \tag{5.7}$$

The Kuhn–Tucker conditions for this objective function are

$$\overline{Q}_{si} = p^i_s q^i - \beta[p^i + s^i p^i_s] - \lambda p^i_s \leq 0, \tag{5.8a}$$
$$s^i \geq 0, s^i \overline{Q}_{si} = 0$$

$$\overline{Q}_\beta = S - \sum_1^{a(.)} p^i (.) s^i = 0 \tag{5.8b}$$

$$\overline{Q}_\lambda = e - \sum_1^{a(.)} p^i (.) = 0. \tag{5.8c}$$

The envelope theorem and equation (5.6) reveals that

$$d\overline{Q}/dS = \beta > 0$$
$$\text{and}$$
$$d\overline{Q}/de = \beta s + \lambda > 0.$$

Hence, β^{-1} is the marginal opportunity cost of quality in terms of forgone tuition revenues and $\beta s + \lambda$ is the incremental effect of one more enrolled student on total quality.

Rewriting equation (5.8a) reveals:

$$s^i[1 + 1/\eta^i]/[q^i - \lambda] \leq \beta^{-1} \; \forall \; i, \tag{5.9}$$

where η^i is the elasticity of p^i with respect to s^i. Then, for all i and j such that $s^i > 0$ and $s^j > 0$, it follows that

$$s^i[1 + p^i/s^i p^i_s]/q^i - \lambda] =$$
$$s^j[1 + p^j/s^j p^j_s]/q^j - \lambda] = \tag{5.10}$$
$$\beta^{-1} > 0$$

Equations (5.9) and (5.10) represent the analogue for price discrimination in the quality maximization model. The numerators in the ratios to the left of the equals sign in (5.10) are positive, while the denominators are positive if and only if $q^i > \lambda$. Therefore, for all i and j such that $s^i > 0$ and $s^j > 0$, it follows that student quality must exceed λ. Lambda (λ) is the highest quality student who does not receive a tuition discount, each student whose quality is less than or equal to lambda is a full pay student. Given tuition and fees and the quality reputation, the institution chooses tuition discounts for each admitted student such that the marginal quality productivity is equal to the marginal cost of quality.

Equation (5.10) leads to the following proposition.

Proposition 5.1) Optimal Scholarship Allocation. If $q^j = q^i$, $\eta^j = \eta^i$, and $p^j = p^i$; then $s^j = s^i$. If $q^j > q^i$, $\eta^j = \eta^i$, and $p^j = p^i$; then $s^j > s^i$. If $q^j = q^i$ and $\eta^j > \eta^i$; then $s^j > s^i$. If $q^j = q^i$, $\eta^j = \eta^i$, and $p^j > p^i$; then $s^j < s^i$. If $q^i \leq \lambda$, then $s^i = 0$.

Given the same student quality, enrollment probability and elasticity, the tuition discount offered to each student will be the same. If everything else is the same except for the fact that the quality of the jth student is higher than the quality of the ith student; then, the tuition discount offered to the jth student will be higher than the tuition discount offered to the ith student. The higher quality student gets a larger discount. If everything else is the same except for the fact that the elasticity of the enrollment probability is higher; then the discount offered to the jth student will be higher than the discount offered to the ith student. If everything else is the same except for the fact that the probability the jth student will enroll is higher than the probability the ith student will enroll, then the discount offered to the jth student will be lower than the discount offered to the ith student. These results are the same as Ehrenberg and Sherman's (1984) results and similar to Rothschild and White's (1995) result.

Enrollment Demand

Let $\hat{s}^i \equiv s^i(T, s, e, q^r)$ be the solutions to the foregoing optimization problem. After substitution into equation (5.4), expected total quality is

$$Q \equiv Q(T, s, e, q^r)$$

and average quality per enrolled student is

$$q \equiv Q(T, s, e, q^r)/e$$
$$\equiv q(T, s, e, q^r). \tag{5.11}$$

Average student quality is decreasing in T and e and increasing in s and q^r. These results follow from the fact that individual student enrollment probabilities decrease in tuition and fees, decrease in student quality, increase in tuition discounts, and increase in quality reputation. The set of all possible q's in equation (5.11) represents a map of constant average quality contours in s, e space.

The enrollment demand function[3] conditional on a constant average quality is the implicit solution to equation (5.11),

$$e = e(T, s, q, q').$$ (5.12)

Since the enrollment probability for each student is decreasing in tuition and fees and decreasing in student quality, the expected enrollment function is decreasing in tuition and fees, $\partial e/\partial T \equiv e_T < 0$, and decreasing in average student quality, $\partial e/\partial q \equiv e_q < 0$. Expected enrollment is also an increasing function of the average scholarship per student, $\partial e/\partial s \equiv e_s > 0$, and increasing in quality reputation, $\partial e/\partial q' \equiv e_r > 0$.

As in Figure 5.1, constant quality expected enrollment contours are projected in the two-space defined by s and e. Average student quality increases as we move northwest in the s, e space. Average student quality increases if we hold e constant and increase s. Or, if we hold s constant and increase e, average student quality declines.

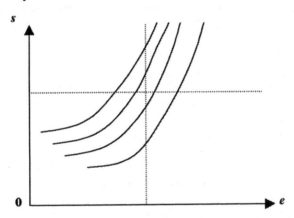

Figure 5.1   Constant quality enrollment demand contours

If the representative institution experiences diminishing marginal returns to tuition discounting, then the constant quality expected enrollment contours will be convex to the origin. Since $e_s > 0$, diminishing marginal returns to discounting implies that $e_{ss} < 0$, and that constant quality e increases at a decreasing rate in s. It is useful to think of this surface as a production function where q is the output and s and e are the inputs, given the constraints imposed by T and q'. In this sense, given an s, e combination any scholarship allocation that yields an average student quality below this surface is x–inefficient.

Quality Reputation

Non-price competition within an oligopoly suggests two effects from improvements in product quality: the successful firm experiences an increase in market share, and product differentiation reduces the effect of substitutes. The demand curve shifts out and becomes more inelastic. The decrease in elasticity reflects greater brand loyalty and increased pricing power for the firm. An increase in quality reputation has similar effects in higher education.

Consider the three-space described by q, s, and e, which is illustrated in Figure 5.1. The iso-quality contours in Figure 5.1 imply a three-dimensional surface, where the quality axis is perpendicular to the page at the origin. The locus of the quality surface depends on the institution's quality reputation, q', which is fixed in the short-run. As quality reputation increases, the surface shifts up for all s and e pairs. In other words, as the institution's quality reputation increases:

1. the institution can achieve higher expected quality for any s, e pair (the quality productivity of the constant scholarship budget and constant enrollment increases);
2. it can attain the same quality and lower its scholarship budget (decreasing s while holding e and q constant);
3. it can attain the same expected quality with a constant average scholarship, while increasing enrollment (hold q and s constant while increasing e); or,
4. any combination of the foregoing options.

In the first instance, net student revenues remain constant as quality increases. The opportunity cost in terms of foregone revenue associated with the increase in quality is zero. In the second case, the institution achieves the same quality level with higher revenues, and in the third case, quality is constant and revenues increase as enrollment increases. Overall, an increase in reputation increases quality productivity for all combinations of s and e.

The increase in quality reputation may also decrease the number and/or the effectiveness of the available substitutes. The impact of this change is reflected by marginal returns to tuition discounting. If the change increases the marginal returns to tuition discounting, the iso-quality contours in Figure 5.1 become less convex. Holding q constant, convexity implies that e increases at a decreasing rate as s is increased. The quality frontier may be convex for the representative institution, but it may not be convex for the institutions at the top of the quality hierarchy.

Consider the point s^o, e^o in Figure 5.2 and assume the constant average quality demand contours are right angles at that point. If an increase in s yields no increase in constant quality enrollment and a reduction in s causes a complete collapse of enrollment, the institution has no pricing power measured by tuition discounting and it is an average scholarship 'taker'. It could be inferred from this condition that the institution has no brand loyalty with respect to its quality reputation and that enrollment depends entirely upon net price.

Alternatively, if any increase in s yields an infinite increase in constant quality enrollment and any reduction in s yields no change in enrollment, the institution's pricing power measured by tuition discounting is total. In this latter case, the institution's pricing power is limited only by the size of the market. The institution can become the sole provider of higher education in its quality niche. Or, if the institution with complete pricing power has a constant target enrollment, it can achieve that enrollment target with the same average student quality by choosing any average tuition discount it desires. The foregoing limiting cases suggest that pricing power increases as marginal returns to discounting increase.

Clearly, most institutions populate the interior between the two pricing power extremes. Therefore, an interesting empirical hypothesis is:

Proposition 5.2) Market Share and Pricing Power. As the institution's quality reputation increases, its potential market share increases and the marginal returns to tuition discounting in terms of constant quality enrollment increase.

Since the elite institutions leave returns to scale in enrollment unexploited (as will be demonstrated in the following subsection), it is clear that the objective of prestige maximization is not greater scale. This analysis suggests that the primary competitive reward to quality reputation and prestige is greater pricing power measured by the ease with which the institution attracts more enrollment of the same quality with higher tuition discounts. For instance, if the institution experiences increasing marginal returns to tuition discounts this suggests it is an elite institution. For this institution, a small increase in the scholarship budget will significantly increase enrollment, which creates higher selectivity with a constant enrollment target.

5.3 MAXIMIZING REPUTATION

The quality dependent expected enrollment demand curve from the annual enrollment cycle provides the foundation for reputation maximization in this section. Since the quality function is the optimal solution for student quality maximization during the annual enrollment cycle, it ensures that the long-run stationary state solution derived in this section is based on the optimal distribution of scholarships across admitted students. During the annual enrollment cycle the institution maximizes the quality of each class enrolled.[4]

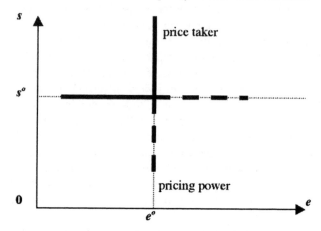

Figure 5.2   Pricing power and returns to discounting

Let $R(q')$ be the net external revenue function derived in Chapter 4, equation (4.3). The external revenue function consists of such revenues as endowment income, grants, annual giving, and auxiliary income. Let $C(e, q')$ be the average variable cost per student[5] derived in Chapter 3, equation (3.13), and F be all other costs (excluding scholarships), such as institutional support, plant maintenance, and auxiliary enterprises. In the short-run F includes fixed costs. The 'other costs' are not fixed costs in the long run; they are threshold costs per period. Threshold costs represent minimum production costs that must be incurred per period before any output takes place. If $e=0$ in the long run, then $F=0$, but for all $e>0$, $F>0$ and is constant. The average variable cost function, $C(e, q')$, is the cost function derived in Chapter 3 during the production cycle, where the institution's objective is to maximize human capital production using the peer production technology. From the foregoing variable definitions, the representative institution's fundamental budget equation is

$$B(T, s, e, q, q') \equiv (T - s)e + R(q') - eC(e, q') - F \qquad (5.13)$$

External revenue and average cost are assumed to be increasing functions of the institution's quality reputation, $\partial R/\partial q' \equiv R_r > 0$ and $\partial C/\partial q' \equiv C_r > 0$. Since $C(e, q')$ is the average cost function, increasing returns to scale in enrollment imply that $\partial C/\partial e \equiv C_e < 0$. Therefore, average cost per student declines as enrollment increases, and increases as the institution's quality reputation increases.

The fundamental budget equation depicted in equation (5.13) represents the economic budget, not the accounting budget. It differs from the accounting budget in two important ways. First, the total cost function, $eC(e, q') + F$, represents the least cost required to educate students, while accounting costs may include both the foregoing costs and rents captured by administrators, faculty, or board members. Secondly, institutions rarely report deficits. Whenever expenditures exceed revenues, the institution increases the payout on the endowment in order to cover the deficit. The accounting budget is balanced in this case, but the economic budget is in deficit even if there are no rents being extracted. Therefore, accounting budgets are not reliable indicators of an institution's financial well-being. The significance of this distinction is that all of the financial equilibriums derived in the following refer to equilibriums where the economic budget is in balance.

I assume quality reputation is an increasing function of the quality of the students the institution enrolls. Higher student quality leads to more successful alumni, and more successful alumni leads to a higher quality reputation. Quality reputation in time period t is an increasing function of expected alumni quality in time period $t-1$. Hence,

$$q_t^r \equiv \theta_t (q_{t-1}),$$

and the law of motion would suggest $\partial q_t^r / \partial q_{t-1} \equiv \theta'_t > 0$. The average student quality function comes from equation (5.11) in section 5.2 and the constrained quality function for time period t is:

$$K_t \equiv q(T_t, s_t, e_t, q_t^r) + \qquad\qquad (5.14)$$
$$\lambda_t[(T_t - s_t)e_t + R(q_t^r) - e_t C(e_t, q_t^r) - F],$$

where $q_t^r \equiv \theta_t(q_{t-1})$. In an intergenerational model, the objective function is:

$$\max \overline{K} = K_t + \alpha K_{t+1}, \qquad\qquad (5.15)$$

where α is the discount factor. The objective function in (5.15) is maximized with respect to T_t, s_t, e_t and λ_t.

The first order conditions for the intergenerational objective function are evaluated at the long-run stationary state equilibrium where all time-subscripted variables are the same. The stationary state equilibrium first order conditions are:

$$\overline{K_T} = q_T\{1 + \alpha\theta' [q_r + \lambda(R_r - eC_r)]\} + \lambda e = 0 \qquad (5.16a)$$
$$\underline{K_s} = q_s\{1 + \alpha\theta' [q_r + \lambda(R_r - eC_r)]\} - \lambda e = 0 \qquad (5.16b)$$
$$K_e = q_e\{1 + \alpha\theta' [q_r + \lambda(R_r - eC_r)]\} + \qquad (5.16c)$$
$$\lambda[(T - s) - eC_e - C] = 0$$
$$\overline{K_\lambda} = (T - s)e + R(q') - C(e, q')e - F = 0 \qquad (5.16d)$$

The second order sufficient conditions require the principal minors of the bordered Hessian determinant must alternate in sign pattern beginning with positive.

After some manipulation of the equations in (5.16a) to (5.16d) and substitution for the derivatives of q with respect to T, s, and e, the four necessary conditions can be reduced to the following three necessary conditions

$$-e_T = e_s \qquad (5.17a)$$
$$[(T-s) - eCe - C]/e = (e_s)^{-1} \qquad (5.17b)$$
$$(T-s)e + R(q') - C(e, q')e - F = 0. \qquad (5.17c)$$

Since these necessary conditions are expressed in terms of the constant quality enrollment demand function in (5.12), they lead to a more intuitive interpretation.

The set of necessary conditions in (5.17) is the same for the short run and the long run. In the short run, the institution maximizes average student quality subject to a break-even budget constraint. That objective function is the same as equation (5.14) and the necessary conditions for maximizing equation (5.14) are the same as those in (5.17). Hence, this set of equations must hold in both the short run and the long run, or the institution is not in financial equilibrium during either planning period.

Equation (5.17b) is a traditional tangency condition. It suggests that the slope of the constant budget contour, $((T-s)-eC_e-C)/e$, must equal the slope of the constant quality enrollment contour, $(e_s)^{-1}$. Equation (5.17c) identifies the break-even constant budget contour as the unique budget contour where stationary state equilibrium is found. This equilibrium is illustrated in Figure 5.3. Hence,

> Proposition 5.3) Equilibrium: short-run and long-run financial equilibrium are found where the institution enrolls the highest possible average student quality consistent with a break-even budget constraint.

All of the constant budget contours lying below the break-even contour represent loci where the budget is in surplus, and the size of that surplus rises as we move southeast in the s,e space. Similarly, all of the constant budget contours lying above the break-even contour represent loci where the budget is in deficit, and the size of the deficit increases as we move northwest in the s,e space. The average student quality increases as we travel northwest in the s,e space. The tangency condition represents the highest quality students the institution can recruit subject to a break-even budget. There are an infinite number of s,e combinations where the budget is in balance, but only one of these combinations is optimal. The optimal solution at point 'a' in Figure 5.3

is the institution's financial equilibrium solution as implied by Hopkins and
Massy (1981).

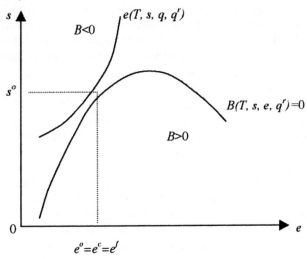

Figure 5.3   Long-run stationary state equilibrium

Note the preference for smaller scale created by the quality modeling. Since
all enrollment levels on the rising portion of the budget curve are preferred to
the corresponding enrollment levels for the same average scholarship on the
declining portion of the curve, the institution will select a lower long-run enrollment target. Assume there are variable returns to scale from enrollment,
which implies the average academic cost function is bowl shaped. $C(e,q')$ is
average academic cost and C_e is the slope of the average cost function. Let e^m
be the minimum 'efficient enrollment' scale implied by $C_e = 0$. The stationary
state equilibrium implies

> Proposition 5.4) Scale. Institutions that use endowment income to subsidize the rep-
> resentative student's education choose a long-run enrollment target that is less than
> the minimum efficient scale, $e^o < e^m$.

Equation (5.17b) reveals that

$$[(T-s)-C]/e > C_e, \qquad\qquad (5.18)$$

and equation (5.17c) yields

$$[(T-s)-C] = [F-R]/e. \qquad\qquad (5.19)$$

The left-hand side of (5.19) is the net tuition price to the representative student less the average academic cost of educating that student. If that expression is negative, it implies the institution requires auxiliary enterprises to be self-sufficient and holds overhead costs below the revenues generated from the endowment and annual giving. If $((T-s)-C)$ is negative or zero,[6] then equation (5.18) implies that C_e is negative and $e^o < e^m$. This result is consistent with empirical observation and occurs as the consequence of the trade-off between quantity and quality.

Equation (5.17a) yields the optimal pricing mix for the sticker price, T, and the average scholarship, s, given the institution's quality reputation and average student quality. The optimal pricing mix yields the following proposition:

> Proposition 5.5) Maximize Net Student Revenues. Given the quality reputation and the average student quality, the optimal mix between sticker price and average tuition discount maximizes net student revenues.

By definition, total net student revenue is $(T-s)e(T, s, q, q')$. The first order conditions for the maximization of this expression yield the same result as equation (5.17a). T and s should be chosen such that the marginal enrollment gain per dollar of reduced sticker price is equal to the marginal enrollment gain per dollar of increased average scholarship. The optimal combination of T and s are found where the elasticity of enrollment with respect to net student revenue from the sticker price and the average scholarship equal one. This solution maximizes net tuition revenue.

The average tuition discount rate is defined as the average scholarship per student divided by gross tuition and fees, $\delta = s/T$. The optimal discount rate implied by financial equilibrium can be derived from equation (5.17c), as follows:

$$\hat{\delta}(e_o) = 1 - C(e_o, q')/T + [R(q') - F]/Te_o. \qquad (5.20)$$

Equation (5.20) implies that optimal discounting capacity increases as non-academic revenues rise relative to non-academic cost, and optimal discounting capacity increases as tuition and fees rise relative to average variable cost. The institution's ability to compete for and educate quality students is enhanced by the efficiency with which auxiliary enterprises are managed. Similarly, maximizing the endowment yield and minimizing administrative costs increases the institution's ability to compete for and educate quality students.

A non-scholarship or full-pay student pays tuition and fees equal to T and the average total cost of educating this student is equal to $C+F/e$, which is the sum of average variable cost plus average fixed cost. Therefore, if $T<C+F/e$,

the full-pay student receives a subsidy from institutional funds in the amount of the difference between $C + F/e$ and T. The revealing part of equation (5.20) is that as long as T is greater than C, the institution uses the difference between T and C to cross-subsidize scholarship students with tuition revenues from full-pay students. Note that as long as T is less than total average cost, $C+F/e$, the full-pay student still receives a subsidy equal to $C+F/e - T$. In summary,

Proposition 5.6) Discounting Capacity. Discounting capacity is determined by the excess of non-student based revenues over fixed costs and the institution's pricing policy with respect to full-pay students.

Let the actual discount rate chosen by the institution be $\delta^a = s^a/T$, where s^a is the actual tuition discount per student. From (5.20) and the definition of the actual discount rate we have:

$$(\hat{\delta} - \delta^a)T \equiv [(T - s)e + R - eC - F]/e. \qquad (5.21)$$

The difference between the maximum and the actual discount rate multiplied by tuition and fees is identically equal to the budget surplus or deficit per student. Therefore, equation (5.13) and the fact that equation (5.21) is an identity suggests that:

$$B \le 0 \text{ if } \delta^a \ge \hat{\delta} \qquad (5.22)$$

$$B > 0 \text{ if } \delta^a < \hat{\delta}.$$

If the actual discount rate exceeds the optimal discount rate, the institution will experience a deficit. Indeed, a deficit implies the actual discount rate exceeds the optimal discount rate for that enrollment. If the actual discount rate is less than the optimal discount rate, the institution runs a surplus. The difference between the optimal discount rate and the actual discount rate is a measure of the institution's reserve financial capacity.

In the short-run when institutions find themselves with excess capacity, the most frequent justification given for additional tuition discounting is based on a comparison of the marginal revenue and the marginal cost of additional students. According to this marginal cost-pricing rule, the institution should continue to enroll students as long as the student's marginal revenue exceeds marginal cost (Hubbell, 1992, 9–10; Breneman, 1994, 48–50; McPherson and Schapiro, 1998, 15–16). The logic of this rule seems impeccable. If a complete new freshman class is not recruited, the college has excess capacity and the relevant marginal cost is the incremental cost per student plus the opportunity cost of tuition discounting. The opportunity cost of tuition discounting is the tuition and fee revenue forgone. If marginal revenue exceeds marginal cost, then it is argued that revenues rise relative to cost and the institution must be better off.

It is well known that marginal cost pricing is inappropriate for public utilities. Hence, public utility regulators employ average cost pricing (rate base regulation) instead. In the presence of increasing returns to scale or significant fixed costs, average cost exceeds marginal cost and if price is set equal to marginal cost, then total revenues will be less than total cost and the enterprise will run a deficit (Mas–Colell, Whinston, and Green, 1995, 570–72). It is important to notice that overlapping tenure contracts and the governance system in higher education lead to high fixed costs. Hence, higher education is subject to both increasing returns to scale and high fixed costs. Just as in public utility rate base regulation, the optimal discount rate comes from an average cost-pricing model, not a marginal cost-pricing model.

The marginal cost-pricing rule implies the institution should continue to discount tuition in order to enroll more students until marginal net revenue equals marginal cost. Hence, the marginal cost-pricing model suggests discounting should cease when

$$T - s = eC_e + C.$$

It follows that the maximum discount rate consistent with the marginal cost-pricing model is

$$\delta^{mc} = 1 - (eC_e + C)/T. \tag{5.23}$$

The optimal discount rate consistent with both short-run and long-run stationary state equilibrium can also be derived from equation (5.17b), as follows:

$$\hat{\delta} = 1 - (eC_e + C)/T - e/Te_s. \tag{5.24}$$

From equations (5.23) and (5.24), we have

$$(\delta^{mc} - \hat{\delta}) = e/Te_s > 0. \tag{5.25}$$

Therefore, the maximum discount rate for the marginal cost-pricing rule is strictly greater than the optimal discount rate from the reputation maximization model. Therefore, these results and equation (5.22) imply

Proposition 5.7) Optimal Discounting Rule. The optimal discounting rule is an average cost-pricing rule, just as in public utility pricing.

Average cost-pricing rules are consistent with short-run and long-run financial equilibrium, while marginal cost-pricing rules can lead to deficits in the short run and shut down in the long run.

There is considerable evidence from individual accounts (Duffy and Goldberg, 1998; McPherson and Schapiro, 1999a) and from objective evidence (Redd, 2000) that aggressive discounting in the 1990s has seriously weakened the financial condition of many higher education institutions. At least part of this damage may be attributable to following inappropriate pricing rules.

5.4 QUALITY CHEATING AND AGENCY COST

Part of the alumni's human capital is represented by their academic degrees and the asset value of those degrees increases or decreases as the institution's prestige increases or decreases. Therefore, the alumni have a principal interest which is served by maximizing prestige. However, since alumni do not participate in decision making at the institution, a potential principal/agent issue exists. The agents who make decisions in the interest of the alumni are administrators, board members, and faculty. It is for this reason that a substantial proportion of the board members are frequently alumni.

The length of the lag between quality choice and any subsequent adjustment in reputation is measured in decades and is more appropriately viewed as an intergenerational problem. The length of time between investments in quality and changes in academic reputation exceeds the expected tenure of most administrators, many members of the faculty, and most board members. The time at which their association with the institution is terminated frequently falls within the period covered by the lag. As a result, the agent's incentive structure may not be properly aligned with the institution's long-run objective.

Of the three agent groups who have the power to influence current decisions, faculty members and board members have the longest association with the institution; indeed, the term of most administrators has been declining. For a substantial proportion of the faculty, their expected employment duration with the institution exceeds 30 years. That is rarely the case for administrators or board members. Therefore, of the three agent groups the administrators' expected length of service is the least compatible with the long-run interests of the institution and the alumni. It is not surprising that we hear more expressions of concern about academic quality from faculty members and board members than from administrators. It follows that any weakening of the role faculty play with respect to the allocation of institutional resources may not be in the long-run interest of the institution. Similarly, any trend that reduces the expected employment duration of faculty members would seem to undermine this incentive compatibility.

Any one of the three primary decision makers (administrators, faculty, or board members) can extract rents from the institution by diverting resources from quality to their own benefit. In theory, shared governance should act as a check on rent-seeking behavior by individual groups. However, it is important to recall that the ultimate discipline that would be imposed by a market for institutional control does not exist. If shared governance is weak, quality cheating may occur.

Since the time lags are such that cause may not be associated with effect, quality cheating may be very difficult to detect. Furthermore, if institutions do not measure outcomes it will be more difficult to detect quality cheating. A decline in academic prestige is the cumulative effect of years of underinvestment in quality. Evidence of quality cheating at a specific point in time will always be arguable. High salaries for administrators and faculty can be portrayed as rewards for excellence and it will be very difficult to determine whether or not high salaries are a reward for productivity or the accumulation of rents. Similarly, lavish administrative offices and expensive public relations events can be explained as necessary marketing.

Let quality cheating be failure to maximize investment in quality through the diversion of resources to agent rents. Let q^m represent the maximum feasible choice and let q^c represent the actual quality chosen; then quality cheating occurs when $q^m > q^c$. Notice that quality cheating can occur even if the institution chooses a quality level that equals its current quality reputation; that is, quality cheating occurs if $q^c = q^r$ while $q^m > q^r$. In this case, the institution is foregoing the opportunity to increase its reputation in the next generation. Alternatively, the institution is not cheating on quality if $q^c < q^r$ and $q^m = q^c$. In this situation, the institution's current quality reputation is not supportable by its competitive and financial condition.

Assume that agents extract rents through higher salaries, excess staffing, or higher perks. Potential rents are measured by the surplus of total revenues over the least academic cost required to enroll and educate students for the quality level chosen. It is important to note that even if agency rents are substantial, accounting budgets will appear to be balanced since rents are captured through institutional expenditures. Hence, potential agency cost equals

$$A = (T-s)e(.) + R - e(.)C[e(.)] - F, \qquad (5.26)$$

where $eC(e)+F$ represents the least academic cost required to enroll and educate e students of quality q; in other words these are the economic costs, not the accounting costs. If agents maximize rents in (5.26) by choosing tuition, scholarships, and quality this implies no interior solution for quality. Maximum rents occur where $q=0$.

Suppose agents can avoid detection of quality cheating only if they choose a quality level greater than or equal to the detection minimum, say q_m. Therefore, the agency cost function under monitoring is:

$$A = (T - s)e(.) + R - e(.)C[e(.)] \qquad (5.27)$$
$$- F + \theta[q_m - q].$$

The Kuhn-Tucker conditions for this optimization problem are

$$A_T = e + [(T - s) - C - eC_e]e_T = 0 \qquad (5.28)$$
$$A_s = -e + [(T - s) - C - eC_e]e_s = 0$$
$$A_q = [(T - s) - C - eC_e]e_q - \theta = 0$$
$$A_\theta = q^m - q \le 0, \theta A_\theta = 0$$

An interior solution for T, s, and q requires that $\theta < 0$ and $A_\theta = 0$. The necessary conditions in (5.28) can be rewritten as

$$e_s = -e_T \qquad (5.29)$$
$$(T - s) - C - eC_e = \theta/e_q > 0$$
$$q = q_m$$

In addition, agent rents are extracted if and only if $A > 0$. Hence, successful rent-seeking implies

$$(T - s)e + R - eC - F > 0. \qquad (5.30)$$

The foregoing results yield:

Proposition 5.8) Agent rents are maximized when net tuition revenue is maximized and the institution chooses the minimum quality to avoid detection.

Since minimum quality is selected and agency costs are positive, we can anticipate that net tuition price, $T-s$, will be higher for the rent maximizing institution. The impact on enrollment is likely to be ambiguous.

5.5 CAPACITY

Traditionally, capacity is measured by physical plant and equipment. In higher education physical plant refers to such things as dormitory space, class rooms, and dining hall capacity. Since faculty members are indispensable quasi-fixed inputs in the short run, capacity is also determined by the level of faculty staffing. The choice of plant, equipment, and faculty are made jointly with respect to targeted enrollment. The intersection of these choices inevitably implies a quality choice, since physical plant constrains the number of enrolled students and a corresponding faculty decision implies choosing a student/faculty ratio, average class size, and the distribution of small and large classes. A quality choice is also made when the institution selects the proportion of terminally qualified faculty and when the institution chooses the mix between tenure track and adjunct faculty. Lower student/faculty ratios imply higher quality, but also higher average cost. The same is generally true for a higher proportion of terminally qualified faculty and a higher proportion of tenure track faculty.

The long-run stationary state equilibrium depicted in Figure 5.3 requires that enrollment and traditional capacity are equal. However, traditional capacity is not the only relevant capacity measure for higher education institutions. It is equally important that the institution's financial capacity to support students is in balance with traditional capacity and enrollment in the long run.

From Proposition 5.6), the primary determinants of the institution's financial capacity are the external revenues available to the institution and the institution's pricing policy with respect to full pay students. External revenue is a function of the endowment, grants, annual giving, and net proceeds from auxiliary enterprises. If all auxiliary enterprises are self supporting and the institution does not use full pay tuition to cross subsidize scholarship students, then endowment, grants, and annual giving are the most important determinants of financial capacity.

In the short-run equilibrium depicted in Figure 5.4, traditional capacity and enrollment may not be balanced. The institution may have excess traditional capacity but financial capacity must be balanced in the short-run equilibrium. If this is not the case, the institution is not maximizing quality and balancing its budget. Again, there is an important difference between accounting budgets and economic budgets. Institutions are hesitant to report deficits. If expenditure exceeds normal revenue, institutions with endowments balance the accounting budgets by increasing the endowment payout. The endowment payout rate is a slack variable used to balance the accounting budget. As a result, accounting budgets are unreliable measures of the financial health of the institution. The financial equilibrium in this chapter requires that the economic budget be balanced.

There are five different capacity and enrollment cases in the short run that are of particular interest. First, traditional capacity, financial capacity, and enrollment are all balanced. This is the equilibrium position in Figure 5.3 that is consistent with long-run stationary state equilibrium. Let this be the 'short-run general equilibrium' scenario. Second, traditional capacity may exceed financial capacity and enrollment may equal financial capacity. Let this be the 'short-run financial equilibrium' scenario.

The next three cases are short-run disequilibrium scenarios. Third, financial capacity exceeds traditional capacity and enrollment equals traditional capacity. Let this be the 'excess financial capacity' scenario. Fourth, enrollment is less than traditional capacity and traditional capacity equals financial capacity. Let this be the 'general excess capacity' scenario. Fifth, enrollment is greater than traditional capacity and traditional capacity equals financial capacity. Let this be the 'general excess demand' scenario. The last four scenarios deserve individual consideration, since no adjustments are called for in the short-run general equilibrium scenario.

Short–run Financial Equilibrium

In this case, traditional capacity, e^c, exceeds current enrollment and financial capacity, e^f, equals current enrollment ($e^c > e^o$ and $e^f = e^o$) as at point 'b' in Figure 5.4. The institution is balancing its budget and maximizing short-run quality; however, the excess traditional capacity that this case implies may lead to additional discounting in order to bring current enrollment up to traditional capacity. Note that current enrollment can be increased to capacity while maintaining a balanced budget only if the institution is willing to lower quality. Technically, this would imply quality cheating according to the definition of quality cheating in the previous subsection. Since the economic budget is balanced at both solutions, there are no potential rents due to this decision. Alternatively, if the institution keeps the average discount constant while increasing enrollment, potential rents are created at the expense of higher quality. Other things being equal, the optimal short-run decision is to continue with the same enrollment level and in the long-run reduce traditional capacity.

The situation where traditional capacity exceeds current enrollment is a likely scenario. In this case the institution has excess traditional enrollment capacity and is constrained by its financial capacity to support students of the desired quality. It is immediately clear in this case that the institution cannot increase enrollment without sacrificing quality. Some may find it attractive to sacrifice quality in the short run, but it is inconsistent with the institution's long-run objective. If the institution increases its enrollment, quality reputation will decline over time. This may precipitate a downward spiral in quality reputation that is hard to arrest.

Excess Financial Capacity

In this case financial capacity exceeds traditional capacity and traditional capacity equals enrollment ($e^f > e^c$ and $e^c = e^o$). If the institution is balancing its budget at this enrollment level and keeping enrollment at traditional capacity, it is forgoing higher quality that can be achieved by expanding enrollment

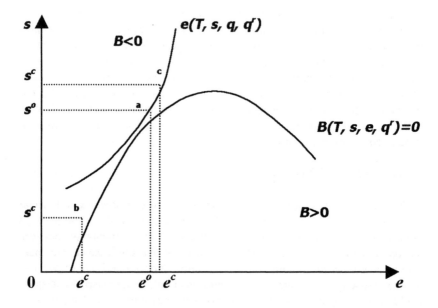

Figure 5.4   Short-run financial equilibrium

through increasing its discount rate. The optimal long-run decision is to increase traditional capacity. This is an ideal situation for an institution to be in prior to enrollment growth: quality and enrollment can be increased at the same time. Tactically, this situation is achieved by an infusion of external revenues (more endowment) before a long-term enrollment expansion.

General Excess Capacity

In this case financial capacity equals traditional capacity and enrollment is less than capacity ($e^f = e^c$ and $e^c > e^o$). This situation describes the optimal tuition discounting model, since the problem here is a pricing problem. The institution can increase enrollment, balance its budget, and increase quality by increasing its discount rate. Enrollment and all capacities can be brought into balance by increasing the discount rate, while quality is increased. It is highly probable that this is the scenario envisioned by most of the aggressive discounters during the 1990s, while the reality was that they faced the traditional excess capacity scenario, where increased discounting and constant quality lead to deficits.

The potential for rent generation in this scenario is substantial. If the institution raises enrollment through higher discounts, while keeping existing quality constant, potential rents are generated because the economic budget is in surplus. It is also possible to increase quality and potential rents at the same time. Detection of quality cheating in this environment will be very difficult.

General Excess Demand

In this case financial capacity equals traditional capacity and potential enrollment is greater than capacity ($e^f = e^c$ and $e^c < e^o$). Even if the institution can find a temporary solution to the traditional capacity constraint, it cannot accommodate this demand without lowering quality, so the optimal policy is to raise admission selectivity and reduce enrollment to the general equilibrium solution.

There are a variety of reasons why we may expect that financial capacity is unlikely to exceed traditional capacity. Most institutions do not have endowments that enable such a solution and the very nature of higher education governance structures makes it extremely difficult for institutions not to spend all revenues that are available.

These cases have implications for enrollment planning. If traditional capacity exceeds financial capacity and the institution cannot expand financial capacity, it should reduce traditional capacity in the long run. If it is determined that on the basis of, say, curriculum requirements or sufficient scale to attract students that the institution should increase its size and maintain its quality level, then the foregoing cases suggest that the institution should accumulate reserve financial capacity to support students before it expands its enrollment. This is easily stated, but it will be very difficult to do, since it requires that the institution must accumulate financial reserves before it begins enrollment growth. In an environment where all constituencies consider themselves under-funded, this will severely tax the leadership skills of the institution.

Optimal short-run quality choice is constrained by the external revenues, and long-run quality reputation depends on short-run quality choice. If costs are rising rapidly, the institution may be unable to raise external revenues fast enough to do anything other than invest in quality sufficient to maintain the institution's current quality reputation. An increase in long-run quality reputation requires an infusion of external revenues large enough to support a sustained investment in higher quality. This type of gift could be 'institutionally transforming'.

Cost Control

Cost control is a contentious issue for those of us in higher education.[7] In the context of this discussion, cost control means minimizing agency costs and using resources efficiently. The foregoing model suggests it is a necessary condition for achieving a long-run stationary state equilibrium that is consistent with reputation maximization. Any expenditure that does not contribute directly to the enrollment of good students, does not improve their educational experience, or place those students on successful career tracks, is a non-essential expenditure, and any inefficient use of resources limits the institution's ability to accomplish its most important objective. The paramount role played by third party subsidies in the economics of higher education also makes cost control critical to the financial well-being of the industry. If higher education does not minimize agency costs and eliminate the inefficient use of resources, third party benefactors are less likely to provide the subsidies required to maintain quality. The result will be declining public support and declining quality in higher education.

If an institution finds itself in the position where its financial capacity to support students is less than its traditional enrollment capacity, the first place the institution can turn for a potential remedy for this problem is more effective cost control. The foregoing model is also a template for explaining to both faculty and staff why cost control is important.

5.6   OPERATING LEVERAGE

The foregoing analysis of traditional and financial capacities reveals an important point in the economics of higher education: enrollment growth is not self financing. In order to increase enrollment and maintain quality reputation, the institution must have an infusion of external revenues. This is due to the unique fact that higher education subsidizes its average patron (Winston, 1999). In the case of the profit maximizing enterprise, capacity expansions are financed by the cash flows directly generated by the production activity of the firm. In that sense, capacity expansions for the profit maximizing firm are self financing. For higher education, the cash flows generated by normal production activity are insufficient to finance capacity expansions due to the average student subsidy. Enrollment growth must be accompanied by an infusion of external revenues from a third party, or quality will decline. The third party may be the government in the case of public institutions, or private benefactors in the case of private institutions.

The conclusion that enrollment growth is not self financing is at odds with conventional wisdom in higher education. Few institutions accumulate reserves before they expand and most view enrollment growth as a way to improve their cash flows. The difference between theory and conventional practice can be explained by the deceptive role played by short-run operating leverage. Higher education institutions have very high fixed costs in the short run. This is the result of significant plant costs per student, the rapid obsolescence of equipment, and the quasi-fixed nature of both faculty and staff. Tenure ensures that there are significant constraints in the variability of faculty in the short run. Similarly, a culture of equity extends these constraints to staff as well. Very few institutions are willing to lay off employees.

High fixed cost ensures that any increase in volume will generate significant surpluses. Institutions do not adjust faculty and staff as soon as enrollment increases, since they hesitate to make such commitments to new quasi-fixed factors until they are certain the increase in enrollment is permanent. This, coupled with high fixed cost, ensures that enrollment growth will significantly improve cash flows in the short run. However, if the institution intends to maintain quality as it expands enrollment, the improvement in cash flows is an illusion. Once the institution adjusts staffing and student quality to restore the targeted quality level, the surpluses will disappear. Unfortunately, the short-run surpluses are a magnet for members of the governance structure. If the surpluses are diverted to agency rents, the institution will run a deficit if it attempts to restore the targeted quality level. Therefore, enrollment growth can initiate a downward quality spiral, if the governance structure is not strong enough to prevent it.

The foregoing analysis suggests the following proposition.

Proposition 5.9) Enrollment growth is not self financing and can create short-run opportunities for agency rents.

In the traditional profit maximizing environment, an increase in demand is followed by an increase in profits and an expansion of output. Due to the subsidy provided to the average student, an increase in demand for the services provided by higher education can result in a decline in quality or deficits. Simply put, an increase in the demand for higher education does not automatically generate the requisite subsidies from third party benefactors. Ironically, the more successful higher education is in attracting customers, the weaker is its financial position. This creates special problems for higher education, since it implies that enrollment growth must be preceded by (or be coincidental with) an infusion of external revenues. The problem arises with the governance structure, since the system abhors temporary surpluses. Expenditures rise as revenues rise.

5.7 SUMMARY

During the annual enrollment cycle, the representative institution maximizes student quality by allocating scholarships among admitted students subject to a scholarship budget and an enrollment target. The optimal scholarship allocation is based on merit, need, and the probability the student will enroll. The expected enrollment demand function is derived from the optimal scholarship offers and the expected quality function. Expected enrollment is an increasing function of quality reputation. An increase in quality reputation increases potential market share and pricing power. Pricing power depends on marginal enrollment returns to tuition discounting.

The long-run stationary state equilibrium model is intergenerational. The representative institution maximizes quality reputation by maximizing quality in the short run. As quality increases and reputation rises, endowment and control of subsidies increase, allowing the institution to increase student quality in the following time period. The control variables in the reputation maximization model are tuition and fees, the scholarship budget, and enrollment. Equilibrium is found where the balanced budget contour is tangent to the highest possible iso-quality contour. Quality maximization leads to equilibrium enrollment levels that are less than traditional 'minimum efficient scale'. The optimal pricing rule is an average cost pricing rule, rather than a marginal cost pricing rule, and tuition/fees and scholarship budgets are chosen in order to maximize net student revenues given enrollment.

Agency cost can arise if administrators, faculty, or board members are rent seekers. Potential rents are created when members of the governance structure cheat on quality choice. The lag between quality investment and changes in reputation is so long that quality cheating is difficult to detect. Potential rent maximization under monitoring leads to the minimum quality required to avoid detection and to higher enrollment.

There are two different types of capacity in higher education: the traditional capacity represented by physical plant, faculty, and staff and the institution's financial capacity to support students. Both capacities must be balanced in long-run stationary state equilibrium, while financial capacity must be balanced with enrollment in the short-run equilibrium. Financial capacity results from the unique higher education characteristic that the average patron receives a subsidy.

In the short run, the institution may be in general equilibrium where all capacities and enrollment are balanced, financial equilibrium where enrollment and financial capacity are balanced, or disequilibrium. If the institution is in short-run financial equilibrium, but traditional capacity exceeds enrollment, any attempt to increase enrollment will result in lower quality. An opportunity to generate potential rents through quality cheating exists in this case. If the institution has general excess capacity (excess financial and traditional capacity), it can increase enrollment and quality at the same time. There are substantial opportunities for rent-seeking behavior in this case, since enrollment, quality, and rents can all be increased at the same time.

Finally, an important characteristic of higher education is that growth in demand (enrollment) is not self financing. As demand increases for the profit maximizing firm, profits rise and the increased cash flows provide the resources to finance an increase in output. This is not the case in higher education, since the average student receives a subsidy. The student-generated revenues flowing from an increase in enrollment are insufficient to finance an increase in output. This essential character of enrollment growth is not widely understood, due to the misleading effect of short-run operating leverage. Since faculty and staff are quasi-fixed inputs in the short run, fixed costs are very high. With high fixed costs, any increase in enrollment has a substantial positive impact on cash flows, giving the appearance that enrollment growth improves the institution's financial position. This is only true if the institution is willing to allow quality to decline.

NOTES

1. Optimality refers to the institution's efficient use of its restricted resources. This is not necessarily the same thing as the social optimal result. From a social perspective, we might be most concerned about obtaining the maximum investment in human capital per dollar of education subsidy. The set of all higher education institutions consists of many independent institutions and agents who pursue their own objectives. Their activities are not directed to the social optimal result by an omnipotent central planner. If the institution's incentive structure is compatible with respect to the social objective, then the institution's optimal solution will be consistent with the social objective. If the institution's optimal solution is not consistent with the social objective, it is said to be incentive incompatible.
2. The possible exceptions to binding short-run constraints may be the institutions at the top of the quality queue whose endowments, reputations, and selectivity give them more degrees of freedom.
3. Since the enrollment demand function, $e=e(T, s, q, q^r)$, is the implicit solution to the constant average quality contour, $q=q(T, s, q, q^r)$, the signs of the derivatives are related as follows:

$$e_q = 1/q_e < 0$$
$$e_T = -q_T/q_e < 0$$
$$e_s = -q_s/q_e > 0$$
$$e_r = -q_r/q_e > 0$$

4. It is appropriate to consider why the institution seeks to maximize average student quality rather than total student quality. There are two reasons for the former approach rather than the latter. First, the metric that enrollment committees use to measure their recruiting success each year is class size and the average quality of the students enrolled. This is how recruiting results are communicated to governing boards and to the faculty at large. Note that 'total student quality' is implicit in the product of class size and average quality. The second reason why this approach is adopted is that average student quality is the signal used to communicate quality in the market for academic reputation. Ranking systems, such as *US News & World Report*, report statistics like average class rank, grade point average (GPA), and standardized test scores. This signal is most valuable to consumers because it measures the central tendency of the quality distribution.
5. Average cost per student includes all student driven costs, such as instruction, boarding,

room, and utilities. Empirical analysis reveals that higher education average cost curves are convex functions of enrollment and they exhibit increasing returns to scale over a wide range of enrollments. Since the price of inputs, p, does not play a role in this analysis, p is suppressed for notational convenience in the cost function.

6.   This condition implies the institution's primary mission is the education of students. If the reverse is true,

$$[(T-s)-C]=[F-R]/e$$

is positive, it means the institution uses revenues from students to subsidize its auxiliary activities. Its primary mission in that case would be the auxiliary activities.

7.   The National Commission's report and, most recently, the Lumina Foundation's report on this question have focused our attention on this important public policy issue.

6. Price and product differentiation

Successful capitalism demands a fusion of cooperation and competition and a means of grafting such a hybrid into the soil of the economic, political and social system.

Will Hutton   (1950 –)

6.1   COLLUSION, COOPERATION, AND COMPETITION

Collusion and cooperation are opposite sides of the same coin. *Webster's New Collegiate Dictionary* defines collusion as a 'secret agreement or cooperation for a fraudulent or deceitful purpose', and it defines cooperation as an 'association of persons for common benefit'. Thus, collusion is a special type of cooperation where the common benefit derived by those who cooperate is at the expense of others.

The negative connotation attached to cooperation among economic agents is clearly expressed by Adam Smith, who observed 'people of the same trade seldom meet together, even for merriment and diversion, but the conversation ends in a conspiracy against the public, or in some contrivance to raise prices' (1976, 144). This theme is an integral part of the modern theory of the firm, where the importance of preventing collusion is demonstrated by the prisoner's dilemma. Cooperation among prisoners leads to both prisoners going free after committing a crime.

Alternatively, cooperation is a necessary condition for the private provision of public goods.[1] Unfortunately, free riding is the dominant strategy Nash equilibrium in such games. Andreoni notes 'the fact that a large fraction of people voluntarily contribute to public goods, despite strong incentives to free ride, has been a long-standing puzzle for economists' (1995, 1). Society's preference for cooperation is observed repeatedly in laboratory experiments and in high levels of voluntary contributions to charities. The results are not explained by pure or impure altruism, since positive or negative framing of the game changes the experimental result (Andreoni, 1995). If the game is positively framed, the 'warm glow' from the provision of the public good leads to significant cooperation among agents. Alternatively, if the game is negatively framed, the 'cold prickle' of not providing the public good does not deter the Nash-equilibrium prediction. In other words, there appears to be 'an asymmetric marginal utility of helping' (Andreoni, 1995, 13).

In the past two decades, the provision of higher education services through both public and private funding has been 're-framed'. Prior to the 1980s, higher education was thought to have significant public good properties. Today, higher education is considered a private good where cooperation among providers should be discouraged. The shift from public good status to private good status is the source of declining public support and growing hostility towards higher education (Winston, 1992). The responsibility for this re-framing rests with the academe itself. Our failure to control costs and to accept the need for reform convinces the public we are no different than any other rent-seeking vested interest group in the country. We are our own worst enemy in this regard.

Clearly cooperation among commercial firms is normally at the public's expense, whereas cooperation among non-commercial organizations may benefit the public interest. If cooperation among commercial firms is always at the public's expense, it is difficult to explain public policy regarding cooperation among these firms. For instance, professional sports leagues are umbrella organizations designed to promote cooperation among profit maximizing commercial enterprises. The umbrella organizations control entry and restrict competition for players. Similarly, professional associations are allowed to restrict competitive behavior in the professions.

A charity is not a commercial enterprise if it provides its services to clients for free. If the charity collects fees from its clients, it is a 'donative-commercial non-profit' (Hansmann, 1981). The non-profit part does not mean these institutions never generate surpluses, it means they are subject to a 'non-distribution constraint'; the surplus cannot be distributed to a residual claimant (Hansmann, 1981). Higher education institutions are donative-commercial non-profit organizations that are subject to a non-distribution constraint.

Cooperation among benefactors is the central purpose of all charities. The cooperation comes at the financial expense of the benefactors and the nature of all charities is that one group makes a sacrifice in the interest of another group. Further, society permits cooperation among charities, some of whom are donative-commercial non-profits, through umbrella organizations such as the United Way. Public approval of cooperation among charities is common and the prohibition of cooperation among commercial firms is not universal, although it is not common.

Is the public interest served by price competition, quality competition, and public relations competition among charities? Or, should public policy discourage price and public relations cooperation, while also encouraging quality competition? Since higher education institutions hold tax exempt status, they are charities. To the extent that price competition lowers the amount paid by students who have the ability to pay, merit subsidies may crowd out private investment in education, and access may be reduced if merit aid is substituted for need based aid. Similarly, if public relations competition among institutions is analogous to an arms race, vigorous competition in this area raises cost without improving quality or access.

Susan Rose-Akerman considered the impact of competition on 'excessive fundraising' among charities (1982). She motivates her analysis by noting its similarity to Schmalensee's argument about advertising competition (1972), where a substantial part of advertising expenditures serve to block competitors' advertising which leads to higher cost and no change in the size of the market or the distribution of market share. To the extent that public relations activities block similar activities by competitors, the resources used in this process are a social waste.

Rose-Akerman considers three charity industry models: in the first, donors are indifferent to fundraising costs; in the second, donors view high fundraising costs as undesirable; and in the third, donors realize that high fundraising costs can lead other donors to contribute (1982, 197). Her overall conclusion is that 'the competition for charitable dollars reduces the level of service provision relative to funds raised for all charities' and she finds that without entry barriers 'the number of charities increases until the fundraising share of the marginal charity approaches one' (1982, 205). In other words, entry continues until almost all service provision is crowded out in the marginal charity. Since net charitable resources in fact do not approach zero, there must be barriers to entry. Entry by new charities is limited by donor brand loyalty and the monopolization of important parts of the 'ideology space' by existing charities. At the margin, a new entrant in these cases would experience very low net service provisions, which render their potential entry ineffective. While the entry barriers serve to limit fundraising expenditures, they also tend to limit the ideological diversity of the charities.

In addition, Rose-Akerman's results suggest that weak entry barriers lead not only to high fundraising expenditures but also to an unstable system and that 'a competitive charity market with no entry barriers does not seem "optimal" in any sense of that word' (1982, 205–206). She then proceeds to consider different regulatory strategies. She concludes that requiring charities to report their fundraising cost proportions (the net service provision), regulating the maximum fundraising cost proportion, or capping fundraising cost will not be enough to prevent the rise of excessive fundraising costs.

In the end, Rose-Akerman finds that 'market structure regulation' may be the most effective way to minimize fundraising costs and maximize net service provision (1982, 206–208). She proposes the formation of a united fund drive that guarantees the share of receipts going to each charity, prohibits charities from soliciting funds independently, and prohibits solicitation of funds without joining the united fund drive. In other words, the proposed public policy is that the charities be encouraged to cooperate in their fundraising activities, rather than compete individually. Hence, competition among charities is an arms race problem, where cooperation is the preferred outcome; rather than the prisoner's dilemma problem, where collusion is to be prevented.[2]

Prior to World War II, the proportion of the population between 18 and 24 years of age attending college was less than 10 percent (Clotfelter et al, 1991, 31). Today, over half of the population in that age bracket attends college. This dramatic increase in access to higher education occurred after the war and as a consequence of a variety of economic influences and public policy initiatives. It was generally understood that a significant increase in the proportion of students who attend college would not be possible without financial assistance. Hence, improving 'access' to higher education became a core higher education policy objective. In an important study prepared by the American Council on Education in 1946, Sharpe et al. argued:

> The award of financial assistance should be, in so far as possible, a coordinated enterprise among colleges of similar type and of similar student clientele...deliberate 'competitive bidding' for students – also undue 'shopping-around' by candidates – should be discouraged. (1946, 29)

This blatant call for higher education 'price fixing' seems anachronistic today, but it is easy to understand in its historical context. World War II followed hard on the heels of the great depression and the end of the war found many families not fully recovered from the economic damage done by the depression. A college education was beyond the reach of those families. If that was going to change, it would have to change through public subsidies. Therefore, it was natural that Sharpe and others would approach the problem as: how to get the maximum investment in human capital from a binding subsidy constraint. They viewed themselves as allocating subsidies, not setting prices in a commercial enterprise. As real family resources have increased over the last six decades, the commercial pricing aspect of higher education pricing has become the primary concern. In light of the price wars of the 1990s and the emergence of a global labor market, the objective of getting the maximum human capital investment from a binding subsidy constraint seems as relevant today as it did in 1946.

Beginning in the 1950s and ending in 1991 a consortium (cartel?) of the top private institutions in the country met to discuss the financial aid awards given to students whose applications 'overlapped' several of the member institutions (Ehrenberg, 2000, 75–84). In these meetings the institutions agreed to a common financial aid award for each overlapping student. The stated purpose was to prevent price competition for gifted students beyond what was necessary to enable the student to attend the institution. Since the net tuition price to the student would be the same at each institution, she could make her final enrollment decision based on the quality differences between the institutions. The member institutions would then be able to follow need-blind admission policies and to compete on the basis of quality rather than price. In 1991, the Justice Department took exception to this arrangement and charged the leaders of the Overlap Group, the Ivy League institutions and MIT, with price fixing. The Overlap Group entered a consent decree with the Justice Department. In 1994, Congress passed legislation that allowed colleges to agree to give only need based aid and to adopt a common definition for that aid (Grossman, 1995, 524–5). This legislation re-opened the door for some cooperation among institutions.

Following the demise of the Overlap Group, the 1990s turned into a 'free-for-all in financial aid' (McPherson and Shapiro, 1999a). Vigorous rounds of tuition discounting characterized the decade, leading some to argue that competitive tuition discounting seriously weakens the financial condition of private institutions, particularly those institutions below the top tier, does not alter the distribution of students, and reduces the quality of higher education (Redd, 2000). The competition has accelerated the shift away from need based aid toward need-blind merit based aid (Carlson, 2001; Brownstien, 2001). The Overlap case and the competitive discounting that followed raise a number of important public policy issues.

Cook and Frank argue that national competition among colleges and universities for the top high school students may best be understood as a tournament (1993). Tournament competition results in many competitors and a small group of contenders. Within the circle of winners, the outcome is very unevenly shared with the contenders who do not 'win, place, or show'.[3] This result is referred to as a winner take all competition.

Competition for gifted students is analogous to competition for gifted professional athletes. It is argued that tournament style competition for players leads to the concentration of the best players in the small number of teams who have the deepest pockets. This is the problem of maintaining 'competitive balance' among the teams (Quirk and Fort, 1992, 240–93). Tournament competition for the most gifted players is said to lead to leagues that are dominated by a few teams. Since losing teams cannot generate as much revenue as winning teams, the losing teams are at a permanent disadvantage in recruiting the best players. If the competitive balance is severely disrupted, revenues for the entire league will decline.

The competitive balance argument is the primary reason why professional sports leagues are considered immune to the anti-trust laws. The league rules for player salaries and collective bargaining are supposed to minimize the impact of tournament style competition for players on the competitive balance. For example, the professional football draft is supposed to reverse this effect by giving losing teams top draft choices. Quirk and Fort argue that the anti-trust exemption actually makes the competitive balance problem worse and results in monopoly rents accruing to the teams (1999, 171–86). Since the leagues are exempt from the anti-trust laws, they restrict entry by expansion teams. Without this restriction, entry would eliminate the dominance of a small number of teams. It is ironic that regulators allow this action by a sports cartel and actively move to prevent it in higher education.

The professional sports analogy suggests that tournament competition for the most gifted students will result in the concentration of those students in a handful of institutions. The empirical evidence suggests that this is the case (Cook and Frank, 1993). The question is: can 'entry' into the top quality tier eliminate the competitive balance problem in higher education? Or, is the threat of entry sufficient to eliminate the competitive balance problem? Any new entrant at the top must duplicate the endowment per student available to the existing institutions and it has to overcome their quality reputations. Quality reputations among the top tier institutions are the result of investments made over many generations. Successful entry might be possible, but it is not probable. Tournament competition widens the quality gap between the top tier institutions and their closest competitors. In the long run, the positions of the top institutions in the quality hierarchy are not contestable, ensuring a perpetual dominance, that is the market power of these institutions becomes complete. Given the purpose of anti-trust legislation, this could only be an unintended consequence.

The public policy issue raised by the Overlap group is: do these activities result in a gain or a loss in social welfare? Clearly, the Justice Department thinks it is a loss. There are potential wealth transfers away from students whose scholarships are less than they would be under competitive pricing. The wealth transfer alone does not guarantee a net welfare loss, since it depends on who receives the transferred wealth and from whom the wealth is transferred. Since high merit students tend to come disproportionately from families with incomes that are higher than the incomes of students who lack access, the 'ability to pay' principle suggests the transfer of wealth from high income students to low income students would be welfare enhancing (Esposito and Esposito, 1995, 448).

Grossman argues that need based aid is problematic in its entirety since it has adverse incentive effects that 'penalize prudence' (1995, 520–21). His point is that families with gifted children are better off if they do not save for their children's college, since any savings will be deducted from need based financial aid. In support of the penalizing prudence position, Feldstein argues that the implicit tax created by need based financial aid reduces savings rates by as much as 50 percent (1995).

Feldstein makes a similar argument with respect to Social Security and the savings rate (1985). In this case he argues that public retirement programs, like

Social Security, create negative incentives for saving. On closer inspection, one can see that there is an important internal inconsistency in these two positions. With regard to need based aid, Feldstein argues that the absence of an academic subsidy for families with higher incomes induces them to save less. In contrast, Feldstein argues that the presence of a retirement subsidy induces the public to save less. One could just as well make this argument with respect to a pure merit based scholarship program: the presence of a pure merit based subsidy induces families to save less.

Over the last two decades, the public's confidence in the ability of Social Security to provide for retirement has declined steadily and merit based aid has progressively replaced need based aid.[4] However, the savings rate has fallen throughout this period. If the foregoing incentive structures for savings are correct, as understood by Feldstein, the savings rate should have risen.

In his dissenting opinion, Judge Weis argued that, other things equal, financial aid is charity and it is not subject to the Sherman Anti-trust Act (Esposito and Esposito, 1995, 449). The wealth used to support students comes from charitable contributions and since these contributions are tax deductible the government has already agreed that they are charity. The wealth does not arise spontaneously from the institution. Again, the irony of this situation is apparent when we consider professional baseball, which is a for-profit industry where no charity is involved. If a benefactor contracts directly with students and makes her awards exclusively on the basis of need, the Sherman Act has no bearing. From the previous discussion of the market for subsidies, it is clear why benefactors choose academic institutions to be their distribution agents.

Judge Weis has identified the critical economic issue: scholarships are charity and the academic institutions are the benefactors' agent. Since student preparation for college is positively correlated with family income, why would the benefactors who support the Overlap Group want to offer charity to the wealthiest families in the country? If the institutions award income-blind merit scholarships, would they be guilty of violating their principal-agent contract? Since academic output is subsidized because it has private and public good characteristics, it seems most likely that pure merit based aid 'crowds out' private investment in human capital (Martin, 2001b). Given that society has a finite quantity of academic subsidy each period (the subsidy constraint is binding), the optimal public policy is to obtain the maximum human capital investment possible with that subsidy. If part of the subsidy is allocated on the basis of merit and independent of need, then some of those subsidy dollars will crowd out private investment in human capital and total human capital output will be lower than it would be if the entire subsidy were allocated according to need.

6.2   COMPETITION IN HIGHER EDUCATION

Like commercial firms, higher education institutions compete on the basis of both price and product differentiation (non-price competition). Price competition in higher education is similar to the pricing practices observed in the automobile and real estate industries, where there is a 'sticker price', or list price (posted tuition), and a negotiated net price (tuition less scholarship). One significant difference between these commercial transactions and colleges and universities is that colleges and universities have considerably more information about their client's ability to pay. Their objectives are a second important difference. Automobile dealerships are profit maximizing institutions, while higher education institutions are charities. The charitable status of higher education institutions does not guarantee, however, that they will not engage in rent-seeking behavior.

Product differentiation can take a variety of forms. It can consist of real improvements in the quality of the service provided and/or it can consist of a marketing campaign to create the perception of higher quality. Since higher education is an experience good, perceptions can be manipulated in the short run. The fact that the purchase decision is more or less irreversible also increases the incentive to focus on perceptions rather than substantial investments in quality. These higher education characteristics create the potential for serious principal/agent problems. Rent-seeking administrators can exploit the lags between perceptions and reality by promising more than the institution is capable of delivering. Short-run gains in enrollment and annual giving follow all marketing campaigns, regardless of the substance behind the claims. The administrator may manipulate perceptions in the short run in order to boost his career and plan to be gone when reality catches up with perceptions.

For example, Ehrenberg tells an interesting story about the Johnson Graduate School of Management (JGSM) at Cornell and the inaugural edition of Business Week's (BW) ranking of MBA programs (2000, 62). The dean of JGSM asked current and recent MBA students in 1988 to give their program very high rankings, explaining that such a high ranking would increase the asset value of their degrees. They responded enthusiastically and the JGSM's MBA program was ranked fifth in the initial rankings. But, that was not the end of the story.

> This in turn led to an improvement in the quality of the students that JGSM was able to attract the next year. Unfortunately, JGSM was not that highly ranked by employers, and so when the newly attracted students graduated, they did not all receive the type of positions that they had expected. This led to some alumni discontent, which adversely affected future ratings, and as deans at other business schools began to play the same 'game', the ranking of JGSM in the *BW* survey fell into the middle

of the second ten schools. When the 1996 *BW* results were announced, JGSM had slipped still further to eighteenth place. (2000, 62)

The campaign to manage perceptions turned out to have a short half-life and it is likely that it did more harm than good. Such tactics can only be employed with experience goods, goods where the consumer cannot determine quality until after the good has been purchased. Administrators with short planning horizons can manipulate these properties at the expense of the institution's long-run reputation.

Real quality differentiation tends to be durable, but harder to quantify and to achieve. Competition in terms of real product differentiation is thought to have beneficial social consequences since it tends to raise industry quality through competition over time. Competition through perceived product differentiation is a zero sum game that captures only first mover advantages that are quickly countered by other competitors. Attempts to manage perceptions can actually damage academic reputations. The social consequence of competition through perceived product differentiation is to add permanent layers of expense that do not contribute to either the quantity or quality of output.

Selective institutions expend considerable effort, time, and financial resources each year to produce applications and to enroll students who are admitted. Parents of highly recruited students are well aware of the volume of material, unsolicited and solicited, that their children receive during their last two years in high school. These institutions may ask alumni to visit prospects or send professional recruiters to visit personally with prospective students. Ehrenberg reports

> When one adds up all the costs that selective institutions incur in recruiting, admitting, and then enrolling their freshman classes, the numbers are mind-boggling. Information provided to me from a confidential study of a set of selective private institutions indicates that in the fall of 1996 the average cost per student was about $1,700 in the universities and $2,500 in the colleges. These numbers actually underestimate the true average cost to the institutions because they do not include the value of the time spent by faculty and alumni in the admission process. (2000, 73)

These expenses have to be recovered through either higher net tuition (higher tuition/lower scholarships) or reduced expenditures elsewhere. So, they very well may come at the expense of educational quality or student access.

An individual institution dare not forgo these expenditures. To do so would ensure a smaller and less qualified class. Hence, any escalation in the public relations aspect of student recruitment by its peer institutions must be met dollar for dollar, just to hold the distribution of students constant. It is ironic in the extreme that our society allows professional sports to avoid this type of 'arms race' for athletes by colluding through annual player drafts. The cost saving due to player drafts is not passed on to sports fans in the form of lower ticket prices. The increase in rents is captured by the owners and the players. Professional sports are profit maximizing industries; higher education is a charity. Society's well-being could be enhanced if these public relations expenses were used instead to raise quality and improve access.

6.3   PRICE COMPETITION

List prices coupled with negotiated discounts are reasonably common.[5]   What is uncommon is the amount of information the seller has about the buyer in higher education and the role the government plays in pricing. The G.I. Bill, state support, Pell Grants, guaranteed student loans, campus work study (CWS), and the processing of the Free Application for Federal Student Aid (FAFSA) forms all reflect the government's active involvement in college and university pricing (Kane, 1999, 20–54).

The discounts have three economic explanations. The first is pure need based discounts. This is the 'access' motivation for tuition discounts (see Chapter 7). The FAFSA form contains a detailed listing of the student's and his family's financial resources, along with the number of siblings currently enrolled, or about to be enrolled, in college. The FAFSA evaluation results in the expected family contribution based on this information. Pure need based aid can then be calculated as the difference between the total of tuition, fees, room, board, books, and travel less the family contribution. Institutions prepare a financial aid 'package' for each student, where the aid is composed of external grants, loans, internal scholarships, and campus work study. The mix between these types of aid is discretionary to some extent. Need based financial aid is a social subsidy designed to increase investment in human capital by making higher education accessible to students who would not otherwise be able to attend.

Pure merit financial aid is growing in popularity. Merit aid represents an implicit wage paid to students who contribute to total human capital output (Chapter 3), where this wage is paid regardless of need. To be pure merit financial aid, the student must receive a discount even though the expected family contribution exceeds or equals the total of tuition, fees, room, board, books, and travel. In other words, it is pure merit aid only if the family has the ability to pay all costs, but the student receives a discount due to merit. The economic justification for this type of financial aid comes from the peer production technology that characterizes higher education (Rothschild and White, 1995). Pure merit financial aid represents compensation for the student's productivity in the process of creating human capital for her and for others. What may be still at issue is whether the externality created by the gifted student is private or public property.

The third economic foundation for tuition discounting is pure price discrimination. Given the detailed information the institution has about each student's ability to pay, maximizing total revenue through price discrimination is a feasible solution. The social impact of this behavior depends on to what end the institution applies the additional resources it collects through price discrimination. Since higher education institutions are not profit maximizing institutions, a wealth transfer to the institution and its agents does not necessarily take place. However, if the institution is maximizing rents, there will be a wealth transfer from students to the agents who control the institution.

The analogy with the commercial monopolist who practices perfect price discrimination is appealing. It is well known that the monopolist who practices perfect price discrimination produces the perfectly competitive output. The wealth transfer from consumers to the monopolist is still a problem, however. The price discriminating monopoly analogy in higher education is revenue maximization subject to a zero rent constraint, which should maximize access, quality, and implicit wages for student productivity. The fact that the government helps provide the tools necessary to practice price discrimination (through the FAFSA forms) suggests that public policy reflects the resource allocation benefits of price discrimination.

Most financial aid packages contain elements of both need based aid and merit aid. The part of the financial aid package reflecting need based aid is the difference between total expenses and expected family contribution. The merit based aid for a student who also receives need based aid can be measured by any aid that relieves part of the family contribution and/or any beneficial composition of the aid package. If the institution replaces all or part of the loan component with grants while meeting all need, this re-composition can be considered merit aid.

Pure need-blind admission is said to occur when the institution admits each class solely on the basis of academic credentials and then guarantees to meet each student's financial need. Only the top tier institutions could follow this policy without also offering merit aid to the incoming class. Most institutions have to offer merit aid or the gifted students elect to go to other institutions. An institution with a limited endowment may not be able to meet all financial need and still enroll a high quality class. The need-blind admission policy can reduce access. The enrollment of students is a portfolio decision; hence, refusing to consider individual student needs (their ability to pay) and the quality of their contributions to the institution will result in forgoing opportunities to cross-subsidize access through the ability to pay of some students.

6.4   PRODUCT DIFFERENTIATION

A recent article in the *Chronicle of Higher Education* documents an emerging competitive trend in higher education (Pulley, 2003). Many institutions are using sophisticated marketing or 'academic branding' campaigns and these institutions report substantial improvements in student quality, increases in contributions to their endowments, and increases in annual giving as a result of these campaigns.

David Kirp provides an example of an apparent academic branding success (2003, 52–65). As was true for many liberal arts colleges, the 1990s were unkind to Dickinson College. The quality of the students they recruited during the decade declined due to their refusal to offer merit aid. The declining enrollment weakened their financial condition and caused their bond rating to fall and, finally, it led to their decline in the national rankings. In 1999, William Durden, an entrepreneurial professor of German from Johns Hopkins was hired 'to turn things around'.

President Durden accomplished this objective by instituting merit aid discounting and an aggressive branding campaign. Self-discovery through strategic planning was the foundation for the branding campaign. The focus was on knowing your own product and communicating what you have to the public. This required both attitudinal and curriculum changes on campus. The near-term results appear very promising.

There are three things missing from this story: what Dickinson's primary competitors are up to, how the college is converting this temporary advantage into permanent reputation, and a view from the year 2010. If they continue to re-invent themselves as their competitors respond and if they follow through with serious and substantial quality enhancements, the view from 2010 will indeed be an important success story.

Academic reputation is a valuable asset, and marketing campaigns do increase public awareness. However, the critical issue is: how does an institution create durable academic reputation at the least cost and in a manner that is most consistent with the service it is commissioned to provide? All academic institutions are ill served by branding campaigns that have an immediate half-life where the benefits end almost as soon as the campaign ends.

Before you dismiss me as another cranky faculty member who is unable to see the big picture, let me say that academic branding is not always a bad idea. However, there is an important pitfall in academic branding. In order to understand the danger, it is important to understand the historical context.

The first institutions to discover the benefits of tuition discounting during the 1980s reaped significant 'first-mover' advantages relative to their less innovative competitors. Out of necessity, other institutions began defensive discounting. The 1990s witnessed a tuition discounting arms race that resulted in the bankruptcy of an increasing number of institutions. Since 1997 over 30 institutions have closed their doors (Van Der Werf, 2002). A recent study suggests that tuition discounting did not alter the distribution of students among institutions but it may have lowered academic quality (Redd, 2000). The most important lesson from the 1990s is that tuition discounting is self-canceling; tuition discounting by one institution can be blocked by the tuition discounting of other institutions.

Administrators and governing boards emerged from the 1990s bloodied but unbowed. In the first decade of the new millennium, they have discovered 'non-price' competition. It is well understood from our experience with commercial firms that perceived product differentiation adds a new and permanent layer to marketing cost, a cost that generates no returns to either the quality of or access to higher education. It is well known that advertising is also self-canceling and that new advertising campaigns are countered by other firms in a manner such that all competitors experience higher cost with no permanent alteration in market share. Given the current public outrage over the cost of higher education and the fact that Congress is threatening to regulate tuition if costs are not brought under control (Burd, 2003), a permanent new layer of marketing costs could become an embarrassment for higher education. In addition, marketing wars frequently take a nasty turn.

Durable non-price competition requires real and substantial improvements in product quality. Enduring reputations can be built only through experience. The value of education is revealed only after it has been purchased. Advertising without substance yields a temporary advantage at best.

Investing in quality and access is a slow and painstaking process. It requires stable cash flows and the production of successful alumni in increasing numbers generation after generation. This strategy requires time and patience, both of which are in short supply. It also requires an intergenerational planning horizon and governing boards willing to make stable investments in long-run goals that are not likely to be met until they are no longer on the board.

There are three leverage points on quality and therefore on academic reputation: the quality of the students, the quality of their educational experience, and the quality of their placement upon graduation. Many institutions focus on the first two and ignore the third. Tuition discounting campaigns were designed to enhance the quality of the students. That turned out to be a zero-sum game.

The primary reason why vigorous tuition discounting failed to alter the distribution of students is because most institutions started with the wrong sequence: they started discounting before they improved the quality of the educational experience and before they improved the quality of their student's placement upon graduation. Had they adopted the right sequence, tuition discounting might have altered the distribution of students. This is part of the adverse incentive effect created by the national ranking systems, such as *US News and World Report*. *USNWR* places too much emphasis on the quality of inputs and too little emphasis on the quality of outputs. The impression is left that permanent quality improvement is accomplished by attracting better students in the short-run, while true quality improvement can only be achieved by improving outcomes.

Academic branding campaigns that lead to durable changes in reputation are a positive step towards improving all of higher education. Quality competition among higher education institutions has positive social effects, while public relations competition among higher education institutions can have negative social consequences. It will be an entirely avoidable tragedy if in 2010 or 2015 the higher education industry looks back on a decade filled with vigorous 'academic branding' campaigns and the distribution of students has not changed, the rankings are the same, and all institutions have a fat new layer of marketing costs.

6.5   REVENUES AND COST

Higher education, both public and private, is more dependent on tuition and fees revenue each year. As Table 6.1 illustrates, the proportion of total revenue derived from tuition and fees for each type of institution has grown steadily since 1980. In 1980, public higher education drew 12.9 percent of its total revenues from tuition and fees, and by 1999 the proportion had risen to 18.5 percent. Similarly, in 1980 private institutions drew 36.6 percent of their total revenues from tuition and fees and by 1996 that proportion was 43.0 percent.

Over the same time period, government support fell for both types of institutions. In 1980, public higher education drew 62.1 percent of its total revenue from federal, state, and local governments and that proportion declined to 50.5 percent in 1999. Once this number goes below 50 percent, it is arguable that these institutions are no longer public institutions; taxpayers will have 'taken them private'. In 1980, private higher education institutions obtained 21.5 percent of their revenues from government sources and in 1995 that number was 16.5 percent. Private external support has grown slightly at public institutions and remained relatively constant at private institutions. These trends reveal that the commercial part of higher education is growing relative to its public and private charitable revenue sources.

In Chapter 1, we considered the factors that are correlated with rising net tuition at both public and private institutions. The analysis revealed that declining public support and rising costs are correlated with rising net tuition in the public institutions. Similarly, we found that rising costs are correlated with rising net tuition at private institutions and that *rising* charitable revenues

Table 6.1   Proportion of total revenues by source of revenue

Year	1980	1985	1990	1995	1999
Public Institutions:					
Tuition and Fees	12.9	14.5	16.1	18.8	18.5
Federal	12.8	10.5	10.3	11.1	10.8
State/Local	49.3	48.5	44.0	39.9	39.7
Private Donations	2.5	3.2	3.8	4.1	4.8
Endowment	0.5	0.6	0.5	0.6	0.7
Other	21.9	22.5	25.3	25.5	25.5
Private Institutions:					
Tuition and Fees	36.6	38.6	40.4	43.0	
Federal	18.8	16.5	15.4	13.8	
State/Local	2.7	2.6	3.0	2.7	
Private Donations	9.3	9.3	8.6	9.1	
Endowment	5.1	5.3	5.2	5.2	

Source: NCES, Digest of Education Statistics, 2002, Tables 330 and 331.

are *positively* correlated with net tuition. Theory suggests that increasing external support for private institutions would moderate the need to raise net tuition
at these institutions; that is, one would expect that external subsidies would be
a substitute revenue source for tuition and fees revenue at private institutions,
just as government support is a substitute revenue source for tuition and fees
at public institutions. Implicit in the analysis in Chapter 1 is the assumption
that the direction of causation is from costs and public/private support to net
tuition. However, there are theoretical reasons that imply the direction of causation may flow in the opposite direction, or flow in both directions.

For example, Bowen argues that higher education institutions eliminate all
budgetary slack by raising expenditures until they equal revenues (1980). Ehrenberg uses the 'cookie monster' analogy to describe the same effect (2000,
11). The tendency of expenditures to rise to whatever revenues are available
is thought to be due to the shared governance structure in higher education and
the fact that each stakeholder group considers their activities under-funded.
Another popular conception among private higher education institutions is the
notion that the relative price of experience goods is a prior indicator of quality
(Martin, 1986). This phenomenon is referred to as the 'Chivas Regal' effect
among the private higher education establishment. It is argued that in an uncertain environment, institutions send quality signals through their list prices.

The foregoing raises specific questions. First, the theory in Chapter 5 suggests that higher tuition and fees increase the institution's financial capacity to support gifted students through cross subsidization. The higher tuition and fees paid by full pay students allow the institution to cross-subsidize scholarship students. This argument suggests the direction of causation is from rising tuition and fees to higher scholarships. If net price competition is the dominant form of competition between institutions, then one expects a feedback relationship between competition for gifted students through higher scholarships and then higher tuition and fees. The Chivas Regal hypothesis implies institutions that compete for gifted students on the basis of net tuition and fees are less hesitant to signal higher quality with higher tuition and fees, since this allows the institution to send the signal and to finance higher scholarships for gifted students. If the institutions are competing on the basis of net tuition and fees and signaling higher quality, then an increase in scholarships should cause higher tuition and fees. The signaling motive for increasing tuition and fees is primarily a characteristic of private higher education institutions. Public higher education institutions typically do not signal quality through their tuition and fees, since the majority of their support comes from government appropriations. Therefore, if there is a feedback relationship, it is more likely to be observed in private institutions.

Second, from the competitive commercial firm model we learn that higher cost leads to higher prices if the demand curve is downward sloped. If this is also true in higher education, then increasing educational and general (E&G) expenses per student should cause higher tuition and fees. On the other hand, if Bowen (1980) and Ehrenberg (2000) are correct, rising tuition and fees will lead to rising E&G expenses per student. Ehrenberg's cookie monster increases expenditures whenever a rise in revenues creates any budgetary slack. Hence, rising revenues cause E&G expenses per student to rise. These issues can be investigated through Granger causality tests (Granger, 1969).

It is generally understood that correlation between two variables does not mean that one variable causes the other variable. It is possible there may be a third unobserved variable that determines both of the variables in question. Even if we can be reasonably assured that no omitted third variable is responsible for the correlation, the direction of causation between the two variables is frequently not certain. Generally, we rely on economic theory to suggest the direction of causation (identify the dependent and independent variables). When considering prices and costs, the theory of the competitive commercial firm establishes the direction of causation from costs to prices. However, there is ample evidence in the preceding chapters that suggests the representative higher education institution does not behave as if it is a perfectly competitive commercial firm.

A limited form of causation through correlation can be established when using time series data. This type of causation is known as Granger or temporal causality (1969). Consider two variables, say A_t and B_t, where conflicting theories suggest the direction of causation may flow in either direction or may flow in both directions. If it can be established that A tends to precede B in time and the reverse is not true, then it can be concluded that A Granger causes B. If there is evidence of Granger causality in both directions this suggests there is some feedback loop between the two variables.

Consider the following two equations:

$$A_t = \sum_1^\rho \alpha_i A_{t-i} + \sum_1^\rho \beta_i B_{t-i} + \varepsilon_t \tag{6.1}$$

and

$$B_t = \sum_1^\rho \alpha_i A_{t-i} + \sum_1^\rho \beta_i B_{t-i} + \varepsilon_t. \tag{6.2}$$

If in equation (6.1) a standard Wald F test reveals that we can reject the null hypothesis that all of the betas are zero, this suggests B temporally precedes A. If also in equation (6.2) a standard Wald F test reveals that we cannot reject the null hypothesis that all the alphas are zero, this suggests B does in fact Granger cause A. If the F test in (6.2) rejects the null hypothesis, then A tends to precede B in time and we conclude that a feedback relationship exists between A and B.

Scholarship Competition and Signaling

In order to test Granger causality between tuition and fees and scholarships, data was collected on tuition and fees per student and scholarships per student from 1967 through 1999 for public institutions and from 1967 through 1996 for private institutions. These data come from the NCES via NSF Web-CASPER. The per student data series were deflated by the service-sector CPI. The number of lags, ρ, was set at four. For each type of institution, a Granger causality test was conducted on the deflated series.

The results of these tests are presented in Table 6.2. In each test, the results suggest that changes in tuition and fees per student tend to temporally precede changes in scholarships, while scholarships do not tend to temporally precede changes in tuition and fees. This result suggests that tuition and fees Granger cause scholarships per student in both public and private institutions. These results are consistent with the hypothesis that institutions increase their financial capacity to support gifted students through increases in tuition and fees. However, the results are not consistent with the notion that scholarship competition drives tuition and fees higher, although there is weak evidence that some feedback effects may take place in private higher education, where the institutions compete heavily on a net tuition and fees basis and where signaling through price is most likely to occur.

Table 6.2   Granger causality tests: tuition and fees/scholarships

Dependent Variable	F Statistic	Significance
Public Institutions:		
Tuition and Fees	0.68	0.42
Scholarships	6.73	0.02
Private Institutions:		
Tuition and Fees	2.16	0.16
Scholarships	6.81	0.02

The Cookie Monster and Disappearing Slack

Bowen's (1980) disappearing budgetary slack and Ehrenberg's cookie monster (2000, 11) suggest that increases in revenues precede in time increases in E&G expenditures per student. The traditional cost/price model from the competitive firm suggests that increases in E&G expenditure precede in time increases in revenues. Since the institutions have some latitude in the setting of their own tuition and fees, we expect that they will rise if E&G expenditures rise. However, public institutions have virtually no control over federal, state, and local government appropriations for higher education, so it seems unlikely that increases in E&G expenditure per student precede in time increases in these government appropriations per student. In the case of private institutions, who are dependent on endowment income and who control the payout ratio on that endowment, we may expect to see E&G expenditure increases per student precede in time increases in endowment income. This may also be the case for the relationship between E&G expenditure per student and annual giving per student, if benefactors respond to rising cost by increasing their donations.

Tuition and fees/E&G expenditures

In the case of tuition and fees and E&G expenditures, there are good reasons to expect that the cookie monster and cost pressure on price create a feedback loop in both sectors of higher education. Using similar data from the same source as the previous Granger causality models, I test this hypothesis using deflated tuition and fees per student and deflated E&G expenditures per student for both public and private higher education institutions. The results from these models are contained in Table 6.3.

Table 6.3   Granger causality tests: tuition and fees/E&G expenditures

Dependent Variable	F Statistic	Significance
Public Institutions:		
Tuition and Fees	5.05	0.04
E&G Expenditures	3.83	0.07
Private Institutions:		
Tuition and Fees	2.62	0.12
E&G Expenditures	6.64	0.02

The overall results in Table 6.3 suggest that feedback effects from E&G expenditures to tuition and fees and from tuition and fees to E&G expenditures are present. In private higher education institutions, increases in tuition and fees tend to temporally precede changes in E&G expenditures. When budgetary slack arises in private higher education, expenditures rise to eliminate the slack. The evidence for this effect in public higher education is weaker. In public higher education institutions, increases in E&G expenditures tend to temporally precede changes in tuition and fees. When costs rise in public higher education they tend to get passed on, at least in part, to students in the form of higher tuition and fees. The evidence for this effect in private higher education is weaker.

The reason for the difference between public and private institutions is probably the fact that real external support per student from government appropriations in the case of public institutions did not rise during the period under study, while real external support for private institutions did rise during the period. The decline in government support for public institutions as a proportion of total support forced them to pass rising costs on to students in the form of higher tuition and fees, while rising real external support for private institutions reduced the imperative to pass increases in cost on to students through increasing tuition and fees.

Government appropriations, endowment income, annual giving, and E&G expenditures

Budgetary slack can also be created by rising government appropriations, rising endowment income, or higher annual giving. Government appropriations are a small proportion of total revenues for private institutions, and endowment income and annual giving are very small proportions of total revenues for public institutions. Hence, it is appropriate to look for evidence regarding budgetary slack effects between government appropriations and E&G expenditures only in public higher education institutions and to look for budgetary slack evidence between endowment income/annual giving and E&G expenditures only in private higher education institutions.

The results are contained in Table 6.4. There is no evidence that increases in E&G expenditures temporally precede government appropriations in public higher education. In other words, the cost per student in public higher education seems to have little bearing on the amounts that are appropriated by government. It would appear that other government budgetary considerations dominate the decisions taken in this regard. The notion that government appropriations temporally precede increases in E&G expenditures draws weak support at best from the results in Table 6.4.

Concerning private higher education institutions, the data reveal a strong feedback loop between endowment income and E&G expenditures per student. Increases in E&G expenditures tend to temporally precede increases in endowment income, suggesting institutions increase payout rates when costs are rising, and increases in endowment income tend to temporally precede increases in E&G expenditures, which suggests the budgetary slack process is at work also. Endowment income at private institutions is a 'soft' budget constraint at best. The results are slightly different for the relationship between annual giving and E&G expenditures, however. Increases in E&G expenditures tend to temporally precede increases in annual giving, but there is no reciprocal temporal precedence. Hence, rising E&G expenditures seem to Granger-cause rising annual giving. The budgetary slack effect appears to be missing between cost and annual giving. Institutions may consider annual giving too volatile a source of revenue to finance permanent increases in cost.

6.6   MARKET SHARE

Enrollment growth since the end of World War II has been substantial. The compound growth rate from 1947 to 2000 in total enrollment in higher education was 1.54 percent per year which brought total enrollment from 2.3 million

Table 6.4   Granger causality tests: government appropriations, endowment income, annual giving, and E&G expenditures

Dependent Variable	F Statistic	Significance
Public Institutions:		
Appropriations	0.01	0.92
E&G Expenditures	2.81	0.11
Private Institutions:		
Endowment Income	22.75	0.00
E&G Expenditures	9.60	0.01
Annual Giving	14.21	0.00
E&G Expenditures	0.54	0.47

students in 1947 to 15.3 million in 2000. This is a 6.6-fold increase in enrollment over the period. While the growth in enrollment has been substantial, the growth has been distributed unevenly between public and private institutions. Figure 6.1 contains a plotting of total enrollment and enrollment at private institutions for the period from 1947 to 2000. Enrollment at private institutions grew at a compound growth rate of 0.90 percent per year, which resulted in an increase in enrollment from 1.2 million in 1947 to 3.6 million in 2000. This is a 3-fold increase in enrollment at private institutions. Public enrollment went from 1.2 million in 1947 to 11.8 million in 2000, which is a 9.8-fold increase in enrollment. Clearly, most of the enrollment growth occurred in public higher education.

In both public and private higher education, the increase in enrollment was accommodated by a combination of increasing the number of institutions offering services and increasing the average size of those institutions. In 1967, there were 829 public institutions and 1274 private institutions. The average enrollment in that year at public institutions was 5809 students and the average enrollment at private institutions was 1645 students. The average public institution was 3.5 times as large as the average private institution in 1967. By 2000, the number of public institutions rose to 1476 with an average enrollment of 7930 students, and the number of private institutions rose to 1746 with an average enrollment of 2010. The scale of the average public institution was four times as large as the scale of the average private institution in 2000. The average public institution increased its scale by over 36 percent during this period, while the average private institution increased its scale by over 22 percent. In addition, the growth in the number of public institutions was 78 percent and the growth in the number of private institutions was 37 percent.

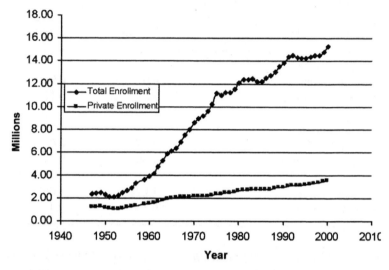

Source: NCES, Digest of Education Statistics, 2002, Table 172.

Figure 6.1   Higher education enrollment: 1947–2000

The trends in higher education enrollment reveal a dramatic shift in market share between public and private higher education during the period from 1947 through 2000. As reflected in Figure 6.2, private higher education's market share declined from 50.7 percent in 1947 to 20.3 percent in 2000. Most of that decline in market share occurred from 1947 to the mid-1970s. Since that time, private higher education's market share has remained relatively constant at around 20 percent of total enrollment.

Given the differences in net tuition rates at public and private institutions, the decline in private higher education's market share is not surprising. What may be unexpected is the relatively constant market share since the mid-1970s. Figure 6.3 contains a plot of the ratio of private tuition to public tuition over the period from 1967 to 2000 and that plot reveals that increases in private tuition have steadily outpaced increases in public tuition. There must be some factors other than relative price that account for private higher education holding its market share since the mid-1970s, particularly since the trend in the tuition ratio appears to be the same before and after the mid-1970s.

Since private tuition has continued to rise relative to public tuition, even though public tuition rose due to declining relative external support over the period, it is not obvious why private higher education's market share stabilized after the mid-1970s. Clearly, factors other than relative price are at play.

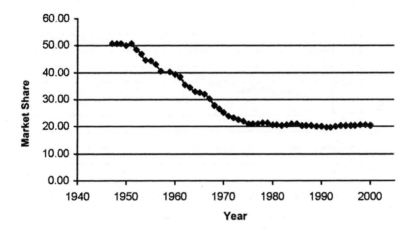

Source: NCES, Digest of Education Statistics, 2002, Table 172.

Figure 6.2   Private higher education's market share

One important unobserved variable is relative quality between public and private higher education. If the public perceives the quality of private higher education to be rising relative to public higher education, their willingness to pay for private higher education would also rise. In 1975, average tuition at private institutions was 2.2 times as high as public tuition; by 2000, that ratio had risen to 2.8, a 27 percent increase in the ratio. If higher education is a normal good, then both public and private enrollments should increase as real wealth and income increase. Furthermore, if enrollment demand at private higher education institutions is more income elastic than public higher education institutions, then, other things being equal, private higher education's market share should rise relative to public higher education's market share as real income rises. The rising relative price ratio and rising real wealth and income would work in opposite directions when it comes to private higher education's market share. The rising relative price ratio seems to have dominated during the period prior to the mid-1970s. Following the mid 1970s, increases in real wealth and income seem to have offset the rise in relative prices. If a shift in quality perceptions in favor of private higher education occurred after the mid-1970s period, this would help stabilize or increase private higher education's market share.

In order to explore the factors that explain private higher education's market share, a simple regression model is presented in Table 6.5. The data covers the period from 1963 through 1999; hence, most of the observations cover the period after private higher education's market share stabilized at around 20 percent.

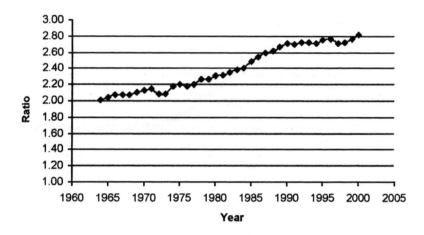

Source: NCES, Digest of Education Statistics, 2002, Table 312.

Figure 6.3   Tuition ratio: private tuition/public tuition

The dependent variable is private higher education's market share, *msp*. The independent variables are the tuition ratio, *tratio*, real per capita income, *rpci*, the unemployment rate, *urate*, and the index of industrial production, *indpro*. The data reveal that private higher education's market share is a decreasing function of the tuition ratio, an increasing function of real per capita income, a decreasing function of the unemployment rate, and a decreasing function of the index of industrial production. The coefficients for all of these variables are significant at the 0.01 or better level.

Given that students from lower income families are more likely to attend public institutions, a slowdown in access to higher education among low income students alone would cause private higher education's market share to rise. The period during which private higher education's market share stabilized coincides with the much-studied decline in the rate of productivity growth in the US economy. It is well known that the productivity slowdown affected high and low skilled workers differently. The real incomes of skilled labor continued to grow over the period, while the real incomes of low skilled workers, particularly males, declined. The real incomes of families at the top of the income distribution grew dramatically during this period. A slowdown in access to higher education, rising returns to skilled labor, and greater dispersion in the income distribution favor private higher education's market share. Alternatively, if society resolves the access problem, the dispersion in the income distribution should decline and one might expect private higher education's market share to continue to decline, since the current wave of new students approaching higher education come predominantly from low income families. In an odd sense, private higher education's market share may be an inverse indicator of access to higher education.

Table 6.5   Private higher education's market share

Variable	Coefficient	t Value
Intercept	86.41	5.27
tratio	−24.39	−2.83
rpci	0.01	3.11
urate	−1.47	−6.28
indpro	−0.70	−3.76
adj R^2	0.75	
n	36	

6.7   SUMMARY

Cooperation among commercial firms is frequently at the public's expense. On the other hand, cooperation is a necessary condition for the private provision of public goods. Similarly, the prevention of an arms race among competing nations requires cooperation among those nations. It is fair to say that public policy with respect to cooperation versus competition among economic entities is deeply conflicted. We vigorously discourage cooperation among commercial firms and routinely expect cooperation among charities, where the United Way is a case in point. The United Way is a cooperative arrangement among numerous charities that pool their fundraising efforts under a single umbrella organization. The conflicted attitude towards cooperation among service providers reflects the double edged nature of competition.

Even among commercial firms, we seem to be of two minds about cooperation and competition. Some public policy supports cooperation among professional sports teams who are profit maximizing enterprises, even though the cooperation is designed specifically to prevent entry and limit competition. Alternatively, the government took steps in the early 1990s to stop cooperation among higher education institutions who sought to limit scholarship competition for gifted students among the overlapping Ivy League institutions.

Higher education is caught in the middle. It is neither a pure commercial enterprise, nor is it a pure charity. Technically, higher education institutions are donative-commercial non-profits that produce a service which is part private good and part public good. It is unlikely that the optimal public policy towards higher education is either zero cooperation (total arm's length competition) among institutions or complete cooperation (zero competition) among institutions. The existence of agency problems and the absence of a market for control of higher education institutions make the discipline imposed by competition more important for the control of agency cost. Given that the optimal solution is a mixture of cooperation and competition, where should public policy encourage competition and where should it encourage cooperation?

Like primary and secondary education, higher education receives substantial government subsidy and significant private charity. Since human capital accumulation is a principal determinant of economic growth, the optimal social policy is to maximize the human capital available from any given subsidy constraint. The substitution of merit scholarships for need based scholarships crowds out private investment in higher education and reduces access for low income students. Price competition among higher education institutions and the growing perception among the public that education is a private good are responsible for rising merit scholarships and declining need based scholarships. When the quality of the institution is measured by the quality of the students the institution recruits, price competition for those students leads to the substitution of merit scholarships for need based scholarships. Vigorous price competition leads to declining access.

Non-price competition in higher education, like advertising among commercial firms, leaves market share undisturbed and adds significantly to higher cost. Cooperation among charities, such as the United Way, leads to lower fundraising costs and higher service provision. Since higher education is an experience good, quality is uncertain prior to purchase. The quality uncertainty is not resolved until well after graduation. Under these circumstances, the opportunities for deceptive non-price competition abound. These deceptive practices lead to the mismatching of students and institutions and a layer of costs that do not contribute to access or to quality.

Real quality competition promotes the public interest. At present, the incentives are not structured to promote real quality competition. The public has too little information about outcomes and misleading information about the quality of the inputs.

The commercial proportion of both public and private higher education continues to rise. Each type of institution is more dependent on tuition and fees revenue each year. The data reveal that public and private institutions raise tuition and fees in order to increase their financial capacity to support students. However, more of that financial capacity to support students is going to merit based support and less is devoted to provide access. There is weak evidence that private institutions may use tuition and fees schedules to signal quality.

The data also suggests that increases in cost per student cause increases in tuition and fees for both types of institution. There is a feedback effect from rising tuition and fees to rising cost per student. This feedback loop is due to the elimination of budgetary slack, which is the tendency of expenditures to fill any slack in the budget created by increases in permanent revenues. This effect is found in both public and private institutions. Increases in government appropriations tend to Granger cause increases in cost per student in public higher education and increases in endowment income tend to Granger cause increases in cost per student among private institutions. There is also strong evidence to suggest that private institutions adjust payout rates on their endowments in response to increases in cost per student.

The foregoing discussion ignores one important player in the competition equation: the for-profit higher education institutions. The University of Phoenix is now the largest university in the country, with an enrollment in excess of 70 000 students. The two trends that make the entry by for-profit institutions possible are rising net tuition rates in excess of the inflation rate and the technology that allows institutions to capture customers in widely dispersed geographic locations. The evidence suggests these trends will continue. To the outside entrepreneur, rapidly rising real prices reveal that existing suppliers are earning rents and those rents are a clear enticement to entry.

In the past, the public and private subsidies made available to non-profit institutions along with their heavy investments in 'bricks and mortar' served as a barrier to entry by for-profit institutions. Declining public support and the tuition increases that are well in excess of the inflation rate have eroded this barrier. The barriers imposed by 'bricks and mortar' are also eroded by technology which holds the promise of making land and buildings a liability rather than an asset. Furthermore, the for-profit institutions are not required to offer a complete curriculum. They can 'cherry-pick' among the programs that are most profitable. This is a serious problem for the non-profit institutions because they rely on the most profitable programs to subsidize programs that are not cost effective.

This trend is likely to cause serious conflict on many non-profit campuses. As non-profit institutions lose more market share to the for-profit institutions, the profitable programs that are capable of being self-sufficient will resent the subsidies paid to other programs on campus even more than they currently resent those subsidies. There will be increasing calls from the profitable programs to reduce the subsidy and/or to become quasi-independent of the rest of the campus. As the for-profit institutions increase their market share, the pressure on non-profit institutions will grow.

The unknown factor with respect to for-profit institutions is how effective they will be at providing a high quality educational experience. Will they ever be able to threaten the upper tier in the quality hierarchy, the part of the quality hierarchy dominated by the elite institutions? It seems unlikely that this could happen in the near future, but it does seem likely that the for-profit institutions will make life very uncomfortable for those institutions in the lower ranks of the quality hierarchy. The for-profit institution's success will be determined by how well their graduates perform in the market test. If they turn out to be productive and successful members of society whose services are highly valued in diverse labor markets, their impact on higher education could be revolutionary.

NOTES

1. Another example of the value of cooperation is found in national security and arms control. In this instance, cooperation prevents an arms race that is expensive, dangerous, and destabilizing. From society's perspective, this form of cooperation is 'good.' So, there are circumstances where arm's-length competition (no pun intended) is not in the public interest.
2. Robert Archibald argues for public policies that reduce competition and increase cooperation among higher education institutions on the basis of the arms race analogy (2002).
3. Tournament competition models are used to explain the widening gap between the salaries received by senior executives and the representative worker on the factory floor.
4. Reports of the decline in need based aid appear regularly in *The Chronicle of Higher Education*. For example, while reporting on a financial aid study prepared by 28 college presidents, the author notes 'The recommendations are an attempt to counteract the growing trend toward giving more money to the most coveted students instead of to those with limited resources. The presidents say their effort is crucial to preserving the practice of need based financial aid'.
5. The two most obvious cases are real estate and automobiles.

7. College access

Small opportunities are often the beginning of great enterprises.
Demosthenes   (384 BC – 322 BC)

Ability is nothing without opportunity.
Napoleon I   (1769 – 1821)

Opportunities are usually disguised as hard work, so most people don't
recognize them.
Ann Landers   (1918 – 2002)

Luck is what happens when preparation meets opportunity.
Darrell Royal   (1924 –)

One can present people with opportunities. One cannot make them equal to
them.
Rosamond Lehmann   (1901 – 1990)

Equality of opportunity means equal opportunity to be unequal.
Iain Macleod   (1913 – 1970)

7.1   INTRODUCTION

Economic opportunity and the social mobility that follows from economic opportunity are at the center of the college access issue. The quotations that
introduce this chapter reflect diverse views regarding both society's and the individual's role in the creation and the pursuit of economic opportunity. Minor
economic opportunities made available to the right people lead to substantial
gains in social welfare. However, before individuals can take advantage of the
opportunities made available to them they must be prepared for opportunity.
Further, individuals must be matched with the appropriate opportunity. Even
if the individual is prepared and is matched with the right opportunity, success
does not necessarily follow unless the individual is willing to put forth the effort required to succeed. These are the central questions for the college access
issue: are college opportunities available to students; are the students prepared
for those opportunities; are the students properly matched with the opportuni-

ties; and will the students make the effort to succeed?

In market economies, an individual's economic status is determined by the quantity and the quality of resources controlled by that individual. Each generation is endowed by the preceding generation through the wealth, natural talents, values, and culture they inherit from their parents and their society. The inheritance lottery is kind to some and cruel to others. Part of this outcome is pure luck; the rest is the result of good and bad decisions made by the child's parents. Since children are not complicit in the inheritance lottery, intergenerational equity is a natural issue. The child is born in a circumstance she did not create and cannot control, so what is society's obligation to this child? As with all policy issues, there are benefits, costs, and potential unintended consequences associated with this question. An important unintended consequence is the disincentive effect that a vigorous public policy might have on parents who may shirk their responsibilities if the state takes too much responsibility for its children. This is the intergenerational equity issue. A Hippocratic answer[1] to the intergenerational equity question is children should not be punished for having bad luck or for having good luck in the inheritance lottery. Each generation should not be punished for the sins (or virtues) of their parents.

Beyond the admonition to do no harm through our public policies toward the young, there are economic reasons why policy should be based on the notion of intergenerational equity. Social mobility is as important to the efficient allocation of resources and economic growth as is wage and price flexibility. Every economy is subject to random shocks that lead to natural volatility in that economy; that volatility can express itself as volatility in prices or volatility in real output. Rigid prices lead to greater volatility in real output, prolonged periods of unemployment, and slower economic growth. Economic mobility is important for the same reasons. Relative wages are market signals that direct human capital investment. The efficient use of labor requires that when returns to different skills change, workers must recognize these changes and they must acquire the preferred labor skills. Without the redirection of human capital investment, real output will be lower and economic growth will be slower. Therefore, economic mobility is as important to the efficient use of resources and economic growth as is wage and price flexibility. Economic mobility is a necessary condition for a prosperous society.

A second economic reason why intergenerational equity is important is because poverty has dynastic properties that perpetuate the ranks of the structurally unemployed and the social costs created by structural unemployment are very high. Permanently removing one family from the ranks of the structurally unemployed can reduce the cost of incarceration, domestic violence, drug abuse, and can lower health care costs for subsequent generations. Since these are social costs rather than private costs, they are not driven by the market mechanism. The direct return to public investment in economic mobility is lower social costs in the future.

Finally, individual attitudes towards economic mobility are shaped by experience, and attitudes can either promote or discourage mobility. Bowles and Gintis report that

> Survey data show that people – rich and poor alike – who think that 'getting ahead and succeeding in life' depends on 'hard work' or 'willingness to take risks' tend to oppose redistributive programs. Conversely, those who think that the key to success is 'money inherited from family', 'parents and the family environment', 'connections and knowing the right people' or being white support redistribution. (2002, 3)

In its extreme form, the belief that success is due to one's inheritance leads to the notion that economic status is imposed externally, and is not the consequence of individual effort. If you are unlucky in the inheritance lottery and there is no public intervention, you are destined to be poor. These are fatalistic attitudes. In contrast, the extreme form of the belief that individual achievement is the result of individual effort holds that the playing field is completely level and there are no significant external constraints on individual achievement. Under this view people remain in poverty because they choose not to put forth the effort required to get out of poverty. Obviously, the truth lies somewhere in between. The significance of this dichotomization is that an individual's attitude determines how optimistic/pessimistic he is about the rewards that will accrue to individual effort, and optimism/pessimism is reflected in each individual's subjective estimation of the probability they will succeed if they put forth the effort. The rising popularity of gambling, particularly state lotteries, suggests that an increasing number of individuals expect an external intervention to alter their economic status. Since those most likely to buy lottery tickets are people in lower income brackets, fatalism appears to be prevalent among those individuals. This should not be a surprise, since the size of the mobility hurdle is higher for low income families.

If the gulf between the wealthy and the poor widens and the obstacles to mobility increase, the proportion of the population who subscribe to the notion that economic success is inherited will grow. In a democracy, rising fatalism leads to more political pressure for more government wealth transfers and less private effort to change one's own economic status. More wealth transfers raise the tax burden on those who produce and this has an adverse impact on incentives and economic growth, the classic outcome in a welfare state. Therefore, the preferred social policy is one that demonstrates specific paths to economic mobility for children from low income families. The demonstration of channels available for economic mobility must be clear and the public support for those willing to accept the opportunity must be unambiguous.

An important part of the demonstration of economic mobility is making the availability of college known to children from low income families at an early age. Fitzgerald and Delaney consider the impact of the availability of financial aid on preparation for college by low income students, their decision to enroll, and their persistence in college (2002, 9–13). As early as the eighth grade low income students who expect aid are more likely to plan for college, more likely to take the courses needed for college in high school, more likely to enroll, and more likely to persist in college. These themes are repeated in Freeman (1997) and Perna (2000), who study minority student attitudes.

The typical student's response to the knowledge that aid is available reflects a simple expected cost/benefit calculus. Any public policy that increases the probability a student in need will be able to attend and be able to complete college increases the expected net benefit from college. The earlier the student and her parents are aware of the opportunity to attend, the more preparation the student makes. Unfortunately, the converse is true; anything that lowers the probability of attendance and/or completion lowers the expected net benefit from college. Unfortunately, the chronic high rate of inflation in college costs lowers the probability a student in need will be able to attend/persist in college and this lowers the net expected benefit from going to college. Failure to control cost lowers access.

Individuals are transported from low economic status to higher economic status by education.[2] By definition, anyone beginning life at a low economic status has been unlucky in the inheritance lottery. They have limited financial resources, they may or may not have been lucky in the natural talents they inherited, and they may or may not have had parents who made good decisions. For those who have been lucky in the inheritance lottery, that luck does not guarantee permanently higher income. Bad luck later in life and poor decisions can lead to lower economic status.

The intergenerational equity (equal opportunity) notion recognizes that all redistribution programs are not the same. Some redistribution programs are used to finance consumption, while others are used to finance social investment. Like government debt, redistribution programs are a burden only if they are used to finance consumption. The critical question for redistribution policies is the nature of the incentives created by the policy. Redistribution policies that finance consumption have adverse consequences on personal effort, while redistribution policies that finance investment have positive consequences for personal effort.

7.2   THE DECISION TO ATTEND COLLEGE

In this section I model the representative student's decision to attend college for an additional period. The results obtained are similar to those reported by Dynarski (2000, 6–11) and Cameron and Taber (2004, 139–144). Important extensions are the addition of the subjective probability of completing the enrollment period and its impact on permanent income. Since the purpose of the model is to provide a framework for discussing the economic issues associated with the access problem, I exclude all of the non-pecuniary effects associated with college attendance and the effect that peer decisions may have on this choice.

The college attendance decision is a sequence of decisions to attend for one more period given that the student has successfully completed e enrollment periods in the past. Assume h is a vector of student characteristics and assume r is the student's discount rate or the student's personal time preference (see Cameron and Taber, 2004, 140). Personal time preference is one measure of the student's degree of self-determination. A student with a high discount rate is fatalistic; he believes there is little he can do to influence his own future. A student with a low discount rate believes he can influence his own future through the actions he takes today. The vector of student characteristics, h, includes inherited traits that have value in the labor market.

The successful completion of one additional enrollment period alters the student's permanent income profile. Let $I(e,h)$ be the uniform annual series[3] that represents the annuity equivalent to the student's permanent income profile and assume that

$$I(e + 1, h) > I(e, h) \forall e \text{ and } h. \tag{7.1}$$

The permanent income profile is monotonically increasing in successfully completed enrollment periods.[4] If the student successfully completes the next enrollment period, his permanent income profile will be $I(e+1,h)$ and if he fails to successfully complete the next enrollment period, his permanent income profile will be $I(e,h)$. I assume $I(e,h)$ is strictly quasi-concave in e, so there are diminishing returns to additional enrollment periods over some values of e.

Let the permanent income profile be an increasing function of the vector of student characteristics, $\partial I(e, h)/\partial h > 0$. This suggests that the student characteristics are productivity indicators and they provide a theoretical foundation for the existence of 'ability bias' in the return to education (see Lang (1993) and Card (1995)). The marginal return to one more enrollment period depends on both the number of enrollment periods and native ability. Hence, there is heterogeneity among the returns to education across students, based on the differences in the vector h. Cameron and Tabor note that 'empirical evidence for this idea has been found in virtually every data set with pre-labor market measures of scholastic ability, such as standardized test scores' (2004, 138).

Suppose terminal time is T; then the present value of the student's permanent income profile if he has successfully completed $e+1$ enrollment periods is

$$I(e + 1, h) \sum_{1}^{T-e} (1 + r)^{-t}, \qquad (7.2)$$

and the present value of his permanent income profile if he has successfully completed e enrollment periods is

$$I(e, h) \sum_{1}^{T-e} (1 + r)^{-t}. \qquad (7.3)$$

If $p \equiv p(e, h)$ is the probability the student will successfully complete the enrollment period, then the expected present value of permanent income given the student enrolls for one more period is equal to p times the expression in (7.2) plus $1-p$ times the expression in (7.3).

The cost of enrolling for one more period depends on the total direct cost of enrollment per period, say c, the subsidy per period, say s, the family contribution per period, say f, and the opportunity income forgone. The opportunity income forgone is one period of annuity income with e enrollment periods successfully completed

$$I(e, h). \qquad (7.4)$$

The direct costs per period (tuition/fees, books, living expenses, etc.), c, must be financed by family contributions, f, the public subsidy per period, s, or by new debt, d. Let the family contribution be a constant proportion of family income, $f=aY$, where Y is family income. Hence, the financing constraint is $c=s+aY+d$ and the present value of new debt for each enrollment period is

$$d = c - s - aY. \qquad (7.5)$$

If $s+aY > c$, then d is negative and the student is being paid a stipend to attend college. The stipend offsets all or part of the opportunity wages forgone by attending college. This was one of the special features included in the World War II GI Bill. Equation (7.5) highlights the difference between grants (either public or parental transfers) and debt that must be repaid (Cameron and Taber, 2004). The present value of the incremental cost of enrolling for one more period is equal to the sum of (7.4) and (7.5).

The expected benefit function for one more enrollment period is

$$\overline{B} \equiv p(e, h)[I(e + 1, h) \sum_1^{T-e} (1 + r)^{-t}] + [1 - p(e, h)]I(e, h) \sum_1^{T-e} (1 + r)^{-t} \quad (7.6)$$

$$- (c - s - aY) - I(e, h).$$

Alternatively, the present value of permanent income if the student does not enroll for one more period is

$$B \equiv I(e, h) \sum_1^{T-e} (1 + r)^{-t}. \quad (7.7)$$

A necessary condition for the student to enroll for one more period is that $\overline{B}$ in (7.6) must be strictly greater than B in (7.7).

The number of completed enrollment periods such that the student is indifferent to enrolling for an additional period is found where the difference between $\overline{B}$ and B is zero. The difference between $\overline{B}$ and B is the net expected benefit function, which is

$$\overline{B}^N \equiv \overline{B} - B \quad (7.8)$$

$$\equiv p(e, h)[I(e + 1, h) - I(e, h)] \sum_1^{T-e} (1 + r)^{-t} - (c - s - aY) - I(e, h),$$

after collecting terms. The student's optimal stopping point, the point where the student is indifferent to enrolling for an additional period, is found where the net expected benefit function in (7.8) is equal to zero. At the optimal stopping point, the expected incremental effect of one additional enrollment period on the present value of the permanent income profile is set equal to the amount borrowed for one more enrollment period plus the opportunity income forgone for one enrollment period.

Consider two students who are identical in all respects except that they have different personal time preferences, r. In order to induce the student with the highest time preference to enroll for the same number of periods as the student with the lower time preference, the student with the highest time preference would have to be offered a higher marginal return to education than the student with a lower time preference. This suggests there will be heterogeneity in the required returns to education for students with different time preferences. These differences are the source of 'discount rate bias' introduced into empirical returns to education (Lang, 1993).

Building on Lang (1993) and Card (1995), Cameron and Taber note instrumental variable techniques are sensitive to the selection of instruments when the returns to education are heterogeneous across students (2004, 133–34). Instrumental variable techniques recover the marginal effects on the income of those students whose results are sensitive to the instrumental variable chosen rather than the average effect over the entire set of students in the sample. This introduces the possibility of two types of bias into the estimation of returns to education: 'ability bias' and 'discount rate bias'. Each one of these biases is associated with heterogeneity across students. In order to recover the independent effect of education on the return to education, both sources of bias must be removed.

Let the implicit solution for $\overline{B}^N = 0$ in (7.8) be $\hat{e} = e(h, r, c, s, Y, T)$. The implicit solution, $\hat{e}$, is the student's optimal number of completed enrollment periods. The optimal solution is found where the net expected benefit function is decreasing in completed enrollment periods; hence,

$$d\overline{B}^N/de < 0. \tag{7.9}$$

Several results follow immediately.

Proposition 7.1) The optimal number of enrollment periods is a decreasing function of the direct cost per enrollment period, a decreasing function of the opportunity cost per enrollment period, an increasing function of the subsidy per enrollment period, and an increasing function of family income.

Given (7.9), the comparative statics with respect to c, s, and Y are

$$\partial\hat{e}/\partial c = (d\overline{B}^N/de)^{-1} < 0,$$

$$\partial\hat{e}/\partial s = -(d\overline{B}^N/de)^{-1} > 0,$$

and

$$\partial\hat{e}/\partial Y = -a(d\overline{B}^N/de)^{-1} > 0,$$

The comparative statics with respect to the opportunity cost is identical to the comparative statics with respect to the direct cost per period. Proposition 7.1) provides the theoretical foundation for the argument that college access decreases whenever costs (direct or opportunity cost) per period increase, and college access increases whenever students receive more family support or more external financial aid.

Time preference is not constant across individuals. This is evident since some people are habitual lenders and some people are habitual borrowers. As the rate of time preference goes to infinity the individual places no value on future consumption and that person might be said to be living entirely in the moment. By contrast, an individual whose rate of time preference is zero places equal value on future consumption and current consumption. This person plans for the future, while the person who lives in the moment assumes the future will take care of itself. The person with a low rate of time preference has a long planning horizon, while the person with the high rate of time preference has a short planning horizon. From the optimal stopping rule, we have

Proposition 7.2) The optimal number of enrollment periods is a decreasing function of the student's time preference.

The derivative of $\hat{e}$ with respect to the student's time preference is

$$\partial \hat{e}/\partial r = \{p(e, h)[I(e + 1, h) - I(e, h)] \sum_{1}^{T-e} t(1 + r)^{-t-1}\}(d\bar{B}^N/de)^{-1} < 0,$$

which is negative due to (7.1) and (7.9).

Proposition 7.2) reveals that the optimal number of enrollment periods for some people is zero, regardless of their ability, the cost of attending college, or the amount of support they may receive from family or from society. For a sufficiently high time preference, the expected incremental effect on the permanent income profile is zero for all e and h. In this case, college attendance is all cost and no benefit. In what follows, I assume the student's time preference does not take such extreme values; that is I assume the students in question have normal time preferences. However, it is worth remembering that there will be students who have very high time preferences and these students may be said to lack motivation to attend college regardless of the probability of success in college.

The student's probability of successfully completing the next enrollment period, $p(e,h)$, is a subjective conditional probability. It is the student's subjective evaluation of the probability he will be successful, and that expectation depends on his experience to date and his personal characteristics. If the student's parents are college graduates, if the student is prepared for college, and if the student is gifted, the student's subjective expectation of success will be higher than another student who does not have any one or all of these characteristics. Therefore, a comparative statics shift in the conditional probability represents all of the foregoing influences.

Proposition 7.3) The optimal number of enrollment periods is an increasing function of the conditional probability of success.

Let k be a multiplicative constant that is initially equal to one; then, multiply p in (7.8) by k and totally differentiate with respect to k and evaluate k at $k=1$. The constant k scales up the conditional probability and the derivative of $\hat{e}$ with respect to k is

$$\partial \hat{e}/\partial k = -\{p(e, h)[I(e + 1, h) - I(e, h)] \sum_{1}^{T-e} (1 + r)^{-t}\}(d\overline{B}^N/de)^{-1} > 0,$$

Any factor that increases the subjective probability the student will succeed increases the number of enrollment periods. Proposition 7.3) suggests that better preparation for college, parental education, cognitive skills, and more certain external support all improve college access.

The incremental effect of an additional enrollment period on the student's permanent income profile is measured by

$$I(e + 1, h) > I(e, h) \forall e \text{ and } h.$$

The incremental effect will vary depending on the quality of the educational experience. For example, one suspects that for the same student the incremental effect of one more semester at the county junior college is not the same as one more semester at an elite private institution. Assume the representative student has multiple higher education opportunities; that is, the representative student has sufficient academic credentials to be admitted to several different higher education institutions. These institutions vary on the basis of cost, c, the subsidy they provide the student, s, and the quality of their educational experience. The quality of their educational experience is reflected by the impact an enrollment period, e, has on the student's permanent income profile. We may also anticipate that the student's probability of successfully completing the enrollment period, p, varies from one institution to the next. At each point in the sequence of attendance decisions, the representative student computes the value of the net expected benefits function in (7.8) for each institution and chooses to enroll in the institution that produces the highest net expected benefits. The student declines to enroll in any institution only if all net expected benefit functions are zero or negative. Hence,

Proposition 7.4) The representative student attends the institution that provides the highest positive net expected benefits, which is not necessarily the highest quality institution available to the student.

Assuming cost and quality are positively correlated, quality choice can be changed by changing the subsidy offered to the student and by changing the student's preparation for college, since this increases the probability of success. Quality matching is a function of both preparation and income.

The model in this section reveals a variety of reasons why an individual student might choose not to attend college or not to complete a degree once enrolled. The most obvious reasons are financial constraints; either the amount of debt required is too high relative to the expected benefits or if the student cannot borrow, then the student may not attend or may not complete a degree. This problem will manifest itself as lower attendance and lower completion rates for low income students. The policy solution in this case is to increase need based financial aid.

However, there are several other reasons why a student may not attend or may not complete a degree. First, if the student is not prepared for college then the probability he will successfully complete the enrollment period is low and the expected benefits are correspondingly low with respect to the cost of attendance. If this student attends, the odds are he will fail and end the experience with debt that he cannot repay. Second, if the inherited characteristics, h, reduce the permanent income profile or reduce the probability the student will successfully complete the enrollment period, then the expected benefits from attendance will be low with respect to the cost and the student will not attend or will not complete a degree. Finally, if the student has a high time preference the expected benefits from attendance will be low even if the student has ample family income, is prepared for college, or has highly marketable inherited characteristics. Note that all three of these alternative reasons not to attend college are rational choices. Further note that all three of these reasons are correlated with family income. Children who are not prepared for college are most likely to be children from low income families. Inherited characteristics create dynastic family income traditions. Dysfunctional family characteristics tend to be transferred between generations. A high time preference suggests a low savings rate and a correspondingly lower family income. Therefore, the three alternative reasons why students may choose not to attend college or to complete a degree will also manifest themselves as a correlation between family income and attendance and completion rates.

These factors create a serious policy dilemma: the root causes of low attendance and low completion rates lead to observationally equivalent empirical evidence, while the optimal public policy solution varies according to the root cause. If it is simply an income problem, then need based subsidies for college attendance are the preferred solution. If the problem is lack of college preparation, then improving the quality of primary and secondary education along with remedial education is the priority. If the problem is dysfunctional inherited characteristics or high time preference, then neither more need based aid nor more investment in primary and secondary education are likely to improve attendance and completion rates. The optimal policy with respect to inherited characteristics and time preference requires a sustained public education program dealing with family cultures and values and that will be politically very controversial.[5]

The information requirements in the decision calculus outlined above are significant, and information determines the subjective probability of success. The children of wealthy families who attend well funded secondary schools with well informed college placement counselors will have more information than the children of poor families who attend under-funded secondary schools. The quality of the secondary school attended determines both academic preparation and information. Wealthy parents make private investments in information that is not available to children from poor families. In other words, college information is very likely to be asymmetrically distributed across families with high and low incomes. The probability that a low income student will be unaware of some college opportunities is higher than the probability that a high income student will be unaware of some college opportunities.

The preceding college attendance model is a traditional human capital model, where students acquire human capital through their attendance decisions and the returns on those investments are reflected in higher permanent income profiles. Apart from human capital, education may also act as a labor market signal when information is asymmetrically distributed (Spence, 2002). In the pure signaling model (ignoring the human capital aspects of education), employers cannot observe individual worker productivity among prospective employees so they use education to sort low productivity and high productivity workers. This is possible only if the cost of additional education is lower for high productivity workers than it is for low productivity workers. In this environment, high productivity workers signal their productivity through their education choice and the model leads to a separating equilibrium with different wage rates for low and high productivity workers. Note that this is the same result one would observe in the human capital model. Since the two types of models lead to similar results, they are more complementary than competitive; however, those similarities make it difficult to empirically discriminate between the two models (Bedard, 2001, 750).

Despite the similar conclusions, there are important differences in the human capital model and the signaling model. Information asymmetry can lead to a pooling equilibrium, where the signal does not allow the employer to sort high and low productivity workers. Kelly Bedard considers how the college access problem may contribute to the failure of education to act as a satisfactory signal (2001). Any factor that prevents high productivity students from acquiring the signal or enables low productivity students to acquire the signal contributes to the increased likelihood that a pooling equilibrium rather than a separating equilibrium will prevail. For example, if high productivity students from low income families are prevented from going to college by credit constraints, the signal quality of education is reduced. Therefore, the greater the access problem, the more noise there is in the signal. When high productivity workers cannot get access to college, they are pooled with low productivity workers who have only a high school education. The wage rate paid to high school graduates is a weighted average of the true productivity wages that would be earned by each type of worker if information was symmetric. Low productivity workers have an increased incentive to complete high school, which leads to a lower high school drop-out rate. If the access problem gets worse over time, the average real wage paid to high school graduates declines (less-productive workers are now getting high school degrees) and the high school drop-out rate declines. The historical trends in high school drop-out rates and in real wages paid to high school graduates fit this profile.

Alternatively, suppose college admission standards fall and grade inflation increases such that more low productivity students (students who have the ability to pay, but are not well prepared for college) are admitted to college and more of those students actually complete college. This trend would create pooling problems in the labor market for college graduates and those problems would raise the incentives for low productivity students to attend college and increase the incentives for high productivity students to find an alternative way to signal their higher productivity. In this situation it would not be surprising to see the quality hierarchy among institutions widen and to see increasing numbers of high productivity students doing postgraduate work. In other words, declining admission standards and grade inflation should lead to more intense quality competition among the top tier institutions and to rising attendance rates in postgraduate programs. The quality competition trends among institutions and rising enrollment in graduate programs are consistent with the signaling theory and the human capital model.

7.3 CRISIS, CHRONIC PROBLEM OR MYTH?

In its pure form the college access issue refers to the simple observation that the rate of college attendance, completion, and/or the quality of the institution attended varies across different groups within society. The access problem is most severe if there are different groups who never have the opportunity to attend college. The problem is less severe if some groups are able to attend college but have difficulty completing a degree program. The access problem is least severe if some groups are able to attend and to complete degree programs but they are not matched with the appropriate institution. The different groups may be defined on the basis of income, gender, ethnicity, race, or any other classification the observer may choose. Given the amount of data available, it would be surprising not to find a longer list of underrepresented groups in college. In fact, we will be able to make a case from the historical data that males are an under-represented group with respect to college attendance. The important question is why these groups are under-represented.

The evidence that attendance and completion rates are lower for low income families than they are for high income families is clear; the current fault line in the college access debate is between those who believe the rate differences are due to income and those who believe the rates are different due to a lack of preparation for college among low income students. The foregoing student choice model reveals a third reason why the rates might be different: family cultures and time preference. The root causes of lower attendance and completion rates, other than income itself, are also correlated with income, so the science suggests that factors other than just income are jointly responsible for the observed differences. Since the other factors are correlated with income, disentangling the independent role of income, preparation, and culture is a significant empirical challenge.

The debate surrounding the college access issue suggests it is a major crisis. The rhetoric employed by some is not constructive.[6] The tone of the debate suggests that things must be getting worse. For example, Sandra Ruppert, author of a report prepared by the Education Commission of the States entitled 'Closing the College Participation Gap: A National Summary' argues that the access situation is deteriorating and that we face a crisis in college access (2003). Similarly, the Advisory Committee on Student Financial Assistance in its report entitled 'Empty Promises: the Myth of College Access in America' takes a decidedly pessimistic and partisan position on the college access question (2002). Most recently, The Institute for Higher Education Policy and Scholarship America in their report entitled 'Investing in America's Future: Why Student Aid Pays Off for Society and Individuals' makes another strong case for increasing need based aid.

In order to gain some perspective, it is appropriate to consider the historical record. What has happened to overall college access during the last three decades? How have minorities and low income students fared during this period? Has any progress been made? Finally, looking forward what can we reasonably anticipate in access trends?

Attendance

Figure 7.1 contains the total number of students enrolled in colleges and universities from 1869 to 2000. This long-run secular growth in enrollment demonstrates a dramatic acceleration that began in the late 1950s and has continued through 2000. Given the near exponential growth in volume, one would be hard pressed to make the claim that the higher education industry has failed to accommodate the rising demand for its services. The near exponential growth in enrollment coupled with the near exponential growth in net tuition and fees over the same period is a bit of a paradox. While these trends suggest that the aggregate demand for higher education is highly price inelastic, econometric studies reveal that aggregate enrollment demand is in fact price elastic (Mazumder, 2003). The rising return to education accounts for the enrollment increases in the face of rising college costs. The rising college costs capture for the education community some of the returns to education that would otherwise accrue to students. If college educations were elastically supplied in a perfectly competitive context, all of the rising returns to education would be captured by students. If the supply of college educations is perfectly inelastic, all of the rising returns are captured by the education community.

Figure 7.2 contains the college attendance rate for the total population who were between 18 and 24 years of age during the period from 1967 through 2002 and the high school drop-out rate for that same period. The data reveal that the college attendance rate rose from 26.7 percent in 1967 to 39 percent in 2002, while the high school drop-out rate declined from 19.8 percent in 1967 to 12.3 percent in 2002. These statistics suggest improvement in both college attendance and high school completion over this period. There does appear to be some slowing in the secular growth rate of the college attendance rate since the early 1990s, however. Together, Figures 7.1 and 7.2 suggest an admirable increase in both the number of students attending and the proportion of the appropriate age cohort attending college. If there is a crisis in college access, one expects to see at least a decline in the rate of growth in the number of students attending college and a constant or declining proportion of students in the 18-to-24-year-old age cohort attending college.

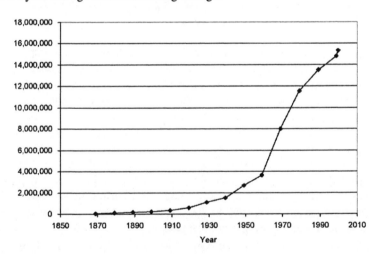

Source: NCES, Digest of Education Statistics, 2002, Table 171.

Figure 7.1   Total enrollment in higher education: 1869–2000

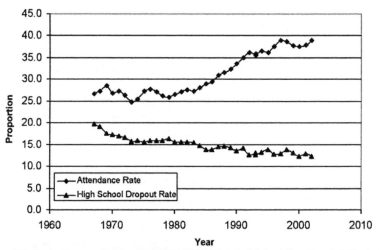

Source: US Census Bureau, October CPS 1967–2002, Historical School Enrollment, Table A–5;
www.census.gov/population/www/socdemo/school.html.

*Figure 7.2   College attendance rates and high school drop-out rates for the
18-to-24-year-old age cohort: 1967–2002*

While the data represented in Figures 7.1 and 7.2 do not suggest there is an
alarming problem, serious issues can be hidden within the aggregates represented by these two figures. Figure 7.3 contains college attendance rates for
female members of the 18-to-24-year-old cohort by race and ethnicity. The
college attendance rates for white, black, and Hispanic females are all trending
upward. There is a clear converging of the trends between white and black
females, while there is some widening of the gap between these two groups
and Hispanic females. In contrast, consider the college attendance rates for
male members of the 18-to-24-year-old cohort by race and ethnicity in Figure
7.4. The college attendance rates for white and Hispanic males show little
trend over the period from 1967 to 2002. However, the gap between white
males and black males does appear to be closing. The nearly flat lined college
attendance rates for white and Hispanic males coupled with the upward trends
in female college attendance rates suggests that the attendance problem is more
of a gender problem than it is a racial problem. This is particularly so since the
gaps between whites and blacks are closing for both genders. Since the white,
black, and Hispanic populations are growing, a more or less constant male college attendance rate means the number of male students by each classification
is growing, and since the black and Hispanic populations are growing faster
than the white population, the number of black and Hispanic males attending

college is growing faster than the number of white males.

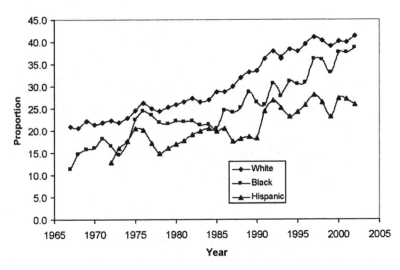

Source: US Census Bureau, October CPS 1967–2002, Historical School Enrollment, Table A–5; www.census.gov/population/www/socdemo/school.html.

Figure 7.3   Female college attendance rates for the 18-to-24-year-old age cohort: 1967 to 2002

The role gender plays in the college access problem is an under-studied issue. Why have college attendance rates for males not risen as have female college attendance rates during the period from 1967 to 2002? The attendance model in the previous section suggests that college attendance varies according to the potential gain in lifetime earnings, the probability of completion, and the student's discount rate. Hence, males may have a lower potential gain in lifetime earnings, be less well prepared, or have a higher discount rate than females. Another possibility is that there is discrimination against males in education (either in primary/secondary school or college). It seems improbable that young males would be subject to more severe financial constraints than young females; so, the financial constraint hypothesis does not seem to be a likely explanation. On the other hand, one may be able to make the case that young males are less prepared for higher education than are young females. The decline in the number of male classroom teachers in primary and secondary schools could contribute to the decline in male role models. This, coupled with higher divorce rates and rising female heads of households could signal an overall decline in the number of positive male role models. These results are also reflected in income trends during the same period. The real incomes

of males who do not attend college have declined the most over the last three
decades.

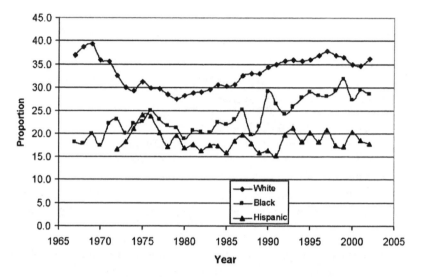

Source: US Census Bureau, October CPS 1967–2002, Historical School Enrollment, Table A–5;
www.census.gov/population/www/socdemo/school.html.

*Figure 7.4   Male college attendance rates for the 18-to-24-year-old age
cohort: 1967 to 2002*

The differential attendance rates for male and female Hispanics also bears
investigation. Before we can conclude whether the gap is rising, we need
to know whether immigration is distorting the results.[7] Young Hispanics are
more likely to immigrate than are older Hispanics and there has been a rising
tide of Hispanic immigrants over the last three decades. Young immigrants are
not likely to be prepared for college and this could distort the attendance rates
for Hispanics.

In the past, one could argue convincingly that under-representation among
groups based on gender, ethnicity, and race were the result of discrimination
against women, Hispanics, and racial minorities. That argument is more difficult today given higher education's demonstrated preference for affirmative
action with respect to groups who have been discriminated against in the past,
and the fact that the attendance data in this section reveals that the attendance
rate for females is rising and the attendance rates for black and white females
and for black and white males are converging. One could conceivably make a
case for discrimination with respect to the under-representation of males and

Hispanics in the college attendance rates.

Completion Rates

College completion rates are defined as the proportion of students starting as freshmen at four-year institutions who complete their degrees within five years. The general trend in completion rates has been down, with one exception. The one exception is the completion rate for students who attend the most selective public and private institutions, where the completion rate was 76.3 percent in 1986 and 80.5 percent in 2003. This trend probably reflects the increasing concentration of the best students in the most selective institutions. The average ACT scores for students at the most selective institutions varies from 27 to 31. The college completion rates for all other quality classifications and by public and private institutions declined or remained approximately constant over the period from 1986 to 2003. Table 7.1 contains completion rates for both public and private institutions by the highest degree conferred by the institution. The completion rate for public bachelors conferring institutions fell steadily from 52.8 percent in 1986 to 41.2 percent in 2003, while the completion rate for private bachelors conferring institutions was approximately constant during this period. The completion rate for public PhD granting institutions fell from 50.9 percent in 1986 to 46.0 percent in 2003, while the completion rate for private PhD granting institutions fell from 70.0 percent in 1986 to 64.9 percent in 2003. Other regularities in these data are that completion rates fall continuously as we move down from the most selective institutions to the least selective institutions and the rate of decline in completion rates is faster as we move down from the most selective to the least selective institutions. Since these trends are in the wrong direction, one can make a case for alarm regarding the role completion rates play in the college access issue.

Table 7.1 College completion rates

Year	Bachelors		PhD Institutions	
	Public	Private	Public	Private
1986	52.8%	55.5%	50.9%	70.0%
1990	51.7	54.9	50.6	67.0
1995	47.8	54.7	49.1	66.3
2000	41.6	53.3	45.6	63.4
2003	41.2	54.5	46.0	64.9

Source: ACT National Graduation Rates, 1983 to 2003, 25 July 2003.

Since ACT scores are positively correlated with family income and minority students are more likely to have lower ACT scores, the foregoing college completion data suggest that lower income and minority student completion rates are lower than high income and white student completion rates. In the previous subsection we found that minority students were attending college at higher rates during this period. Unfortunately, it appears that those higher attendance rates are not being translated into higher completion rates for minority students.

A further indication of college completion rates can be obtained by considering the proportion of the population who are 25 years of age and older who have completed four or more years of college. This is an imprecise measure of college completion because completing four years of college does not imply the student completed a degree program. The data in Figure 7.5 reveal that the proportion of both males and females who completed four or more years of college rose steadily from 1964 through 2002. It also reveals that the gap between males and females has been closing. The closing of the gap between males and females is primarily due to the slowdown in the male proportion that began in the early 1980s. The slowdown in the male proportion is the natural consequence of the nearly constant male attendance rates discussed in the previous subsection.

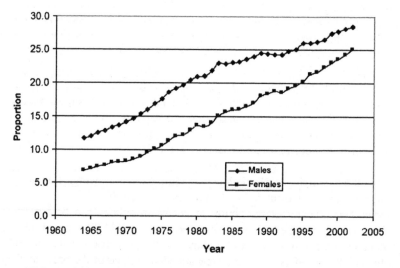

Source: US Census Bureau, March CPS 1964–2002, Historical Educational Attainment Table A–2. www.census.gov/population/www/socdemo/educ–attn.html.

Figure 7.5   Proportion of 25 and older population completing four or more years of college: 1964 –2002

The proportion of females by race and ethnicity who are 25 years of age or older and have completed four or more years of college for the period from 1964 through 2002 is recorded in Figure 7.6. The completion rate for white females shows a steady progress along a stationary secular trend. The secular trend for black females is slightly more shallow, suggesting a widening of the gap between white and black females, and demonstrates more volatility from one year to the next. It is apparent that the higher attendance rates by black females are not being transformed into higher completion rates for black females. The gap between white and Hispanic females is widening. Again, we do not know what role immigration plays in this process. The completion rates for males who are 25 years of age or older and by race and ethnicity for the same period are contained in Figure 7.7. The gaps between white males and black or Hispanic males are rising. Again, the secular trend for white males appears to have slowed down beginning in the early 1980s.

Unlike the attendance data, the completions data suggest the access problem does vary by race and ethnicity. The lower completion rate for racial and ethnic minorities may be the result of financial constraints, lack of preparation, or the effect of differences in culture. It is very likely to be a combination of all three of these factors. These results are consistent with Kevin Carey's conclusion

> America's colleges and universities have a serious and deep-rooted problem: far too many students who enter our higher education system fail to get a degree. Even among the students most likely to succeed – those who begin their college career as full-time freshmen in four-year colleges and universities – only six out of every ten of them, on average, get a BA within six years. This translates into over *half* a *million* collegians every year, a group disproportionately made up of low-income and minority students, who fall short of acquiring the credentials, skills and knowledge they seek. ... There is a large graduation rate gap between low-income and high-income students, and the *majority* of African American and Latino students don't complete their degree within six years. (2004, 1–2)

The college completion problem is real, chronic, and growing. It is one rung on the economic mobility ladder that needs our attention.

Another indicator of the ability to persist in college can be constructed using the proportion of the population between 25 and 29 years of age who completed four or more years of college and the proportion of the population between 18 and 24 years of age who attended college in the preceding time period. The ratio of these two proportions in any one year provides a measure of the persistence of students attending college who complete four or more years of college. Recall from the previous subsection that the proportion of the 18-to-24-year-olds who attend college grew throughout this period; therefore, if the ratio is constant, the ability of students to persist until they have four or

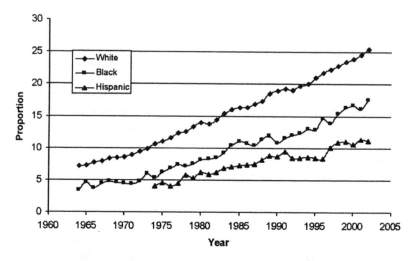

Source: US Census Bureau, March CPS 1964–2002, Historical Educational Attainment Table A–2. www.census.gov/population/www/socdemo/educ–attn.html.

Figure 7.6   Females by race and ethnicity completing four or more years of college: 1964 –2002

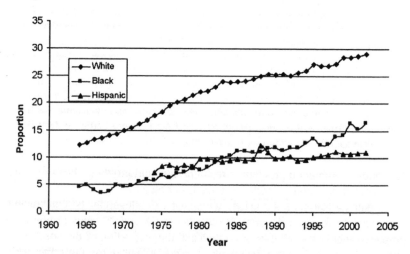

Source: US Census Bureau, March CPS 1964–2002, Historical Educational Attainment Table A–2. www.census.gov/population/www/socdemo/educ–attn.html.

Figure 7.7   Males by race and ethnicity completing four or more years of college: 1964 –2002

more years of college has remained constant. When the ratio rises, completion must be improving relative to the previous year and when it falls, completion must be declining relative to the previous year. Figure 7.8 contains the plotting of this ratio from 1968 through 2001. The data reveal that a larger proportion of students who were attending college succeeded in completing four or more years of college from 1968 until the mid-1970s. Following that time, the ratio declined. With rising enrollment this reveals that increasing numbers of students are not completing four or more years of college. Progress towards completion appears to have stopped and have begun to backtrack in the mid-1970s.

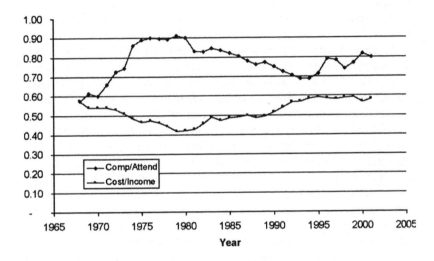

Source: US Census Bureau, October CPS 1967–2002, Historical School Enrollment, Table A–5. March CPS 1964–2002, Historical Educational Attainment Table A–2. CPS Historical Income Tables, Table P–2. NCES, Digest of Education Statistics, 2002, Table 312.

Figure 7.8   Completion/attendance ratio and college cost/income ratio

Of equal interest is the ratio of college costs to per capita income, which is also plotted in Figure 7.8. Note that the college cost/income ratio is almost the inverse image of the completion/attendance ratio. When college cost was declining as a proportion of income, the completion/attendance ratio was rising, and when college cost was rising as a proportion of income, the completion/attendance ratio was falling. These data suggest that the college completion decision is more sensitive to college cost than is the decision to attend college.

The relationship between the completion/attendance ratio and the college cost/income ratio deserves further analysis. The attendance model in section

7.2 reveals that the student's total cost of attendance depends on direct cost and opportunity cost. Further, the model suggests that the completion/attendance ratio should be a decreasing function of the ratio of the direct cost and income, and it should also be a decreasing function of the opportunity cost of attending college. Let the completion/attendance ratio be the variable *ratio* and let the direct cost/income ratio be the variable *cost*. The *cost* variable is defined to be the weighted average direct cost for tuition, fees, room, and board from public and private institutions divided by per capita income. The weights are computed on the basis of enrollment in the public and private institutions.

The opportunity cost of attending college is measured by wages forgone during attendance. I choose the unemployment rate, *ur*, and the index of industrial production, *ipi*, as proxy variables for opportunity wages. As unemployment increases, the opportunity cost should decline, so the anticipated sign for the unemployment rate is positive – persistence in college should rise as the unemployment rate increases. The reverse should be true for the index of industrial production. Finally, the representative student's college persistence depends on the distribution of income. There are two competing effects associated with the distribution of income and college persistence: the financial incentive effect and the discouraged student effect. As the income distribution becomes more uneven, the financial incentives to persist in college rise; so, the completions/attendance ratio should rise as the income distribution becomes more uneven. Alternatively, the impact of financial incentives to persist in college may be sensitive to the process by which the income distribution becomes more uneven. For example, if the income distribution becomes more uneven because the process 'hollows-out' the middle class; then the gap between rungs on the income ladder can become so wide that lower income students are discouraged. The forces that are pushing some families out of the middle class towards lower incomes must also be at work on lower income students. The GINI coefficient[8] is the traditional measure of the distribution of income; as it increases, the distribution of income becomes more uneven. Therefore, the hypothesized empirical model is

$$ratio_t = \beta_0 + \beta_1\ cost_t + \beta_2 GINI + \beta_3 ur_t + \beta_4 ipi_t + \varepsilon_t.$$

Since there are no controls for preparation and culture, this model clearly has some omitted variable problems and the results should be approached with caution. Using data from 1968 to 2001, three empirical models were estimated. The first model is for the total population, the second is for the white population, and the third is for the black population. Each model was estimated using general method of moments (GMM) with Newey-West corrections for the standard errors. The Newey-West technique is the preferred technique in the presence of autocorrelation and/or heteroscedasticity of an unknown origin. The results are contained in Table 7.2.

Table 7.2   College persistence models: dependent variable = Ratio

Variable	Total	White	Black
int	1.88	1.98	0.46
	(8.79)*	(9.01)*	(2.86)*
cost	−1.11	−1.29	−0.56
	(−5.35)*	(−6.02)*	(−2.71)**
GINI	−3.06	−3.23	0.93
	(−3.29)*	(−3.80)*	(0.96)
ur	0.03	0.03	0.01
	(3.32)*	(3.85)*	(2.45)**
ipi	0.01	0.01	0.00
	(5.97)*	(6.62)*	(0.66)
adj R^2	0.84	0.85	0.58
n	35	34	30

Notes:
* significant at the 0.01 or better level.
** significant at the 0.05 or better level.

In the total model, all variables are significant at the 0.01 or better level and each variable except *ipi* has the anticipated sign. College persistence declines as the financial burden measured by *cost* increases, and it declines as the distribution of income becomes more uneven. It appears that the discouraged student effect is dominant in the total model. College persistence increases as the unemployment rate increases. In the white and black models, the cost variable is computed using white per capita income and black per capita income respectively. In addition, the unemployment rate used in the white model is the unemployment rate for whites and the unemployment rate used in the black model is the unemployment rate for blacks. The white model is structurally the same as the total model in terms of signs and significance levels. In the black model, neither the GINI variable nor the industrial production index variable are significant. The signs for the intercept, *cost*, and the unemployment rate are the same as in the total and white models. The most significant influences on black college persistence appear to be the direct financial burden and the opportunity cost.

A measure of the significance of the financial burden imposed by direct college costs on black students can be obtained by using the parameter estimates from the black college persistence model and the white values for the *cost* variable each year. The assumption here is that the estimated model parameters in each model capture the cultural and preparation differences between whites and blacks, while the actual *cost* variable values reflect the direct financial burden. Since white incomes are considerably higher than black incomes, the relative college cost burden is less for whites than it is for blacks. Figure 7.9 contains plots of the actual white and black ratios along with the predicted ratio for blacks assuming the direct financial burden was the same for blacks as it was for whites. The results suggest that most of the college persistence gap between blacks and whites could be closed if the relative direct cost financial burden were equalized across blacks and whites.

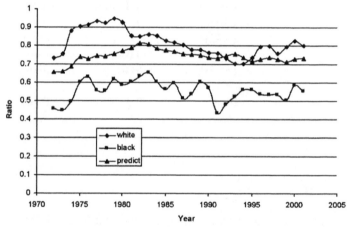

Note: a. Assumes the financial burden imposed by direct college costs for blacks and whites is the same during the period of study.

Source: US Census Bureau, October CPS 1967–2002, Historical School Enrollment, Table A–5. March CPS 1964–2002, Historical Educational Attainment Table A–2.

Figure 7.9   Actual white/black completion/attendance ratios and the predicted black ratio[a]

Income, Race, Ethnicity, and Quality

The third type of college access issue is the problem of matching students with the appropriate college opportunity. Mismatching can arise whenever gifted students attend low quality institutions or when less-gifted students attend high quality institutions. Private and social opportunities are lost whenever a gifted student settles for an institution that does not challenge her abilities. This type of mismatching can occur if the student lacks information about the available opportunities or she has insufficient financial resources to attend and complete a degree at a high quality institution. Although it may not be the most frequent type of matching problem in college access, mismatching gifted students with low quality institutions is the most frequently cited example of student/college matching problems. Vigorous quality competition, affirmative action programs, and aggressive tuition discounting throughout the late 1980s and all of the 1990s made it easier for gifted students from all races and ethnicities to attend high quality institutions. The studies that reveal an increasing concentration of top students in the elite institutions document this trend (see Chapter 2).

Private costs and social costs are created whenever less-gifted students are matched with high quality institutions. Since racial and ethnic preferences in college admissions are relevant only when minorities are granted admission in spite of their academic preparation, they must necessarily result in some degree of quality mismatching between the student and the institution. Aggressive affirmative action programs lead to proportionally more mismatching. Consider the quality hierarchy among academic institutions and then picture aggressive affirmative action programs at each level of the hierarchy. The impact of these programs will be to pull each college-bound minority student up at least one step in the quality hierarchy, such that virtually every minority student is quality mismatched. If a student is unprepared for the institution he attends but is admitted for reasons independent of preparation, the institution may be setting the student up for failure, a failure that can leave him with high debt and little means to repay that debt. The higher rate of failure, or at least being in the lower half of the grade distribution, and the longer time required to graduate among minority students may reinforce negative stereotypes, lower the probability of graduation, and it may substantially lower the rate of postgraduate studies among minorities. On the other hand, success breeds success and minority students who are properly matched with institutions are more likely to be in the top half of the grade distribution, graduate on time, and pursue postgraduate studies.

Racial and ethnic preferences in college *admissions* do not have the same consequences as racial and ethnic preferences in *financial aid*. Racial and ethnic preferences in college admissions can mismatch students and institutions, while racial and ethnic preferences in financial aid do not per se lead to mismatching of students and institutions. Supporters of minority preferences in *admissions* argue that eliminating affirmative action will reduce minority access to the elite institutions and adversely impact the economic prospects of all minorities (Bok and Bowen, 1998; Bowen and Rudenstine, 2003). Critics of minority preferences in admissions argue that the practice discriminates against non-minority students, imposes a stigma on the minority students, and leads to a mismatching of students and institutions (Thernstrom and Thernstrom, 1997; Graglia, 2003; Cole and Barber, 2003). Since minority students are not properly matched with the institutions they attend, they do poorly relative to their non-minority peers, they are less likely to graduate, and their lower academic performance limits their opportunities for graduate studies. It would be a cruel example of the law of unintended consequences if affirmative action admissions programs are actually at the expense of minority students.

Some opponents of all types of minority preferences seek to bundle all activities and programs in higher education that are designed to serve, or to be sensitive to, minority backgrounds with the University of Michigan cases recently before the Supreme Court (Schmidt, 2003). While there may be legal, social, and economic reasons why *admission* practices should be minority neutral, it does not imply that all minority sensitive policies in higher education should be eliminated. These policies should be considered on their own merits. This is particularly true for minority preferences in *financial aid*. Since minority populations are the fastest growing portion of the US population and they are the most under-represented groups in higher education, there is a compelling national interest in increasing minority access to higher education. It is very difficult to see how that can be accomplished without racial and ethnic sensitive financial aid.

There are several important economic differences between minority preferences in admissions and minority preferences in financial aid. First, minority sensitive financial aid is not price discrimination, since minority students contribute to the education of all students through the diversity benefits only they can provide. Potential theoretical support for this argument comes from Rothschild and White's human capital production model where students are inputs as well as customers (1995). The individual student contributes to her own education as well as to the education of other students; it is a joint effort by the student, other students, and the instructor. Students who generate positive production externalities are rewarded for their contributions through scholarships and tuition discounts. Conceptually, there is no difference between a student who provides positive production externalities through superior academic skills and one who provides positive production externalities through diversity experiences. Unfortunately, the production externalities from any source are difficult to measure.[9]

Second, minority preferences in financial aid do not create the same unintended consequences[10] as one finds with minority preferences in admission. If admission is minority neutral, the minority students who receive differential financial aid will be properly matched with the institutions they attend: there should be no stigma and no material difference in their academic performance.

Third, it can be argued that minority preferences in financial aid increase minority access to higher education. Institutions are currently bidding for minority students when they are not completely confident these students are academically qualified to attend their institutions. It would seem plausible that they would be less hesitant to bid for minority students when they know the students are qualified to attend. At present, financial aid bids by lower ranked institutions for qualified minority students are not competitive because those students are given preferred admission and financial aid to institutions one rung above in the academic rankings. A better match between the student's academic preparation and the institution he attends can result in greater minority student access to higher education, improved academic performance, and a greater frequency of graduate enrollment by minority students.

Finally, government regulation of the distribution of financial aid in higher education can prevent welfare enhancing transactions. For a variety of reasons,[11] higher education institutions act as agents who administer the subsidies provided by private individuals, private institutions, and government programs (see Chapter 4). Many of these subsidies have different social objectives. Charitable contributions by benefactors who value diversity are allocated to institutions that employ those contributions to benefit minority students. It is hard to see how prohibiting those transactions could be welfare enhancing. A court decision to remove minority status from any consideration in the allocation of financial aid is in fact price regulation. Net prices to students are determined by financial aid offers and these decisions are an important part of the price mechanism by which minority students are matched with higher education institutions.

The data on attendance and completion rates in the foregoing subsections reveal that larger proportions of the college age population are both attending college and completing at least four years of college. This is true in the aggregate and within racial and ethnic classifications. All of this has occurred despite the rapid rise in net tuition and fees for both public and private higher education. The foregoing does not reveal what has happened to the quality of higher education made available to low income students. Table 7.3 contains the percentage distribution of students by family income quartile by type of institution for the beginning and end of the 1990s. These data reveal a significant increase in students from the lowest family income quartile enrolled in public two-year institutions along with a significant decline in the students from the lowest family income quartile enrolled in private four-year institutions. These two statistics suggest that the quality of higher education made available to students with family incomes in the lowest quartile declined in the 1990s. There is considerable quality variation among the public four-year institutions, particularly between state flagship institutions and satellite campuses. The proportion of students from the lowest quartile who attended public four-year institutions was constant, but it would not be surprising to find that fewer students from the lowest family income quartile are attending flagship institutions. If these trends are due to insufficient financial resources and not because of preparation; then we have evidence of quality mismatching among low income students.

Table 7.3   Percent distribution of students[a] by type of institution[b] and family income: 1989–90 and 1999–2000

Family Income/Quarter	Public two-year		Public four-year		Private four-year	
	89–90	99–00	89–90	99–00	89–90	99–00
Lowest	16.4	24.7	47.0	47.4	28.0	22.9
Lower middle	19.7	22.3	53.5	51.9	22.8	23.8
Upper middle	15.5	18.6	56.4	51.7	25.2	28.0
Highest	10.6	12.6	52.4	53.9	35.7	32.6
Total	15.5	19.4	52.4	51.3	28.0	27.0

Notes: [a] Full-time, full-year dependent undergraduates.

[b] The private for-profit institutions are omitted.

Source: Choy, Susan P. 'Paying for College: Changes Between 1990 and 2000 for Full–Time Dependent Undergraduates.' NCES, June 2004, 7.

In order to understand these shifts in the distribution of students by family income, it is necessary to consider the impact of shifts in financial aid by family income over the same period. Table 7.4 contains data on the percentage of students with aid and the percentage of the price of attendance covered by aid by family income quartile. The first thing to notice about these data is that the proportion of students with aid increased in all family income quartiles and the size of the shifts in proportions are all statistically significant. Second, the proportion of the price of attendance covered by that aid increased for all family income quartiles and the size of the shifts are all statistically significant. More students received aid, and the aid the average student received covered a larger share of the price of attendance. Third, the increase in the proportion of students from the lowest family income quartile who received aid was the smallest increase of all four income quartiles. For instance, the lowest quartile increased by about 5 percent, while the highest quartile almost doubled from 29.4 percent to 57.9 percent. The largest gains in student populations receiving aid occurred in the higher income quartiles. Finally, the increase in the proportion of the price of attendance covered by aid for the lowest quartile was the smallest of all four income quartiles. The proportion covered for the lowest income quartile went from 55.6 percent to 62.0 percent, while the proportion covered for the highest income quartile went from 32.9 percent to 43.4 percent. In other words, the real burden of college attendance lifted from families in the highest income quartile was larger than the real burden lifted from families in the lowest income quartile. It is clear that these trends are regressive.

Table 7.4   Percentage of students[a] with financial aid and the percentage of the price of attendance covered by that aid by family income: 1989–90 and 1999–2000

Family Income/Quarter	Percentage with Aid		Percentage of Price	
	89–90	99–00	89–90	99–00
Lowest	81.1	86.8	55.6	62.0
Lower middle	58.3	73.4	45.3	53.3
Upper middle	49.5	68.0	38.1	50.1
Highest	29.4	57.9	32.9	43.4
Total	53.8	71.1	45.5	52.9

Note: a. Full-time, full-year dependent undergraduates.

Source: Choy, Susan P. 'Paying for College: Changes Between 1990 and 2000 for Full-Time Dependent Undergraduates.' NCES, June 2004, 17.

Since the burdens of higher college costs are distributed differently across family income quartiles, it is appropriate to consider what is happening to the families' ability to bear those burdens across the income distribution. The regressive nature of the distribution of aid might not be a serious problem if the distribution of income was becoming progressively more equal across the income quartiles. If real family incomes are rising rapidly in the bottom quartile while real family incomes are falling in the top quartile, one might not consider the regressive distribution of aid to be a problem. Unfortunately, that is not what is happening. Figure 7.10 contains the ratio of real average household income and real median household income from 1967 to 2001. The data reveal that average real income has risen steadily with respect to median real income over this period, continuing a long term trend. In 1967 the ratio was 1.31 and the ratio ended the period at 1.46 in 2001. As the mean rises relative to the median, the distribution of real income becomes more skewed towards the higher income quartiles. This conclusion is also reflected by the historical trends in Gini coefficients. Hence, the higher income quartiles are more able to bear the burden of higher college attendance costs than they were before the shifts occurred. The real income gap between the bottom and top income quartile is growing; indeed, it appears to have accelerated in the mid-1990s.

These trends in real income and in the distribution of financial aid by income quartile suggest that the financial burden that society is asking lower income families to bear in order to finance their children's college education is increasing while the financial burden that society is asking higher income families to bear is decreasing. These are regressive policies that are very likely to reduce economic mobility at a time when increasing economic mobility through higher education should be a national priority. While this is an important and chronic problem, it would be inappropriate to call this a crisis. Attendance and completion rates are still rising and more aid is flowing to all students in all income quartiles. The first priority is to bring college costs under control, before any substantial increases in aid are made available. A second priority (see Chapter 6) would be to encourage price discrimination based on income among higher education institutions. A policy of revenue-neutral price discrimination based on ability to pay would have a beneficial effect on the current regressive nature of the financial aid distribution.

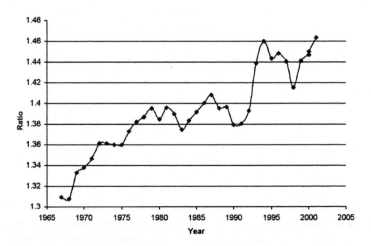

Source: US Bureau of the Census, Tables H–13 and H–14.

Figure 7.10   Ratio of average and median household income: 1967 to 2001

7.4   FINANCIAL CONSTRAINTS, STUDENT PREPARATION, AND THE RESIDUAL

The notion that college access is adversely impacted by financial constraints is the conventional justification for need based aid programs, either public grants or subsidized loans. Financial constraints arise from either low family incomes or credit market imperfections that prevent the student from borrowing (hard constraint) or force the student to borrow at interest rates that reduce access (soft constraints). If lower college access among low income and minority students is the result of financial constraints, then the apparent solution to this problem is a redistribution program that reduces the direct cost of college attendance for lower income students through either grant or subsidized loan programs.

Note that the size of the redistribution program needed to close the college access gap increases in direct proportion to the rate of increase in the cost of college to students and their families. Hence, one can make a case that current need based aid programs, such as Pell Grants and Stafford loans, did not close the access gap because the education establishment failed to control higher education costs. As a community, we bear at least partial responsibility for the failure of need based programs to resolve this problem.

Cameron and Taber's review of the existing access literature reveals that the

> Evidence favoring the idea that borrowing constraints hinder educational attainment, particularly at the college level, is based almost entirely on well-documented correlations between schooling attainment and family income and other family characteristics. The step from correlation to causation is precarious since family income is also strongly correlated with early schooling achievement, where direct costs of schooling have little role. (2004, 136)

It is well known that correlation does not imply causation, that two variables that are highly correlated may in fact be driven by a third unobserved variable. Free public primary and secondary education eliminates the possibility that credit constraints are a factor in schooling achievement among students who attend public schools; yet it remains true that school achievement is positively correlated with family income among those students. This clearly suggests that factors other than financial constraints are at work in determining schooling achievement and that whatever those factors are, they are correlated with family income.

A growing body of important recent work suggests that the fundamental college access problem is not financial constraints. Cameron and Heckman (1998, 2001), Shea (2000), Keane and Wolpin (2001), and Cameron and Taber

(2004) all find that college access is not restricted by borrowing constraints. Their results are supported by Bound and Turner (2002) and Stanley's (2003) work on the GI Bills, which were not means tested, since those programs had a larger effect on higher income students than on low income students. This conclusion is also supported by the dynastic poverty studies such as Bowles and Gintis (2002), where we find that culture plays an important role in the intergenerational transfer of poverty. The implication is that when we observe the correlation between income and college access what we are actually observing is the relationship between college preparation and access; that is, college preparation is highly correlated with income and college preparation begins at home and in primary school. Therefore, directing a large flow of public resources towards need based aid will misdirect the flow from where it is needed if the access problem is in fact a problem with student preparation. Furthermore, if the question is inadequate college preparation, it is both a public and a private problem and that makes it inherently more complex. Directing more public resources to primary and secondary education without addressing the institutional problems in education and without addressing the family culture problems associated with college preparation is also unlikely to have a beneficial effect on college access.

Those who believe achievement is inherited argue that differences between groups can be explained by externally imposed constraints, while those who believe achievement is the result of individual effort argue that differences between groups can be explained by lack of preparation for college. The appropriate public policy depends critically on the source of the observed difference in college access. The fact that access rates are different from one group to another is not in question. If access is low due to financial constraints then more need based aid is required. If access is low because preparation is poor, then additional need based aid will not help, and society should invest more in remedial education (the two-year college system) and in primary/secondary education. If access rates vary because of cultural factors, then more need based aid or more investment in remedial education is unlikely to improve access.

Finally, there is considerable evidence that the intergenerational transmission of poverty is the result of more complex factors than just credit constraints and poor preparation in primary and secondary school. To the extent that poverty is transmitted across generations, economic and social mobility has failed. Indeed, credit constraints and poor preparation may be two of many interconnected factors that prevent college access. Once we control for financial constraints and preparation, there is still a substantial residual that remains unexplained. The problem is similar to the multifactor productivity residual in economic growth theory that led to the development of endogenous growth models. Endogenous growth theory seeks to explain economic growth as the complex interaction of economic, political, and cultural forces. Higher education access depends on the same complex combination of factors. The threads that determine higher education access must be untangled in order to avoid unintended public policy consequences.

Credit Constraints

Michael Keane and Kenneth Wolpin consider the impact of credit constraints and parental transfers on college attendance (2001). Starting with the regular empirical result that shows a strong correlation between the educational attainment of children and the educational attainment of their parents, Keane and Wolpin seek to separate the effects of credit constraints from the effects of parental transfers. There are two types of parental transfers: 'the heritability of traits', such as 'abilities, personalities, and preferences', and the financial investments parents make in their children (2001, 1051). Keane and Wolpin are concerned with parental financial transfers versus credit constraints on student access. The credit constraints are measured by the availability of uncollateralized loans made to students; credit constraints exist if these loans are not available to students. Keane and Wolpin formulate a dynamic optimization model where the student jointly chooses to attend college, work, and to save. The model is tested on young men using data from the National Longitudinal Surveys of Labor Market Experience.

Keane and Wolpin conclude that parental financial transfers are more important in determining college attendance than are credit constraints (2001, 1053). Since parental transfers are small for children from low income families, their impact on attendance rates for low income students is small. The relaxation of even severe credit constraints has little impact on the attendance decision, even among students from low income families, although credit constraints may have a significant effect on the student's work and consumption decisions. These results are consistent with the argument that preparation for college among low income students is the constraining factor, but they are also consistent with the argument that parental financial transfers are also a constraining factor. From the student's perspective, parental financial transfers and public grants are the same; the student incurs no obligation to repay the parental transfer or the public grant. On the other hand, even subsidized loans have to be repaid, so the rational student who is unprepared for college knows that the probability he will complete college and find rewarding employment is low; hence, incurring debt to attend college is not a rational decision and the availability of debt financing is not an inducement to attend college. Alternatively, a grant either from the public or from parents does not require repayment, so the unprepared student is likely to attend if grants are available. If the student is unprepared for college, the likelihood he will complete college does not change. Higher Pell grants should result in higher college attendance rates among low income students who are not well prepared for college, but they are unlikely to have significant effects on college completion rates.

In a related article, Stephen Cameron and Christopher Taber explore the impact of credit constraints on education attainment (2004). They note that the total cost of attending for one period is equal to the direct cost plus the opportunity cost. The direct cost must be financed with debt, public grants, or family transfers, while the opportunity cost is not an actual cash outflow, so it does not have to be financed. The direct costs impose a greater burden on low income students than do the opportunity cost, while the direct costs are less of a burden for high income students. These differences help identify the impact of credit constraints on low income students. The authors use four different econometric approaches to the problem; all of these approaches yield essentially the same conclusions. They find no evidence that borrowing constraints impede attendance in any of their four different approaches.

Dynastic Poverty

Casual observation and conventional wisdom ('the apple does not fall very far from the tree') reveals that personality, attitudes, skills, and wealth are passed from parents to their children. The significance of these transfers in determining economic status in subsequent generations is an empirical question. Are these intergenerational transfers destiny[12] or are they minor obstacles/enablers that are easily overcome by subsequent generations? If the parental endowments are destiny, then economic status is exogenously determined and if they are minor obstacles, then economic status is endogenously determined. The more important parental transfers are in determining economic status, the less social and economic mobility one should observe. The early evidence suggested the power of parental transfers to determine economic status was quite limited.

In a survey of the earlier work, Becker and Tomes (1986) reported that the intergenerational correlation between parents and their children's income was about 0.15. Becker and Tomes concluded that the earnings effect between generations would disappear within three generations. The implication from this conclusion is that social mobility is available to all those who apply themselves. Later research revealed serious problems with the earlier studies. In a more recent survey of the new literature, Bowles and Gintis find the earlier work suffered from two types of measurement error:

> mistakes in reporting income, particularly when individuals were asked to recall the income of their parents, and transitory components in current income uncorrelated with underlying permanent income... The high noise-to-signal-ratio in the incomes

of both generations depressed the intergenerational correlation. When corrected, the intergenerational correlations for economic status appear to be substantial, many of them three times the average of the US studies surveyed by Becker and Tomes. (Bowles and Gintis, 2002, 4)

According to Bowles and Gintis, the new empirical literature on the intergenerational transmission of economic status suggests several 'empirical regularities':

1. brothers' incomes are more strongly correlated than the incomes of comparably and randomly chosen males;
2. the correlation between the incomes of identical twins is higher than the correlation between the incomes of fraternal twins or non-twin brothers;
3. children from high income families get more and better schooling; and
4. the wealth of high income parents and that of their children are strongly correlated (2002, 4).

From all of this they conclude that income, wealth, genetics, and culture do matter in dynastic studies.

After controlling for income, education, and cognitive skills, approximately two-fifths of the variation in economic status between generations remains to be explained. Bowles and Gintis conclude that the unexplained residual is due to factors such as wealth, race, and 'noncognitive behavioral traits' (2002, 5). The non-cognitive behavioral traits are factors such as 'a sense of personal efficacy, work ethic ... a rate of time discount' and fatalism (2002, 20). Fatalism has proven to have a strong negative correlation with earnings. Similarly, measures of social 'maladjustment' in parents have a negative correlation with their children's income (2002, 21). One of the curiosities in this literature is that the genetic transmission of IQ is weak and it does not have a significant bearing on intergenerational economic status. The genetic/environmental transmission of appearance, height, weight, and personality are more important in determining intergenerational economic status than raw cognitive ability as measured by IQ. Being homely, short, overweight, ill-tempered, uneducated, and having low income parents is a near perfect recipe for a lifetime of low earnings.

The impact of parental transmission on economic mobility is vividly demonstrated by Hertz (2002). Hertz calculates the entire probability map for the conditional probability a child will be in a certain income decile given the income decile of the child's parents. The horizontal axis of the three dimensional 'transition matrix' contain children's income on one axis and the parents' income on the other axis. The vertical axis contains the conditional probability that a child will be in that income decile given the parents' income decile. The transition matrix has two peaks: one for the probability a child from low income parents will also have low income and one for the probability a child from high income parents will also have high income. The first high probability is the traditional poverty trap and the second is the 'affluence trap'.[13] Bowles and Gintis report the following conclusions from the Hertz study:

> A son born to the top decile has a 22.9 percent chance of attaining the top decile... and a 40.7 percent chance of attaining the top quintile.... the son of the poorest decile has a 1.3 percent chance of attaining the top decile and a 3.7 percent chance of attaining the top quintile. ... children of the poorest decile have a 31.2 percent chance of occupying the lowest decile and a 50.7 percent chance of occupying the lowest quintile, while ... the probability a child of the richest decile ends up in the poorest decile is 2.4 percent, with a 6.8 percent chance of occupying the lowest quintile. (2002, 7)

These results suggest that the poverty trap has a tighter grip on its children than does the affluence trap. Hertz also reports that downward mobility differs by race. Black children from families in the top quintile are five times more likely to end up in the bottom quintile than white children from families in the top quintile. The affluence trap is less of a trap for black children than it is for white children.

The policy implications one draws from the new studies of dynastic poverty are both comforting and a cause for concern. While the intergenerational transmission of poverty/prosperity is strong, it is clearly not a genetically imprinted imperative. Furthermore, a successful interdiction of the transmission of poverty from one generation to the next will repeat itself in subsequent generations. On the other hand, persuading children to be more self-reliant and less fatalistic than their parents is not something easily accomplished by any society. The current preoccupation with victim culture does not help this task. There are family traditions or parts of family cultures that are self-destructive and there are those that are constructive. The long term solution to dynastic poverty requires candid discussions about culture and its role in perpetuating poverty. The solution for individuals and society is the elimination of the parts of each culture that undermine economic mobility while retaining the positive aspects of each culture. The doctrinaire attitudes of multiculturalism, those that insist all cultures are equally valid, work against the economic interests of the very people the advocates of multiculturalism seek to protect.

The most important conclusion to be drawn from this evidence is that a rising tide will lift a lot of boats, but it definitely will not lift all boats. Public policy towards poverty should encompass more than stimulating economic growth. The growth is a necessary condition for economic mobility, but it is not sufficient. Bowles and Gintis suggest that public policy should focus on the unfair mechanisms that are responsible for the intergenerational transmission of poverty (2002, 23). Some of these mechanisms work through race and ethnicity. Discrimination is a patently unfair mechanism; others are associated with the cultures attached to different races and ethnicities. Parental income and wealth have unfair consequences as well. For example, low parental income is associated with lower health care for children and lifetime health profiles play an important part in economic mobility. Similarly, low parental income means children have access to less education and to poorer quality education.

Ensuring economic mobility does not mean the 'playing field must be level'. Making each member of every generation start at the same point regardless of their parents' contribution would have significant adverse incentive effects. The economy grows by creating wealth. If all wealth is confiscated at death, the incentive to create wealth is significantly reduced. A more constructive public policy would be to use redistributive programs to maximize the probability that children from lower income families will be able to improve their economic status.

Merit Aid

In its most general form, 'merit aid' is any financial assistance made available to students that is not means tested. The recipient of merit aid may deserve the financial assistance as a reward for academic achievements, as a reward for military service, or as a reward for any characteristic chosen by the public. Indeed, merit refers to any reason for providing financial aid other than the recipient's income. By this definition, minority financial aid is a form of merit aid. The economic justification for pure merit based aid rests on the proposition that human capital investments have public good properties. The role of human capital accumulation in increasing economic growth and in reducing social costs is cited as a reason for public support for private investment in human capital. Given the existence of social benefits from higher education, then total benefits exceed private benefits, and private investment in higher education, even by the wealthiest families, will be lower than the social optimal investment in higher education.

The National Merit Scholarship program is the most prestigious and well-known such merit program. Since the demise of the 'overlap group' in the early 1990s (see Chapter 6), merit aid for gifted students has become a central competitive strategy for institutions seeking to improve their academic standing. There are also several federal financial aid programs that are not means tested. The two federal tax incentive programs are called the Hope Scholarship and Lifetime Learning Credit; these programs allow families to shelter taxes using their expenditures for education. Dynarski notes that these federal programs are of limited value to low income families because the income caps for eligibility are set very high[14], the benefits are offset by need based aid, and the benefits are in the form of a non-refundable tax credit (2000, 2). The federal Education Individual Retirement Account (IRA) allows families to make IRA contributions that are tax free with respect to the interest income from those IRAs. Since higher income families save more and are in higher tax brackets, the Education IRAs benefit high income families more than they benefit low income families.

There are two primary issues regarding merit aid. First, is merit aid effective or does it merely crowd out private human capital investment? If there is no change in attendance rates or degree completion rates for middle and higher income students as a result of merit aid programs, it can be argued that merit aid simply crowds out private investment in higher education. The crowding out question is not relevant for low income students since they do not have the resources to make private investments in education. Hence, the degree of crowding out is inferred by the efficacy of these programs with respect to middle and higher income students. The second question deals with the relationship between need based aid and merit aid: are need based aid dollars diverted to merit aid? If merit aid comes at the expense of need based aid and there are diminishing marginal returns to the social benefits from higher education for each student, then the marginal social benefit of each aid dollar is reduced by the shift from need based aid to merit based aid.

The GI Bills

Sidney Burrell concludes that the World War II and the Korean War GI Bills are the most successful education policies ever adopted (1967). Researchers invariably refer to the importance of these programs, as have I in Chapter 1. The GI Bills have been described as 'a kind of domestic Marshall plan' (Stanley, 2003, 671) and as being responsible for 'the "democratization" of American higher education' (Bound and Turner, 2002, 784). While the circumstantial evidence that justifies this reverence seems convincing, a closer analysis will reveal that most of the incremental impact was on veterans from middle and higher income families (Stanley, 2003). The twin GI Bills did encourage large numbers of veterans to attend college and their investments in human capital contributed to economic growth. The people who took advantage of the GI Bills were those who were most prepared to benefit from the programs. The programs were not that successful with respect to low income veterans who were not prepared for college.

The popular perception surrounding the mid-century GI Bills is based on the rising proportion of the population attending four or more years of college and the contemporaneous rise in real per capita GNP that followed the war years. It is the casual empirical association of these two secular trends that sustains the popular belief that the GI Bills made a major contribution to post-war prosperity. The new endogenous growth models explored in Chapter 1 confirm the importance of human capital formation in the generation of sustained economic growth.

The original GI Bill became law on June 22, 1944. The scale was unprecedented; it covered all those serving from September 1940 through July 1947, over 10 million soldiers. The grants were made to individuals rather than institutions and they provided for tuition and books and a monthly living allowance. Bound and Turner report that the tuition grants were enough to cover tuition and fees at the most expensive institutions, the living allowances covered about 70 percent of the opportunity cost of going to college, and the grants 'were neither means nor ability tested' (2002, 790). While about half of those eligible for the GI Bill drew benefits from the program, only about 2 million were enrolled in traditional four-year institutions (Stanley, 2003, 674). The majority of those drawing benefits used them for vocational training.

The number of service men and women that qualified for the Korean War GI Bill was substantially smaller than the WWII bill due to the smaller number of soldiers mobilized for that war and to its shorter duration. Stanley reports that

> the Korean War GI Bill was passed by congress in July 1952 and was consciously modeled after the WWII GI Bill. ...the generosity of the bill was similar to but somewhat less than that of the WWII GI Bill. Again, response was strong: out of around 5.3 million Korean conflict veterans, about 2 million drew on educational benefits under the bill within five years of passage, and more than a million used it for college. (2003, 674)

The surge in enrollment associated with these two veterans programs is vividly displayed in Figure 7.1, which contains total enrollment in higher education from 1869 through 2000. Total enrollment growth from 1869 through 1939 displayed a gradual acceleration. A break in the old trend and the establishment of a much faster secular trend after 1949 is clearly discernible in the data. The circumstantial evidence contained in Figure 7.1 clearly indicates the 1940s and 1950s were watershed decades for college enrollment growth. If the two GI Bills were the only factors that changed, the data would present a perfect natural experiment. Unfortunately, there were other substantial changes before and during the 1940s and 1950s. The most significant development was the emergence of the Cold War and then the surprise launching of sputnik in 1957. The sputnik launch led to the National Defense Education Act of 1958 and subsequently to the Elementary and Secondary Education Act of 1965. The country was in a near panic over the perceived science and technology gap between the USSR and the US.

The Great Depression followed immediately by World War II brought significant changes in society and in government. The combined experience provided powerful motivation for many to find new careers that did not rely on hourly wages or agricultural production. World War II accelerated urbanization, while full employment and rationing forced considerable savings on the economy, and gave rise to rapid technical progress. The near-death experiences for millions of men and their families must also have provided powerful motivation for the survivors. Given this context, it is easy to understand why post-war college enrollment growth would accelerate. Most of this could have happened without the GI Bills. Furthermore, a closer inspection of Figure 7.1 reveals that the real tipping point in the enrollment trend occurs around 1959, when the children of the veterans were reaching college age and after the sputnik launch. Therefore, it is appropriate to take a close look at the empirical evidence regarding what role the two GI Bills played in post-war enrollment growth.

John Bound and Sarah Turner consider the impact of the two GI Bills on both college attainment and college persistence (2002). Using age cohort data for veterans and non-veterans, they measure the incremental impact of the World War II and Korean War bills on attendance and completion. They also measure these effects on different age cohorts, where the different age cohorts represent those who were subject to induction and those who were not subject to induction. If the wartime experience and the GI Bills are responsible for the changes we observe in Figure 7.1, we should see differences in college attendance and completion rates between veterans and non-veterans within the same age cohort and across age cohorts. Bound and Turner state:

> Our results indicate that the combined effect of military service and the GI bill was to increase postsecondary educational attainment among World War II veterans above that of their non-veteran peers, with particularly large effects on college completion. These results suggest that the behavioral effects were quite large – our estimates suggest war service increased college completion rates by close to 50 percent. (2002, 786)

They find similar effects across age cohorts and as a result of the Korean War GI Bill. Bound and Turner are careful to note that these effects are the joint impacts of the veteran's wartime experience and the GI Bill, not just the extra incentive provided by the GI Bills (2002, 808). Disentangling these two influences is beyond their data's ability to differentiate. However, the enrollment trend established after the two wars continued well past the lapse of the GI Bill benefits and continued for those who had no wartime experiences when they attended college. The sustained trend in enrollment may represent dynastic effects from the post-war education experience passed on to their children by those parents from the wartime era. Bound and Turner also note that their results do not identify the effect of income and academic preparation on enrollment and persistence (2002, 809).

In a later article, Marcus Stanley considers the differential impact of the GI Bills on veterans relative to their incomes (2003). Using the abrupt cut-off date for the Korean War bill he concludes:

> Most of the effects of the legislation on higher education seem to have been concentrated among men from families in the upper half of the distribution of socioeconomic status. This suggests that the perceived ability to benefit from college was a more important determinant of college attendance during the period examined than credit constraints were. ... Because of the independent negative impact of WWII on education, much of the effect of the WWII GI bill was probably compensatory; it maintained the prewar trend of rapid growth in higher education and moderately accelerated it. (2003, 673)

In other words, the GI Bills were primarily middle class benefit programs. A moment's reflection reveals why this would be the likely outcome. None of the young men eligible for the draft during either war could have known they were going to be given this opportunity. Therefore, they could not prepare to take advantage of the opportunity: either their parents made the investments in their primary and secondary educations that made them ready to take advantage of the generous benefits or they did not make those investments. So, when the opportunity was thrust upon them, they were either ready or not.

The impact of the GI Bills reveals an important interaction between financial constraints, low socioeconomic status, and college access: overcoming financial constraints and achieving college access requires planning and preparation by prospective students and their parents. Students from low socioeconomic families must be guaranteed subsidies for college as early as possible. The guarantees need to be conditional on their performance in primary and secondary school; but the financial uncertainty has to be removed.

State sponsored merit scholarship programs

The prototype for state merit programs is Georgia's HOPE scholarship program[15] which began in 1993. Georgia's program is funded by a lottery and provides free tuition at any state institution for any student with a B or better average in high school. It is no surprise that the Georgia program is extremely popular with the families of college-bound students. It has the additional political benefit of keeping a larger proportion of the state's gifted students enrolled within the state. Since student grade point averages are positively correlated with the parents' income and higher for whites than minorities, Georgia's program has been criticized as an aid program for middle and higher income whites. Students must maintain a B or better grade point average in college in order to continue to receive the scholarship and as a result minority students are more likely to lose the scholarship than are white students.[16] The political popularity of such programs spread to other states whose politicians saw considerable wisdom in pleasing middle class families and in keeping their own gifted students enrolled within the state.

Susan Dynarski estimates that the Georgia HOPE program raised the college attendance rate among 18- and 19-year-olds by almost 8 percentage points, from around 30 percent to almost 38 percent (2000, 18). She uses data from the Current Population Survey before and after the introduction of the HOPE program for Georgia and surrounding states in the Southeast. She also finds that most of these effects are on middle and upper income white students. The attendance rates for black students did not increase. Dynarski reports that the impact on middle and upper income students is 'surprisingly large', which suggests that the crowding out effects from merit scholarship programs are small (2000, 4). The HOPE program seems to have altered the choice of institutions away from two-year colleges towards four-year institutions. In addition, the Georgia students are more likely to attend college in Georgia as a result of the HOPE program.

As Susan Dynarski states, the results she reports may be the short term effects from the HOPE program (2000, 32–33). There are two competing longer term effects. There is some indication that attendance rates have peaked and begun to decline. This is attributable to a discouraged student effect among those students who are not well prepared for college. Many students who have B averages in high school are not able to maintain a B average in college, so they lose the aid after their freshman year. For those students, having the aid for one year is insufficient incentive to attend. Alternatively, primary school students who are guaranteed tuition-free college educations may be motivated to become better prepared for college. This effect is likely to be stronger for low income students than for high income students. In a later paper Dynarski reports evidence that seems to suggest that the incentive effect dominates the discouraged student effect so that the positive impact of these programs grows over time (2002, 25). It may take another decade of experience with the state sponsored merit programs before we know how they impact low income families.

Thomas Dee and Linda Jackson report that approximately half of the students receiving HOPE scholarships lose them at the end of their freshman year (1999). They also note that when one controls for student ability, the attrition rate is the same across race and ethnicity lines. The interesting result in Dee and Jackson's study is the fact that students who enroll in science, engineering, and computing courses are from 21 to 51 percent more likely to lose their scholarships than are students who enroll in the humanities and the social sciences (1999, 389). In other words, the HOPE scholarship program may adversely steer students away from rigorous course work to courses of study that have 'historically different grading standards' (1999, 380). It is important to bear in mind that the prior selection bias that exists in this case tends to underestimate the impact of differential grading standards, since the more able students are likely to choose course work in the sciences, engineering, and computing.

Dynarski also reports that the HOPE program caused tuition increases to accelerate in Georgia as higher education institutions took steps to capture the subsidy. Specifically, she notes:

> Public college costs were relatively flat in Georgia before HOPE, with costs in 1993–94 only about six percent higher than their level in 1986–87. Real prices in Georgia actually dropped during the years immediately preceding HOPE. By contrast, real public schooling costs in the US rose steadily between 1986–87 and 1993–94, for a total increase over this period of around 15 percentage points. After HOPE was introduced, the situation was reversed, with public college costs in Georgia rising at a rate higher than that of the US. (2000, 31)

These results are consistent with the Granger causality results and budgetary slack model in Chapter 6. For those students who do not qualify for merit aid, the tendency of costs to rise as merit aid increases will lower attendance and completion rates for students who do not qualify for merit aid. Therefore, low income and minority students who are not as well prepared for college face higher tuition with no offsetting subsidy.

Susan Dynarski reconsiders the Georgia HOPE program along with six[17] other southern state merit aid programs modeled after the original HOPE program in a subsequent paper (2002). She finds that the other six programs also increase college attendance rates by five to seven percentage points and they tend to encourage enrollment at four-year institutions at the expense of two-year institutions. An important difference between the other six southern state programs and the Georgia program is that the other six programs seem to have a beneficial effect on black and Hispanic enrollment while the HOPE program appears to have little if any impact on black and Hispanic enrollment. Dynarski attributes the differences in these programs to two characteristics of the HOPE program: first, the GPA requirements for the HOPE program are significantly higher than the GPA requirements for the other programs and second, the HOPE program reduces the aid award dollar-for-dollar for any other aid received by the student (2002, 28). The combination of these two characteristics renders the HOPE program of little help to the average black or Hispanic student. The other state programs set the bar lower and in essence are saying we accept responsibility for all students who are capable of succeeding in college, not just those who are capable of excelling in college. She also makes an interesting observation on the political economy of state merit aid programs when she notes that it is easier for the voting public to accept aid to higher education when it is packaged as a merit aid program that is available to all rather than the equivalent amount of aid packaged as direct appropriations for higher education (2002, 35–36).

Recently Susan Dynarski considered the impact of another non-need based financial aid program on attendance and completion rates (2003). The termination of the Social Security Student Benefit Program in 1982 provides variation in financial aid benefits that are unrelated 'to unobservable attributes that influence college attendance' (2003, 279). This orthogonal variation is very useful in identifying the unique impact of variations in financial aid on attendance and completion rates. Remarkably, she found that the elimination of the SS benefit reduced the attendance probability by more than a third (2003, 279).

Patterns in the Empirical Access Literature

A strong correlation between parental income and children's school attainment is the dominant regularity in the empirical access literature. The literature also reveals that family characteristics have important dynastic effects, both for good and bad results. The evidence from the GI Bills reveals that veterans from middle and higher income families benefited most from those merit aid programs, suggesting that college preparation is a precondition for financial aid programs to improve college access. Credit constraints have little influence on school attainment. Analysis of the Georgia HOPE program reveals that merit programs designed only to benefit the gifted do exactly that: high grade point requirements and awards that deduct other sources of aid benefit middle and higher income families most. High grade point requirements can have other adverse effects such as grade inflation, adverse curriculum selection, and discouraged student effects. Other state merit programs with lower grade point requirements and that do not reduce awards for other sources of aid have a more beneficial effect on minority and low income students in terms of both attendance and completion. Unlike the GI Bills, low income students can plan on the state merit aid programs and that planning has a beneficial impact on their preparation for college.

Collectively, these results imply that attendance and completion rates are dependent on both preparation and financial access. Family financial constraints appear to be very important with respect to college completion. Academic preparation and financial access are necessary conditions for attendance and completion. The top priority for improving access is to bring college costs under control, since that directly impacts financial access at all income levels. College preparation depends on both public and private investments in student preparation. Improvements in primary and secondary schools can increase college access for minority and low income students and more public investment in remedial education will also increase college access. The most difficult part of this complex puzzle will be the parental non-financial transfers. The absence of parental financial transfers can be offset by public financial transfers. Non-financial parental transfers can enable a student's economic mobility or they can hinder that mobility. The empirical evidence suggests that the more important non-financial parental transfers are *not* genetic imperatives, they are values and culture. Therefore, students who have benefited from public investments in their preparation and have financial access to college may not either attend or complete college if they have received the wrong type of non-financial parental transfers. In the end, public investments in preparation and in financial access are necessary conditions for economic mobility, but they do not compose a set of sufficient conditions for economic mobility.

7.5 FINANCIAL CONSTRAINTS, PREPARATION, AND UNMET NEED

The college access problem can be subdivided into three types: no opportunity to attend college (attendance), no opportunity to complete a college degree (completion), and no opportunity to attend and complete a degree at the appropriate institution (quality matching). The most severe form of access problem is never having the opportunity to attend, while the least severe form is when a gifted student attends and completes a degree at a low quality institution. Each type of access problem can occur because of financial constraints and/or lack of preparation for college. Severe financial constraints can prevent any attendance, moderate financial constraints can prevent the completion of the degree, and mild financial constraints can cause a mismatching of students and institutions. The severe lack of preparation will prevent attendance, inadequate preparation will prevent completion of degrees, and a lack of preparation will prevent an otherwise gifted student from attending the right institution.

There are two types of financial constraints: inadequate family financial resources, or credit market imperfections that prevent students from borrowing. By definition all students from low income/low wealth families are subject to inadequate family financial resources. Credit market imperfections can result in either hard or soft constraints. A hard constraint occurs whenever a student cannot borrow in order to finance higher education. Given hard constraints and low family income/wealth, the student has no college access, he cannot attend, so he cannot complete a degree, and the quality mismatching is complete. Pell grants and Stafford loans are designed to place low income students who are subject to inadequate family financial resources and credit market constraints on the first rung of the higher education ladder.

Lack of preparation for college is the result of at least three different factors. A student may be unprepared for college because society failed to provide the student with adequate preparation in primary and secondary school. The remedy here is primary and secondary school reform. Next, the student may be unprepared for college because his family made too few financial and in-kind investments in the student's preparation for college. Not buying educational toys and books, allowing the child to spend too much time watching television, and not teaching the child the value of learning frequently lead to students who are unprepared for college even in families with abundant financial resources and access to high quality primary and secondary schools. Finally, a student may be unprepared for college due to their peer group culture. Students who come from families that place a high value on education can be led to a different path by their peers who place very little value on education. Minority families who place a high value on education are confronted with a hopeless situation when their school options are restricted to dysfunctional public schools where discipline problems occupy 90 percent of the teacher's time and where most of the other students place little value on education. These families want and need school vouchers because that is the ticket to an educational environment that works.

The college access problem is in fact several different problems with multiple origins. The optimal policies required to improve access depend critically on the problem's origin. Consider two student scenarios. The first student comes from a low income family where the parents made personal sacrifices to invest in their child's preparation for college throughout that child's life, the child is well prepared for college, but the family's financial resources are exhausted. This is a pure financial access problem, higher Pell grants, abundant Stafford loans, and state sponsored merit aid will be of significant private value to the student and of great social value to society. Alternatively, consider the second student who comes from a low income family where the parents were unwilling to make any sacrifices for their child's college preparation. The child is unprepared for college and the family may not have any savings either. Pell grants and Stafford loans may allow this student to attend college for a short duration, but the lack of preparation will lead to a failure to complete college. There may also be unintended consequences from encouraging large numbers of unprepared students to attend college: the quality of higher education may decline and the budgetary slack model may lead to faster inflation in college costs. Given the existence of college preparation problems, it does not follow that a significant expansion of non-merit based aid will improve low income and minority student access to college.

Alternatively, assume there are no college preparation problems among low income and minority students. Does this imply that the first priority for public policy is to expand financial aid? In other words, if all access problems arise as a result of financial constraints, is the first best policy to increase financial aid in order to increase access? In order to answer this question it is necessary to consider 'unmet need', which is the marker for financial access problems. When the college access problem is due only to financial constraints, then the size of the access problem is measured by the number of students with unmet need and the amount of the representative students' unmet need. Unmet need is defined as 'the amount of money students and families must procure to afford college after all financial aid and the expected family contribution are considered' (Fitzgerald and Delaney, 2002, 15). Fitzgerald and Delaney also report that

> On average, the lowest-income students in 1995 faced $3,200 of unmet need annually at community colleges. At four-year public institutions, they faced average unmet need of $3,800, and at four-year private institutions this amount was over $6,000. In comparison, middle- and high income students faced much lower levels of unmet need at each type of institution. (2002, 15)

From the attendance model in section 7.3, the total direct cost of college is c, the public subsidy or grant is s, the family contribution is f, and the amount borrowed is d. Unmet need occurs when the student cannot satisfy the financing constraint; that is, when

$$c > s + f + d,$$

and unmet need is then equal to

$$n = c - s - f - d.$$

A constraint on borrowing (Stafford Loans), family contribution, or public grants (Pell Grants or state sponsored merit aid) can result in unmet need. Note, however, that these are not the only source of unmet need. Unmet need increases as college cost, c, increases. If college costs are out of control, unmet need will rise no matter what public policy with respect to s and d might be.

Average unmet need can rise substantially even if real public support per student is rising or is constant. Since unmet need is the student's total cost less expected family contribution, grants, loans, and scholarships; unmet need per student will rise as long as the student's total cost rises faster than expected family contribution, grants, loans, and scholarships. Hence, the representative student's family can experience growth in its real income, public grants, loans, and scholarships can rise significantly and the student will still be worse off as measured by unmet need if higher education costs rise at a faster rate. Recent reports[18] show that the annual increase in new federal tax breaks and new state sponsored merit aid programs since 1998 has been about $22 billion each year and this increase in aid has reduced the net cost of college for the average student by about a third over the period. By definition rising public support increases the average student's ability to pay for college. If the budgetary process in higher education follows its historical pattern, the student's increase in ability to pay will soon be reflected in a corresponding rise in cost per student at colleges and universities: the increased ability to pay leads to higher tuition and fees, and rising revenues lead to budgetary slack that is soon filled by rising college and university expenditures. As tuition/fees and college costs rise, the access problem worsens again. In other words, the recent inflow of financial aid may provide only a temporary improvement in college access; adding more public aid to the system is not a permanent fix.

NOTES

1. The Hippocratic admonition to 'first, do no harm...' is the motivation for this interpretation of intergenerational equity.
2. The competing means of transportation is a criminal career.
3. The uniform annual series is the annuity value that corresponds to a specific lifetime earnings profile. Take the lifetime earnings profile, discount it at the discount rate r; then, find the annuity value for the same time period that when discounted at the same discount rate corresponds to the present value of the lifetime earnings profile. This simplifies the analysis by avoiding the introduction of time indexed earnings.
4. One might also consider e as courses completed rather than time periods.
5. Speaking at a Constitution Hall event commemorating the 50th anniversary of the Brown vs. Board of Education decision, the actor/comedian Bill Cosby raised the issue of family and individual responsibility for their own economic status. His comments were not warmly received, but he did perform an important service by focusing public attention on one aspect of the problem of economic status among minorities. It is clearly not the only determinant of economic status and it may not be the most important part, but it is part of the overall puzzle.
6. See Stephen Burd's reporting on the debate in *The Chronicle of Higher Education* (2001).
7. The author is indebted to Will Young for raising this point.
8. The GINI coefficient is the difference between the area of a cumulative income distribution function assuming a perfectly even distribution of income and the actual cumulative income distribution function. If the actual cumulative income distribution function is perfectly even, the GINI coefficient equals zero. If the actual cumulative income distribution function is perfectly uneven (one person has all the income), then the GINI coefficient equals one.
9. The benefits of diversity reported by Bok and Bowen (1998) are based primarily on responses to surveys and do not lend themselves to rigorous statistical analysis. It is also not easy to measure the production externalities created by academically gifted students either, although anyone who has spent much time in a college classroom knows the value of a cohort of gifted students in each class.
10. There may be other as yet unidentified consequences of minority preferences in financial aid.

11. The two most important reasons are economies of scale in the allocation and monitoring of subsidies and asymmetric information regarding the qualifications of the recipients of subsidies.
12. This issue is the updated version of the role nature versus environment plays in human development. As one would expect, the correct answer is some combination of the two effects. What is in question is the degree to which one dominates the other.
13. Bowles and Gintis remark that the term 'affluence trap' is unlikely to catch on (2002, 7).
14. Ninety percent of those who apply qualify for the program.
15. Helping Outstanding Pupils Educationally.
16. Critics have also argued that the HOPE program encourages grade inflation in secondary schools and lowers academic standards in college since students must maintain a B average in college in order to retain their scholarship.
17. Arkansas, Florida, Kentucky, Louisiana, Mississippi, and South Carolina.
18. See *USA Today*, 'Tuition Burden Falls by a Third,' 28 June 2004; 'Grants more than offset soaring university tuition,' 27 June 2004; and 'Merit awards make college affordable,' 27 June 2004.

8. Overview

8.1 PROSPERITY AND THE SOCIAL CONTRACT

The difference between the developed countries and the less developed countries might be described as the difference between dynastic prosperity and dynastic poverty. The process by which one society achieves prosperity and another society remains mired in poverty is not fully understood. Recent studies suggest that social prosperity or poverty is the complex result of the interaction between technology, human capital, culture, and the rule of law. Broadly understood, the study of the economics of higher education is the study of the relationship between technical change, human capital, economic mobility, and culture. In this sense, it is an integral part of what can be described as the most important question facing the economics profession: why do some societies achieve dynastic prosperity and others face dynastic poverty?

Growth studies reveal that the rate of technical change, investment in education, the distribution of income, and mobility are positively correlated with faster economic growth. At any point in time, the optimal distribution of labor skills depends on technology, and more rapid technical change means faster shifts in the optimal distribution of labor skills. The shifts in the labor skills required by the market are signaled by fluctuations in relative wage rates and the distribution of income. These signals are an indispensable part of the resource allocation mechanism.

The marketplace can send signals, but there is no guarantee that workers will or can respond to the signals. Education is the vehicle by which workers respond to market signals. If that vehicle is in good working order, society provides those willing to make the effort with economic opportunities – another essential link in dynastic prosperity. Since rapid technical change means frequent shifts in the labor skills required, rapid technical change means education's state of repair is ever more important to economic mobility.

The social contract between the older generation, the younger generation, and the education community is the institution responsible for preserving economic mobility in prosperous societies. That contract calls for the older generation to repay society for the advantages they received by subsidizing the educations of the younger generation. The younger generation is obligated to use these opportunities efficiently and to pass the benefits on to succeeding generations when their time comes. The education community is the steward of this contract. It is responsible for maintaining quality and for keeping the cost of the obligation between generations reasonable. The social contract can fail if the older generation does not honor its obligation, if the younger generation does not use the opportunities efficiently, or if the education community does not maintain quality and control cost. The social contract is a valuable public asset. The shift in public attitudes towards higher education and the persistent calls for reform suggest the social contract is in jeopardy.

When the mechanism that creates economic opportunity is functioning well, people are able to respond to shifts in the income distribution and their response tends to make the income distribution more even. If there are no restrictions on economic mobility, a rise in income inequality will be quickly followed by a return to a more even distribution of income as workers acquire skills with higher market value. Hence, a secular decline in income equality suggests there is something amiss with economic mobility. Trends in college access are symptomatic of problems with economic mobility. A prosperous economy can generate economic opportunities, but the ability to exploit those opportunities depends on college access.

The US economy has experienced a secular decline in the equality of its income distribution. The most direct evidence of this decline is the persistent rise in GINI coefficients since World War II. The exponential increase in the ratio of CEO salaries to average employee salaries in the US relative to other industrialized countries is further evidence of this persistent trend. The same thing is observed in the relationship between presidential salaries and average faculty salaries in higher education. There is a persistent rise in tournament style results in many labor markets. This type of wage differential could not persist if there was real mobility across skill levels. In order for the differentials to persist, there have to be barriers to mobility.

College access is adversely impacted by college cost. The analysis of cost increases in higher education in Chapter 1 suggests that higher education and health care have been the most inflationary sectors of the economy for decades. There are a variety of factors that contribute to rapid inflation in higher education costs. Two of the factors that are beyond the control of the higher education community are the public's demand for additional services from higher education and unfunded government mandates. The costs of these new services and the cost of the mandates are bundled with traditional education services, making it appear that costs are increasing faster than they are.

On the other hand, there are factors under the control of the education community that contribute significantly to higher real cost. The most important cost drivers are mission creep, declining faculty/staff productivity, rising real faculty/staff wages, proliferating overhead costs, rising administrator salaries, and a general failure to innovate.

8.2   ENTERPRISE BEHAVIOR

Effective public policies and successful management of higher education institutions require solid economic foundations, and those foundations depend on a coherent economic model of the representative institution. A primary purpose of this book is to advance research on a model of the representative higher education institution. More work is required beyond what I provide here; this is clearly not the last word on enterprise models for higher education. Towards this end, I examine the primary economic factors that influence all types of enterprise forms that engage in production in Chapter 2.

The starting point for the influence of basic economic factors is with the theory of the profit maximizing firm. How much does the theory of the firm tell us about the representative higher education institution? The answer to this question depends on the similarities between firms and higher education institutions and it depends on which theory of the firm we are talking about. The theory of the perfectly competitive firm bears little resemblance to the representative higher education institution, but the perfectly competitive firm also bears little resemblance to almost all commercial firms. When we consider the imperfect market structures, where information is asymmetrically distributed and reputations matter, the similarities between the firm and higher education institutions increase.

The most important similarity between firms and higher education institutions is that they must cover their long-run cash outflows with cash inflows. Furthermore, their long-run survival suggests they both have some optimal properties. It follows that the basic economic forces that explain the existence and internal structure of the firm must also have implications for the existence and internal structure of the representative higher education institution. The basic economic forces of interest are risk bearing, transaction costs, technology, and asset ownership. Both firms and higher education institutions minimize transactions cost, and since the costs of internal and external transactions are not stable over time, the optimal structure for the firm and for higher education institutions is not constant over time.[1] There is an imperative for both types of institution to innovate. A failure to innovate leads to higher social cost.

The production surplus generated by inseparable team production also helps explain the existence of the firm and its internal structure. Team production gives rise to monitoring problems that are best solved by a central monitor who has claim to the residual profit generated by the firm. The role of the central monitor in the firm is reinforced by the distribution of the ownership of assets within the firm. The need for team production is much weaker in higher education and there is a more diverse distribution of the ownership of the indispensable assets in higher education: the academic reputations of faculty are a critical component of the institution's overall reputation, and reputation is the institution's most valuable asset. The minimization of transaction costs requires a central contractor in higher education, just as it does in the firm; but, the weak team production technology, the distribution of asset ownership, and the fact that higher education produces a public good means that there is no single residual claimant. Without a residual claimant, there are monitoring problems that lead to agency costs. The monitoring problems are partially addressed by a complex governance structure.

The public good character of education and the absence of a residual claimant mean the institution does not have access to organized equity markets. Without access to equity markets there is no market for control of higher education institutions and this creates more agency problems. It also complicates risk bearing in higher education institutions and explains the emphasis on the accumulation of endowments as a hedge against risk.

In the economics literature the notion that higher education institutions seek to maximize academic quality, reputation, or prestige is almost universal. In addition, these discussions of the representative institution's objectives invariably cite the role that good students and successful alumni play in this process.[2] Since reputation and prestige are constant in the short run, it is clear that these discussions are focused on the institution's long-run objective. Therefore, an integrated model of the representative enterprise must include goal oriented models of short-run behavior that are incentive compatible with the long-run objective. The short-run behavior has to be linked directly to the long-run objective.

Finally, quality, reputation, and prestige are subjective concepts that are difficult to represent by a real valued metric such as dollars. If for example we assume there is a prestige function that the institution seeks to maximize subject to a break-even budget constraint, the model will bear a strong resemblance to traditional utility theory. This will complicate the connection between short-run behavior (enrolling students, educating students, and fundraising), since there are real valued metrics for these activities. Therefore, I assume the long-run objective of the institution is to maximize prestige since this maximizes the flow of external resources that follow from prestige in the long-run. Prestige also leads to greater market power with respect to recruiting high quality students.

The dynamic of the relationship between short-run activities and long-run reputation is a reinforcing loop across generations. Subject to the institution's current reputation, its competitive constraints, and its existing resources, the institution enrolls the highest quality students it can during each annual enrollment cycle. During the production cycle (four years for the undergraduate degree program), the institution maximizes its human capital output subject to a Rothschild and White (1995) production technology and places its newly minted alumni on the fastest career track possible. This yields the institution's cost function which depends on enrollment and its reputation. Alumni success drives the institution's reputation across generations. Better students and more efficient human capital output lead to more successful alumni and a better reputation. Rising reputation leads to a larger endowment, a greater flow of external resources into the institution, and more market power in recruiting good students. The ability to recruit better students establishes a reinforcing loop over succeeding generations. Long-run stationary state equilibrium is found where reputation is maximized. The formal modeling of the foregoing process is contained in Chapters 3, 4, and 5.

Production and Cost

The cost function is derived in Chapter 3. The absence of a formal enterprise model for higher education has led some to argue that higher education cost functions do not exist. If decisions are not based on rational behavior in higher education, then costs are not minimized, the regularity conditions required for cost minimization do not hold and the cost function does not exist. Alternatively, a necessary condition for achieving any rational economic objective is the minimization of costs.

In Chapter 3, the institution is assumed to maximize human capital output subject to a cost constraint. The production technology is peer production with spillover effects between students. The model reveals that maximizing total human capital and maximizing value added lead to the same optimal solution. The point here is that if the institution's reputation depends on the value it adds to students' lives rather than the quality of the students enrolled, the production solution is the same. The faculty takes whatever set of students are enrolled and maximizes their accumulation of human capital. The difference between reputations based on value added and reputations based on the quality of the students enrolled will be reflected in the nature of the students enrolled during the enrollment period.

Additional results follow from the cost/production model. First, the cost function implied by this optimization is a function of enrollment, the average human capital produced per student, and the institution's quality reputation. Second, education inputs are allocated more intensively to students with positive production externalities than to students with negative production externalities. Since good students are complementary teaching inputs to faculty, the institution allocates more faculty time to these students. Finally, if average cost per student is elastic with respect to human capital per student, then minimum efficient scale for human capital output occurs at a lower enrollment level than minimum efficient scale with respect to enrollment. This explains why so many institutions appear to leave returns to scale in enrollment unexploited.

Net Charitable Revenues

The fundraising process and the role of endowments are explored in Chapter 4. Endowments are an unusual feature of charities and their importance in higher education has been growing. The most frequent justification for endowments one hears from institutions is that they promote 'intergenerational equity'. A careful analysis of this argument reveals that it makes little economic sense, and that the most plausible motives for accumulating endowments are for liquidity, security, and a barrier to competition from other institutions. These motives for accumulating endowments create some agency issues.

Chapter 4 also contains a discussion of the literature regarding why individuals donate to charities. The traditions in this literature are pure altruism, impure altruism, and signaling wealth and status. A formal fundraising model is presented in Chapter 4 where the representative institution maximizes the net revenue from fundraising where donors wish to signal wealth and status. Since the quality of the signal depends on the institution's reputation, the net revenue function depends on the cost of fundraising inputs and the institution's quality reputation. The model also reveals that demonstration expenses (the amount expended by the institution in producing the donor's signal) are an increasing function of the amount the donor contributes. Net charitable revenues are an increasing function of the institution's quality reputation and a decreasing function of solicitation costs. Finally, high quality charities carry fundraising to the point where the marginal influence on donations is approximately equal to zero. This means high quality charities behave as if they are maximizing charitable revenues rather than net charitable revenues.

The Annual Enrollment Cycle

During each enrollment cycle the institution seeks to enroll the highest quality students possible subject to a financial constraint and the constraint imposed by its quality reputation. The institution maximizes expected total student quality by the allocation of scholarship awards to individual students. The probability an individual student will enroll is a decreasing function of tuition and fees and student quality, while it is an increasing function of the scholarship offer and the institution's quality reputation. This optimization yields the institution's expected enrollment demand function which depends on tuition and fees, the scholarship budget, average student quality, and the institution's quality reputation.

Analysis of the scholarship distribution reveals that higher quality students are offered higher scholarships, students who are more likely to enroll are offered lower scholarships, and the students with more elastic enrollment probabilities are offered higher scholarships. These results are consistent with results from earlier studies of the optimal scholarship allocation. An improvement in the institution's quality reputation increases not only the institution's potential market share (longer waiting lists) but also increases its market power as measured by marginal returns to tuition discounting. Like the cost function from Chapter 3 and the net fundraising revenue function from Chapter 4, the expected enrollment demand function in Chapter 5 is employed in the intergenerational reputation model.

Maximizing Reputation

The institution's current reputation depends on alumni quality from the previous generation. The accomplishments and success of those alumni determine the institution's quality reputation and provide the foundation for its ability to raise external funds in the current period. These alumni constitute a portfolio of valuable and irreplaceable assets. Within every generation the institution is either enabled or constrained by the enrollment and academic decisions taken by the institution in previous time periods. I assume the institution's quality reputation is monotonically increasing in the quality of those alumni. The institution maximizes quality reputation subject to a budget constraint by choosing tuition and fees, the scholarship budget, and enrollment. In long-run stationary state financial equilibrium, the institution maximizes net tuition revenue from students and maximizes average student quality subject to a break-even budget.

Among other results, the reputation maximizing institution chooses an enrollment scale that is less than the enrollment scale suggested by traditional minimum efficient scale. The institution trades potential cost reductions from enrollment scale for higher quality. The institution's capacity to discount tuition depends on the excess of net fundraising revenues over the costs not driven by enrollment (threshold costs) and its pricing policy with respect to full–pay students. If the institution chooses tuition and fees such that they are greater than the average variable cost of educating students, it increases its discounting capacity and is able to cross subsidize students from this difference. The optimal discounting rule is an average cost pricing rule just as it is in public utility pricing. Since the representative institution has unexploited returns to scale and high threshold costs, marginal cost pricing can lead to chronic losses and bankruptcy.

Quality Cheating and Agency Cost

The intergenerational reputation maximizing model represents the result one should observe in the absence of any agency problems. The break-even budget result refers to the optimal resource allocation associated with a balanced economic budget. The existence of agency problems suggests the administration and/or the faculty may award themselves rents by allocating expenditures to perks, reduced workloads, or higher than market salaries. The fact that education is an experience good, where the quality of the service cannot be determined until after it is purchased, and the time lags are very long before students can make an informed judgment about quality, creates ample opportunity for administrators and faculty to cheat on the quality of service delivered in the short run. Lower quality delivery frees financial resources that can be used for agency rents.

Budgets will be balanced in both the reputation maximization model and the agency model. The difference is that the economic budget will be balanced in the reputation maximization model while it is the accounting budget that will be balanced in the agency model. In order to make comparisons between the reputation maximization model and the agency model, I use the economic cost function from Chapter 3, the net fundraising revenue function from Chapter 4, and the expected enrollment demand function from Chapter 5 and assume agency rents are maximized subject to an accounting budget constraint in the agency model. The choice variables are tuition and fees, the scholarship budget, and enrollment. The agency model reveals that rent maximizing agents maximize net tuition revenue and choose the minimum quality level that avoids detection; they do not maximize quality.

Traditional Capacity, Financial Capacity, and Operating Leverage

Stationary state financial equilibrium requires balancing both traditional enrollment capacity and the institution's financial capacity to support students. Traditional capacity is defined by physical plant and staffing. Financial capacity is derived from the institution's financial ability to offer subsidies to students. For any given endowment and full pay student pricing policy, the institution's financial capacity decreases as the quality of the students it wishes to support increases. Since the average student receives a subsidy from the institution, then a target enrollment and target student quality level implies a scholarship budget required to meet those targets.

In the short run, the representative institution can face a variety of capacity imbalances. Actual enrollment may equal traditional capacity, but financial capacity can be less than or greater than actual enrollment. Or the inverse may be true; financial capacity is in balance but traditional capacity is not in balance. General excess capacity occurs when traditional and financial capacity exceed actual enrollment. General excess demand occurs when potential enrollment exceeds both traditional and financial capacity.

A popular conception among higher education administrators is the notion that the institution's financial condition can be improved by increasing enrollment. This proposition is true only if the institution is prepared to lower quality. The popular misconception is the result of short-run operating leverage. Since fixed costs are high in higher education, any increase in volume has a positive effect on net cash flow. The benefit only occurs in the short run. If the institution adjusts its capacity to reflect its original quality target, expenditures must rise and it must have new external revenue sources to subsidize the new students. Pure enrollment growth is not self-financing since the average student receives a subsidy and the average scholarship per student has to rise just to maintain the same quality level.

8.3   COLLEGE ACCESS

Since some groups are chronically under-represented in the higher education student population, some argue that a college access problem exists. That chronic under-representation can be with respect to the students who attend higher education, those that complete higher education degrees, and/or those that attend high quality institutions. The most severe form of college access problem is never having the opportunity to attend. The college access question is important on at least two levels, because it is an equity issue and because college access determines economic mobility.

The under-representation of some groups in higher education, investment in education, and long-run economic growth are all related. Dynastic prosperity within any society depends directly on access to economic opportunities that result in economic mobility for all of its citizens. Economic mobility is as important to continued prosperity as is wage and price flexibility. Economic mobility also lowers social costs.

The Student's Attendance Decision

The representative student's decision to attend college is modeled in Chapter 7. The student is assumed to make this decision on the basis of the probability he will successfully complete the enrollment period, the impact of that enrollment period on his permanent income profile, his personal time discount rate, his inherited characteristics, college cost, grants, loans, family support, and the opportunity cost of attending college. The model yields an optimal stopping rule for college enrollment based on the foregoing factors. The optimal stopping point is found where the present value of the expected impact on his permanent income profile equals the direct and opportunity cost of attending for one more period.

The model suggests that the number of enrollment periods is a decreasing function of the direct cost and the opportunity cost per enrollment period and an increasing function of the subsidy and the family's contribution per period. These results provide support for the notion that financial constraints lower student access to college. The number of enrollment periods is an increasing function of the student's subjective probability of completing the enrollment period. Since the probability of success is a function of preparation, lower preparation means fewer enrollment periods attended. The model also reveals that the number of enrollment periods is a decreasing function of the student's time preference. A sufficiently high time preference alone will prevent some students from ever attending college.

The Historical Record

A review of the historical evidence in Chapter 7 reveals that total enrollments and the proportion of the college age cohort attending college have grown robustly and continuously. The lagging attendance trends are among male college age students. The evidence with respect to program completion rates is alarming. In general students are taking longer to complete programs and the proportion of those who attempt college and who complete their programs of study appears to be declining, particularly among low income and minority students. The evidence regarding the quality of education made available to different groups of students is also not comforting. It appears that the quality gap between high income students and low income students is widening. The completion and quality gap appear to be particularly sensitive to income.

The major fault line among researchers on the college access issue is with respect to what causes lower attendance and completion rates. The fact that attendance rates and completion rates are different is not in debate. Some argue that the rates are different because the students are not prepared for college, while others argue that the rates are different because students have financial constraints. The controversy has its origin in a statistical issue. No one disputes the statistical relationship between income and college access. Those who argue that preparation is the primary problem note that preparation and the factors that lead to a lack of preparation are a function of income; hence, the positive correlation between college access and income could be a simple lack of preparation.

The college access debate is more important than a simple disagreement among academics. If the financial constraints advocates are correct, the public policy solution is simple: provide more need based aid to students and college access will rise. If the preparation advocates are correct, then more need based aid can actually cause college access to decline. Colleges will raise net prices to capture the increase in subsidies, the unprepared students will still not complete their degrees, and the prepared low income students will be in worse financial condition than before the subsidies were increased. If the college access problem is due to lack of preparation, then new public resources should be directed towards reform of primary and secondary education where the preparation problem begins.

The polarization of the college access issue is not productive. The evidence is consistent with both sides of the debate. Furthermore, the dynastic poverty studies suggest that culture plays an important role in low college access. A permanent fix for the chronic college access problem requires that society address all three: financial constraints, lack of preparation, and family cultural barriers. Unfortunately, a successful solution to all three would still not be sufficient, since college access also depends on college cost control. In other words, the college access problem will not be eliminated until colleges learn to control their costs.

8.4   OPTIMAL PRICE AND QUALITY COMPETITION

The difference between cooperation and collusion is intent: agents are said to cooperate when they act collectively with the intent to promote social objectives, while agents are said to collude when they act collectively with the intent to promote private interests at the expense of public interests. Cooperation among producers of private goods invariably leads to collusion, while cooperation among producers of public goods is a necessary condition for the private provision of public goods. For charities that produce services that have both private and public good characteristics, such as higher education, it is not obvious that the optimal public policy should be to promote unrestricted competition or to promote complete cooperation among institutions. The existence of unresolved agency problems in higher education suggests that some form of competition among higher education institutions is desirable. Alternatively, unrestricted competition among charities can lead to the complete elimination of the provision of public goods in the marginal charity. Furthermore, the empirical evidence suggests that the public prefers cooperation among charities; however, that preference depends on how the game is framed.

Public policy with respect to competition among higher education institutions has changed in the last six decades. It can be argued that at the end of World War II, the public considered higher education a public good where society's interests were best served by cooperation among higher education institutions. Today, it seems the public considers higher education a private good where competition among institutions should be encouraged. This cultural change is best reflected by the history of the 'Overlap Group' and the Justice Department's prosecution of these institutions in the early 1990s. It seems likely that the higher education community is responsible for this shift in the public's perceptions regarding higher education. The failure to control costs and the use of aggressive lobbying techniques to defend the cost increases leaves the impression that higher education is just one more vested interest group that pursues its own self-interests at the public's expense.

Competition among institutions can arise on the basis of any combination of price and product differentiation. For the past decade and a half, private higher education institutions have been engaged in vigorous net price competition. There were first mover advantages for those institutions that began to discount tuition early, but the data suggests the competition has had little effect on the distribution of students. Collectively, the price competition was self-canceling. The price competition was at least partially responsible for the shift away from need based aid towards merit aid and responsible for a decline in college access among low income and minority students.

The financial stress created by tuition discounting is a powerful motivation for institutions to look for new policies that generate an advantage. A new program for product differentiation called 'academic branding' is drawing increasing attention. It will, in all probability, create first mover advantages for those institutions that adopt the new advertising programs early. Unfortunately, advertising is an arms race. The advertising advantage created by one institution will be blocked by the advertising efforts of other institutions precipitating another round of advertising expenditures by the institution. In the end, all participants wind up with higher costs and no change in the distribution of students. This is particularly dangerous for higher education since the service provided is an experience good where the length of time required for consumers to judge the quality of the service they purchased is very long. The long lag creates ample opportunities for institutions to make mischief with the public's perception of the quality of the service provided. This is a serious agency issue because marketing programs do generate short-run returns and the average tenure among most administrators is short enough for them to be gone before the long-run costs of ill-conceived marketing programs manifest themselves.

In contrast, the type of product differentiation that has a durable impact on reputation is real quality differentiation. Investing in real quality differentiation requires a willingness to take risks and to innovate. Unfortunately, investment in higher quality does not have an immediate payoff and the lag exceeds the average tenure of most administrators and many board members. The risk, the requirement to innovate, and short tenure among administrators creates incentives for administrators to adopt forms of competition that generate a short-run advantage. The type of competition adopted may or may not have long-run benefits. Therefore, a public policy that seeks to increase general competition among higher education institutions may in fact make college access worse and may make costs rise faster.

8.5   THE STATE OF THE ACADEME

At the July 2004 annual meeting of the Council for Advancement and Support of Education the president of Smith College, Carol T. Christ, made a public plea for more disclosure, accountability, and a proactive stance with respect to higher education reform (Strout, 2004). President Christ is concerned about the 'erosion of public trust' and the prospect that the government will insert itself further into the administration of higher education institutions. Her concerns are quite valid and her comments on this topic are timely. The academe should lead the reform movement rather than hire lobbyists to resist reform. Being driven to reform by the public will result in more Draconian changes than are necessary. After all, objective analysis, experimentation, and an open minded attitude towards change are all core academic values.

As an institution, we have never failed to apply analytical methods to every other institution within our society. Our critical analysis of government, business, political parties, and culture are abundant. We have been less diligent in the application of these critical skills to introspection. It is time to acknowledge our own failings and admit there are agency problems in higher education that are responsible, in part, for chronic college access problems.

The public should be aware that the higher education establishment has a strong financial incentive to promote more direct financial aid to low income students. Any increase in the students' ability to pay for college will be captured, at least in part, by the institutions through higher net tuition and fees and through higher expenditures: the increase in ability to pay increases potential rents. Furthermore, it will be easy for education lobbyists to defame anyone who argues against more financial aid to low income students and for them to position themselves as advocates for these students. After all, any increase in aid to low income students must have some positive benefit at the margin. The same thing can be said about any increase in the return to higher education. As the return to a college education rises relative to the return to a high school education, the willingness and ability of students to pay for a college education increases. Lax cost control ensures that part of that return will be captured by higher education institutions rather than the students themselves, resulting in chronic underinvestment in higher education.

A permanent solution to the higher education access problem can be achieved only if higher education's culture is changed. The current culture is hostile to the very notion of cost control and it freezes the distribution of resources in place. The current inertia prevents any active response prior to a financial emergency. An institution has to be in serious trouble before any action is taken; as a consequence missed opportunities are common in higher education. The essential structure of higher education has not changed in 50 years. The rapid increase in college costs is compelling evidence that reform is necessary. Unfortunately, cost control is a profoundly boring and dismal issue. As a result it is going to be very difficult to engage the academe in a constructive dialogue about why this issue is a vital public policy question and why it is critical to the permanent resolution of college access problems.

NOTES

1. Changes in technology also require a response from both types of institution. The structure of the organizations cannot remain static and minimize social cost as technology changes.
2. As an exercise, try to describe a plausible objective function for a higher education institution that does not include quality, reputation, prestige, good students, or successful alumni.

References

Acosta, Rebecca J. (2001), 'How Do Colleges Respond to Changes in Federal Student Aid?', Working Paper, Department of Economics, UCLA, October.

Advisory Committee on Student Financial Assistance (2002), *Empty Promises: The Myth of College Access in America*. June.

Akerlof, G. (1970), 'The Market for Lemons: Quality Uncertainty and the Market Mechanism', *Quarterly Journal of Economics*, 89, 488–500.

Alchian, Armen A. and Harold Demsetz (1972), 'Production, Information Costs, and Economic Organization', *American Economic Review*, 62, 777–95.

Andreoni, James (1995), 'Warm-glow versus Cold-prickle: The Effects of Positive and Negative Framing on Cooperation in Experiments', *The Quarterly Journal of Economics*, 110(1), 1–21.

Andreoni, James (1998), 'Toward a Theory of Charitable Fund-Raising', *Journal of Political Economy*, 106(6), 1186–213.

Andreoni, James and A. Abigail Payne (2003), 'Do Government Grants to Private Charities Crowd Out Giving or Fund-raising?', *The American Economic Review*, 93(3), 792–812.

Archibald, Robert B. (2002), *Redesigning the Financial Aid System*, Baltimore: The Johns Hopkins University Press.

Bartolome, C. de. (1996), 'Equilibrium and Inefficiency in a Community Model with Peer-group Effects', *Journal of Political Economy*, 623–45.

Basinger, Julianne (2001), 'When a President Quits Early, the Damage Can Linger On', *The Chronicle of Higher Education*, July 27.

Basinger, Julianne (2004), 'High Pay, Hard Questions, *The Chronicle of Higher Education*, November 19.

Bates, Laurie J. and Rexford E. Santerre (2000), 'A Time Series Analysis of Private College Closures and Mergers', *Review of Industrial Organization*, 17, 267–76.

Becker, G. (1975), *Human Capital*, New York: Columbia University Press.

Becker, G. and Nigel Tomes (1986), 'Human Capital and the Rise and Fall of Families', *Journal of Labor Economics*, 4(3), 1–39.

Bedard, Kelly (2001), 'Human Capital versus Signaling Models: University Access and High School Dropouts', *Journal of Political Economy*, 109(4).

Berube, Michael (1998), 'Why Inefficiency Is Good for Universities', *The Chronicle of Higher Education*, March 27, B4–B5.

Blakemore, A. E. and S. A. Low (1983), 'Scholarship Policy and Race/Sex Differences in the Demand for Higher Education', *Economic Inquiry*, 21(4), 504–19.

Boehner, Rep. John A. and Rep. Howard P. McKeon (2003), *The College Cost Crisis*, US House Subcommittee on Education and the Workforce.

Bok, Derek and William G. Bowen (1998), *The Shape of the River: Long-Term Consequences of Considering Race in College and University Admissions*, Princeton, N.J.: Princeton University Press.

Bound, John and Sarah Turner (2002), 'Going to War and Going to College: Did World War II and the G.I. Bill Increase Educational Attainment for Returning Veterans?', *Journal of Labor Economics*, 20(4), 784–815.

Bowen, Howard (1980), *The Cost of Higher Education*, San Francisco: Jossey-Bass.

Bowen, William G. and Neil L. Rudenstine (2003), 'Race-Sensitive Admissions: Back to Basics', *The Chronicle of Higher Education*, February 7.

Bowles, Samuel and Herbert Gintis (2002), 'The Inheritance of Inequality', *Journal of Economic Perspectives*, 16(3), 3–30.

Boyes, William J., Dennis L. Hoffman, and Stuart A. Low (1989), 'An Econometric Analysis of the Bank Credit Scoring Problem', *Journal of Econometrics*, 40(1), 3–14.

Breneman, David W. (1994), *Liberal Arts Colleges: Thriving, Surviving, or Endangered?*, Washington, DC: The Brookings Institution.

Brewer, Dominic J., Susan M. Gates, and Charles A. Goldman (2002), *In Pursuit of Prestige: Strategy and Competition in US Higher Education*, New Brunswick: Transaction Publishers.

Brinkman, Paul T. (1989), 'Instructional Costs per Student Credit Hour: Differences by Level of Instruction', *Journal of Educational Finance*, 15, 34–52.

Brinkman, Paul T. (1990), 'Higher Education Cost Functions', in Stephen A. Hoenack and Eileen L. Collins (eds) *The Economics of American Universities*, , Albany: State University of New York Press.

Bronner, E. (1998) 'College Tuition Rises 4%, Outpacing Inflation', *New York Times*, October 8.

Brownstien, Andrew (2001), 'Upping the Ante for Student Aid', *The Chronicle of Higher Education*, February 16.

Brueckner, J. and K. Lee (1989), 'Club Theory with a Peer-group Effect', *Regional Science and Urban Economics*, 19(3), 399–420.

Burd, Stephen (2001), 'US Education Faces "Access Crisis" if Need Based Aid Programs Are Not Revived, Report Says', *The Chronicle of Higher Education*, February 2.

Burd, Stephen (2002), 'Report on College Access Angers Private Institutions', *The Chronicle of Higher Education*, January 18.

Burd, Stephen (2003), 'Republican Leaders Stress Accountability and Cost Issues in Hearing on Higher Education Act', *The Chronicle of Higher Education*, May 14.

Burrell, S. (1967), 'The G.I. Bill and the Great American Transformation', *Boston University Graduate Journal*, 15, 3.

Cameron, Stephen V. and James J. Heckman (1998), 'Life Cycle Schooling and Dynamic Selection Bias: Models and Evidence for Five Cohorts of American Males', *Journal of Political Economy*, 106(2), 262–333.

Cameron, Stephen V. and James J. Heckman (2001) 'The Dynamics of Educational Attainment for Black, Hispanic, and White Males', *Journal of Political Economy*, 109(3), 455–99.

Cameron, Stephen V. and Christopher Taber (2004), 'Estimation of Educational Borrowing Constraints Using Returns to Schooling', *Journal of Political Economy*, 112(1), 132–82.

Card, David (1995), 'Earnings, Schooling, and Ability Revisited', in Solomon W. Polachek, (ed.) *Research in Labor Economics*, 14, Greenwich, Conn.: JAI.

Card, D. and A. Krueger (1992), 'Does School Quality Matter? Returns to Education and the Characteristics of Public Schools in the United States', *Journal of Political Economy*, 100(1), 1–39.

Carey, Kevin (2004), *A Matter of Degrees: Improving Graduation Rates in Four-Year Colleges and Universities*, The Education Trust, May.

Carlson, Scott (2001), 'Harvard Increases Size of Financial-Aid Packages by $2,000 a Student', *The Chronicle of Higher Education*, February 22.

Carmichael, H. Lorne (1988), 'Incentives in Academics: Why is there Tenure?', *Journal of Political Economy*, 96(3), 453–72.

Cawley, John, James Heckman, and Edward Vytlacil (1999), 'On Policies to Reward the Value Added by Educators', *The Review of Economics and Statistics*, 81(4), 720–27.

Choy, Susan P. (2004), *Paying for College: Changes Between 1990 and 2000 for Full-Time Dependent Undergraduates*, NCES, June.

Clotfelter, Charles T. (1996), *Buying the Best: Cost Escalation in Elite Higher Education*, Princeton University Press.

Clotfelter, Charles T. (1999), 'The Familiar but Curious Economics of Higher Education: Introduction to a Symposium', *Journal of Economic Perspectives*, 13(1), 3–12.

Clotfelter, Charles T., Ronald G. Ehrenberg, Malcolm Getz, and John J. Siegfried (1991), *Economic Challenges in Higher Education*, Chicago, Ill: The University of Chicago Press.

Coase, Ronald H. (1937), 'The Nature of the Firm', *Economica*, 4, 386–405.

Cohn, Elchanan and Terry G. Geske (1990), *The Economics of Education*, 3rd edition, Oxford, UK: Pergamon.

Cohn, Elchanan, Sherrie L. W. Rhine, and Maria C. Santos (1989), 'Institutions of Higher Education as Multi-Product Firms: Economies of Scale and Scope', *Review of Economics and Statistics*, 71, 283–90.

Cohn, E. and S. T. Cooper (2004), 'Multiproduct cost functions for universities: Economies of scale and scope' in G. Johnes and J. Johnes (eds), *International Handbook of the Economics of Education*, Cheltenham, UK and Lyme, US: Edward Elgar.

Cole, Stephen and Elinor Barber (2003), *Increasing Faculty Diversity: The Occupational Choices of High-Achieving Minority Students*, Cambridge, Mass: Harvard University Press.

Coleman, James S. (1973), 'The University and Society's New Demands Upon It', in Carl Kaysen (ed.), *Content and Context*, New York: McGraw-Hill.

Commission on National Investment in Higher Education, Council for Aid to Education (1997), *Breaking the Social Contract: The Fiscal Crisis in Higher Education*, RAND.

Cook, Phillip J. and Robert H. Frank (1993), 'The Growing Concentration of Top Students at Elite Institutions', in Charles T. Clotfelter and Michael Rothschild (eds), *Studies of Supply and Demand in Higher Education*, Chicago: University of Chicago Press.

Crawford, Elizabeth (2003), 'Americans Give Higher Education High Marks in All Areas Except Cost, Survey Finds', *The Chronicle of Higher Education*, June 19.

Daniere, Andre and Jerry Mechling (1970), 'Direct Marginal Productivity of College Education in Relation to College Aptitude of Students and Production Costs of Institutions', *Journal of Human Resources*, 5, 51–70.

Dee, Thomas S. and Linda A. Jackson (1999) 'Who Loses HOPE? Attrition from Georgia's College Scholarship Program', *Southern Economic Journal*, 66(2), 379–90.

De Gregorio, Jose (1996), 'Borrowing Constraints, Human Capital Accumulation, and Growth', *Journal of Monetary Economics*, 37(1), 49–71.

Docquier, F. and P. Michel (1999), 'Education Subsidies, Social Security and Growth: The Implications of a Demographic Shock', *Scandinavian Journal of Economics*, 101(3), 425–40.

Duffy, Elizabeth A. and Idana Goldberg (1998), *Crafting a Class: College Admissions and Financial Aid*, 1955–1994, Princeton, N.J.: Princeton University Press.

Dynarski, Susan (2000), 'Hope for Whom? Financial Aid for the Middle Class and its Impact on College Attendance', *NBER Working Paper Series*, NBER, June.

Dynarski, Susan (2002), 'The Consequences of Merit Aid', *NBER Working Paper Series*, NBER, December.

Dynarski, Susan (2003), 'Does Aid Matter? Measuring the Effect of Student Aid on College Attendance and Completion', *American Economic Review*, 93(1), 279–88.

Edlin, A. S. (1993), 'Is College Financial Aid Equitable and Efficient?' *Journal of Economic Perspectives*, 7(2), 143–58.

Ehrenberg, Ronald G. (2000), *Tuition Rising: Why College Costs so Much*, Cambridge, Mass: Harvard University Press.

Ehrenberg, Ronald G., and Daniel R. Sherman (1984), 'Optimal Financial Aid Policies for a Selective University', *Journal of Human Resources*, 19, 202–30.

Ehrenberg, Ronald G. and C. L. Smith (2003), 'The Sources and Uses of Annual Giving at Selective Private Research Universities and Liberal Arts Colleges', *Economics of Education Review*, 22, 223–35.

Epple, D. and R. Romano (1998), 'Competition Between Private and Public Schools, Vouchers and Peer-group Effects', *American Economic Review*, 88(1), 33–62.

Esposito, Frances Ferguson and Louis Esposito (1995), 'Monopolization, Social Welfare, and Overlap', *The Antitrust Bulletin*, Summer, 40(2), 433–51.

Evans, W., W. Oates, and R. Schwab (1992), 'Measuring Peer Group Effects: A Study of Teenage Behavior', *Journal of Political Economy*, 100, 966–91.

Feldstein, M. (1985), 'The Optimal Level of Social Security Benefits', *Quarterly Journal of Economics*, 100(2), 303–20.

Feldstein, M. (1995), 'College Scholarship Rules and Private Saving', American Economic Review, 85(3), 552–66.

Fernandez, Raquel and Richard Rogerson (1995), 'On the Political Economy of Education Subsidies', *Review of Economic Studies*, 62, 249–62.

Ferris, James M. (1991), 'Contracting and Higher Education', *Journal of Higher Education*, 62(1), 1–24.

Ferris, James M. (1992a), 'School-based Decision Making: A Principal–Agent Perspective', *Educational Evaluation and Policy Analysis*, 14, 333–46.

Ferris, James M. (1992b), 'A Contractual Approach to Higher Education Performance: With an Application to Australia', *Higher Education*, 24, 503–16.

Fish, Stanley (2004), 'Make 'Em Cry', *The Chronicle of Higher Education*, March 5.

Fisman, Raymond and R. Glenn Hubbard (2003), 'The Role of Nonprofit Endowments', in Edward L. Glaeser (ed.), *The Governance of Not-for-Profit Organizations*, Chicago: The University of Chicago Press, 217–33.

Fitzgerald, Brian K. and Jennifer A. Delaney (2002), 'Educational Opportunity in America' in Donald E. Heller (ed.), *Condition of Access: Higher Education for Lower Income Students*, Westport, CT: American Council on Education Praeger Series on Higher Education, 3–24.

Freeman, Kassie (1997), 'Increasing African Americans' Participation in Higher Education', *Journal of Higher Education*, 68(5), 523–50.

Freeman, Richard B. (1996), 'Toward an Apartheid Economy?' *Harvard Business Review*, 74, 114–21.

Galor, Oded and Joseph Zeira (1993), 'Income Distribution and Macroeconomics', *Review of Economic Studies*, 60(1), 35–52.

General Accounting Office (2002), *Tax-Exempt Organizations: Improvements Possible in Public, IRS, and State Oversight of Charities*, Washington, DC: GAO, April.

Getz, Malcolm and John J. Siegfried, and Hao Zhang (1991), 'Estimating Economies of Scale in Higher Education', *Economics Letters*, 37(2), 203–08.

Getz, Malcolm, John J. Siegfried, and Kathryn H. Anderson (1997), 'Adoption of Innovations in Higher Education', *The Quarterly Review of Economics and Finance*, 37(3), 605–31.

Glazer, Amihai and Kai A. Konrad (1996), 'A Signaling Explanation for Charity', *The American Economic Review*, 86(4), 1019–28.

Glomm, G. and B. Ravikumar (1992), 'Public versus Private Investment in Human Capital: Endogenous Growth and Income Inequality', *Journal of Political Economy*, 100, 818–34.

Golden, Daniel (2001), 'Opening Arguments: As Law School Begins, It's Columbia vs. NYU', *The Wall Street Journal*, August 28, 1.

Graglia, Lino A. (2003), 'Why Race Preferences in Admissions Aren't the Answer', *The Chronicle of Higher Education*, March 7.

Granger, C. W. J. (1969), 'Investigating Causal Relations by Econometric Models and Cross-Spectral Methods', *Econometrica*, 37(3) 24–36.

Grossman, Herschel (1995), 'Scholarships: Need or Merit?', *Cato Journal*, 14(3), 519–25.

Grossman, Sanford J. and Oliver D. Hart (1986), 'The Costs and Benefits of Ownership: A Theory of Vertical and Lateral Integration', *Journal of Political Economy*, 94(4), 691–719.

Hansmann, Henry (1981), 'The Rationale for Exempting Nonprofit Organizations from Corporate Income Taxation', *Yale Law Journal*, 91, 54–100.

Hansmann, Henry (1990), 'Why do Universities Have Endowments?', *Journal of Legal Studies*, 19, 3–42.

Hanushek, Eric (1979), 'Conceptual and Empirical Issues in the Estimation of Education Production Functions', *Journal of Human Resources*, 14(3) 351–88.

Hanushek, Eric (1986), 'The Economics of Schooling: Production and Efficiency in Public Schools', *Journal of Economic Literature*, 24(3) 1141–77.

Hanushek, Eric (1992), 'The Trade-off Between Child Quantity and Quality', *Journal of Political Economy*, 100(1), 84–117.

Harbaugh, William T. (1998), 'What Do Donations Buy? A Model of Philanthropy Based on Prestige and Warm Glow', *Journal of Public Economics*, 67, 269–84.

Hare, Paul and Geoffrey Wyatt (1992), 'Economics of Academic Research and its Implication for Higher Education', *Oxford Review of Economic Policy*, 8(2), 48–66.

Harford, J. D. and R. D. Marcus (1986), 'Tuition and US Private College Characteristics: The Hedonic Approach', *Economics of Education*, 5(4), 415–30.

Harrison, Lawrence E. and Samuel P. Huntington (eds) (2000), *Culture Matters: How Values Shape Human Progress*, New York: Basic Books.

Hart, Oliver (1995), 'Corporate Governance: Some Theory and Implications', *The Economic Journal*, 105(430), 678–89.

Hart, Oliver and John Moore (1990), 'Property Rights and the Nature of the Firm', *The Journal of Political Economy*, 98(6), 1119–58.

Henderson, Vernon, Peter Meiszkowski, and Yvon Sauvageau (1978), 'Peer Group Effects and Educational Production Functions', *Journal of Public Economics*, 10(1), 97–106.

Hertz, Thomas (2002), 'Intergenerational Economic Mobility of Black and White Families in the United States', Paper presented at the Society of Labor Economists Annual Meeting, May.

Hoenack, S. A. (1990), 'An Economist's Perspective on Costs within Higher Education Institutions', in *The Economics of American Universities*, Stephen A. Hoenack and Eileen L. Collins (eds), Albany: State University of New York Press.

Hoenack, S. A. and D. J. Pierro (1990), 'An Econometric Model of a Public University's Income and Enrollments', *Journal of Economic Behavior and Organization*, 14(3), 403–23.

Holmstrom, Bengt and Paul Milgrom (1994), 'The Firm as an Incentive System', *American Economic Review*, 84(4), 972–91.

Honan, W. H. (1994), 'Cost of 4-year Degree Passes $100,000 Mark', *New York Times*, May 4.

Hoover, Eric (2001), '28 Private Colleges Agree to Use Common Approaches to Student Aid', *The Chronicle of Higher Education*, July 20.

Hopkins, David S. P. and William E. Massy (1981), *Planning Models for Colleges and Universities*, Stanford, California: Stanford University Press.

Hubbell, Loren Loomis (1992), 'Tuition Discounting: The Impact of Institutionally Funded Financial Aid', NACUBO.

The Institute for Higher Education Policy and Scholarship America (2004), *Investing in America's Future: Why Student Aid Pays Off for Society and Individuals*, May.

James, Estelle (1990), 'Decision Processes and Priorities in Higher Education,' in Stephen A. Hoenack and Eileen L. Collins (eds), *The Economics of American Universities*, Buffalo, NY: State University of New York Press.

Jensen, Michael C. (1986), 'Agency Costs of Free Cash Flow, Corporate Finance, and Takeovers', *American Economic Review*, 76(2), 323–29.

Johnes, Geraint (1997), 'Costs and Industrial Structure in Contemporary British Higher Education', *The Economic Journal*, 107, 727–37.

Johnes, Geraint (1999), 'The Management of Universities', *Scottish Journal of Political Economy*, 46(5), 505–22.

Johnson, Bruce K. (2000), 'An Overlooked Implication of Baseball's Antitrust Exemption' in Paul D. Staudohar (ed.), *Diamond Mines: Baseball & Labor*, Syracuse, N.Y.: Syracuse University Press.

Kane, Thomas J. (1994), 'College Entry by Blacks since 1970: The Role of College Costs, Family Background, and the Returns to Education', *Journal of Political Economy*, 102(5), 878–911.

Kane, Thomas J. (1995), 'Rising Public College Tuition and College Entry: How well do Public Subsidies Promote Access to College?', *NBER Working Paper Series*, NBER July.

Kane, Thomas J. (1999), *The Price of Admission: Rethinking how Americans pay for College*, Washington, D.C.: Brookings Institution Press.

Kaplan, Ann E. (2003), *2002 Voluntary Support of Education*, New York: Council for Aid to Education.

Keane, Michael P. and Kenneth I. Wolpin (2001), 'The Effect of Parental Transfers and Borrowing Constraints on Educational Attainment', *International Economic Review*, 42(4), 1051–103.

Khanna, Jyoti and Todd Sandler (2000), 'Partners in giving: The Crowding-in Effects of UK Government Grants', *European Economic Review*, 44, 1543–56.

Kipp, Samuel M., Derek V. Price, and Jill K. Wohlford (2002), *Unequal Opportunity: Disparities in College Access Among the 50 States*, Lumina Foundation, January.

Kirp, David L. (2003), *Shakespeare, Einstein, and the Bottom Line: The Marketing of Higher Education, Cambridge*, Massachusetts: Harvard University Press.

Koshal, R. K. and M. Koshal (1995), 'Quality and Economies of Scale in Higher Education', *Applied Economics*, 27(8), 773–78.

Koshal, R. K. and M. Koshal (1999), 'Demand and Supply of Educational Service: A Case of Liberal Arts Colleges', *Education Economics*, 7(2), 121–30.

Koshal, R. K. and M. Koshal (2000), 'Do Liberal Arts Colleges Exhibit Economies of Scale and Scope?', *Education Economics*, 8(3), 209–20.

Kremer, Michael (1993), 'Population Growth and Technological Change: One Million B.C. to 1990', *Quarterly Journal of Economics*, 108(3), 681–716.

Lancaster, Kelvin J. (1966), 'A New Approach to Consumer Theory', *Journal of Political Economy*, 74(2), 132–57.

Lang, Kevin (1993), 'Ability Bias, Discount Rate Bias, and the Return of Education', Manuscript, Boston: Boston University, Department of Economics.

Larson, E. (1997), 'Why Colleges Cost too Much', *Time*, March 17.

Leibenstein, H. (1965), 'Allocative Efficiency and X–efficiency', *American Economic Review*, 56, 392–425.

Leslie, L.L. and G. Rhoades (1995), 'Rising Administrative Costs: On Seeking Explanations', *Journal of Higher Education*, 66, 197–212.

Levin, Henry M. (1997), 'Raising School Productivity: An X–Efficiency Approach', *Economics of Education Review*, 16(3), 303–11.

Lewis, Ethan G. and Gordon C. Winston (1997), 'Subsidies, Costs, Tuition, and Aid in US Higher Education', Unpublished working paper, Williams Project on the Economics of Higher Education, April.

List, John A. and David Lucking-Reiley (2002), 'The Effects of Seed Money and Refunds on Charitable Giving: Experimental Evidence from a University Capital Campaign', *Journal of Political Economy*, 110(1), 215–33.

Loury, Linda Datcher, and David Garman (1995), 'College Selectivity and Earnings', *Journal of Labor Economics*, 13, 289–308.

Lucas, R. E. (1988), 'On the Mechanics of Economic Development', *Journal of Monetary Economics*, 21, 3–42.

Mabry, T. (1999), 'College Tuition Outpaces Inflation Again', *The Wall Street Journal*, March 12.

Malani, Anup, Tomas Philipson, and Guy David (2003), 'Theories of Firm Behavior in the Nonprofit Sector', in Edward L. Glaeser (ed.), *The Governance of Not-for-Profit Organizations*, Chicago: The University of Chicago Press, 181–215.

Manski, Charles F. and David A. Wise (1983), *College Choice in America*, Cambridge, Mass: Harvard University Press.

Martin, Robert E. (1986), 'On Judging Quality by Price: Price Dependent Expectations, Not Price Dependent Preferences', *Southern Economic Journal*, 52, 665–72.

Martin, Robert E. (2000), 'Enrollment Management as a Portfolio Investment Problem', *College & University*, 76(1), 25–9.

Martin, Robert E. (2001a), 'Dangerously Denying Deficits', *Trusteeship*, AGB, January/February, 20–23.

Martin, Robert E. (2001b), 'The Vicious Spiral of Tuition Discounting', *Trusteeship*, AGB, May/June.

Martin, Robert E. (2002) 'Tuition Discounting: Theory and Evidence', *Economics of Education Review*, 21(2), 125–36.

Martin, Robert E. (2004), 'Tuition Discounting Without Tears', *Economics of Education Review*, 23, 177–89.

Martin, Robert E. and David J. Smyth (1991), 'Adverse Selection and Moral Hazard Effects in the Mortgage Market: An Empirical Analysis', *Southern Economic Journal*, 57(4), 1071–84.

Mas–Colell, Andreu, Michael D. Whinston, and Jerry R. Green (1995), *Microeconomic Theory*, New York: Oxford University Press.

Massy, William F. (1998), 'Remarks on Restructuring Higher Education' in *Straight Talk About College Costs and Prices*, Report of the National Commission on the Cost of Higher Education, Phoenix: Oryx Press.

Mazumder, Bhashkar (2003), 'Family Resources and College Enrollment', *Federal Reserve Bank of Chicago Economic Perspectives*, 27(4), 30–41.

McPherson, Michael S. and Morton Owen Schapiro (1991a), 'Does Student Aid Affect College Enrollment? New Evidence on a Persistent Controversy', *American Economic Review*, 81(1), 309–18.

McPherson, Michael S. and Morton Owen Schapiro (1991b), *Keeping College Affordable: Government and Educational Opportunity*, Washington, DC: The Brookings Institution.

McPherson, Michael S. and Morton Owen Schapiro (1998), *The Student Aid Game: Meeting Need and Rewarding Talent in American Higher Education*, Princeton, NJ: Princeton University Press.

McPherson, Michael S. and Morton Owen Schapiro (1999a), 'Gaining Control of the Free-for-all in Financial Aid', *The Chronicle of Higher Education*, July 2, A48.

McPherson, Michael S. and Morton Owen Schapiro (1999b), 'Tenure Issues in Higher Education', *Journal of Economic Perspectives*, 13(1), 85–98.

McPherson, Michael S. and Morton Owen Schapiro (2002), 'Changing Patterns of Institutional Aid: Impact on Access and Education Policy', in Donald E. Heller (ed.), *Condition of Access: Higher Education for Lower Income Students*, Westport, CT: American Council on Education Praeger Series on Higher Education, 73–96.

McPherson, Michael S., Morton Owen Schapiro, and Gordon C. Winston (1993), *Paying the Piper: Productivity, Incentives, and Financing in US Higher Education*, Ann Arbor: University of Michigan Press.

Meyer, Robert H. (1997), 'Value-Added Indicators of School Performance: A Primer', *Economics of Education Review*, 16(3), 283–301.

Mumper, Michael (2001), 'The Paradox of College Prices: Five Stories with No Clear Lesson', in Donald E. Heller (ed.), *The States and Public Higher Education Policy: Affordability, Access, and Accountability*, Baltimore: The Johns Hopkins University Press.

National Commission on the Cost of Higher Education (1998), *Straight Talk About College Costs and Prices*, The Report of the National Commission on the Cost of Higher Education, Phoenix, AZ: Oryx Press.

Newhouse, Joseph F. (1970), 'Toward a Theory of Nonprofit Institutions: An Economic Model of a Hospital', *American Economic Review*, 60, 64–74.

Ortmann, Andreas and Richard Squire (2000), 'A Game-Theoretic Explanation of the Administrative Lattice in Institutions of Higher Learning', *Journal of Economic Behavior & Organization*, 43, 377–91.

Perna, Laura Walter (2000), 'Differences in the Decision to Attend College Among African Americans, Hispanics, and Whites', *The Journal of Higher Education*, 71(2), 117–41.

Perotti, Roberto (1996), 'Growth, Income Distribution, and Democracy: What the Data Say', *Journal of Economic Growth*, 1(2), 149–87.

Pope, Loren (2000), *Colleges That Change Lives: 40 Schools You Should Know about Even if You're Not a Straight-A Student*, Penguin Press.

Posnett, John and Todd Sandler (1989), 'Demand for Charity Donations in Private Non-profit Markets', *Journal of Public Economics*, 40, 187–200.

Pulley, John L. (2003), 'Romancing the Brand', *Chronicle of Higher Education*, October 24.

Quirk, James and Rodney D. Fort (1992), *Pay Dirt: The Business of Professional Team Sports*, Princeton, N.J.: Princeton University Press.

Quirk, James and Rodney D. Fort (1999), *Hard Ball: The Abuse of Power in Pro Team Sports*, Princeton, N.J.: Princeton University Press.

Redd, Kenneth E. (2000), 'Discounting Toward Disaster: Tuition Discounting, College Finances, and Enrollments of Low-Income Undergraduates', *New Agenda Series*: USA Group Foundation, 3(2), December.

Rizzo, Michael J. (2004), 'A Less Than Zero Sum Game? State Funding for Public Education: How Public Higher Education Institutions Have Lost', dissertation, Economics Department, Cornell University.

Romer, Paul M. (1994), 'The Origins of Endogenous Growth', *Journal of Economic Perspectives*, 8(1), 3–22.

Rooney, P. M. (1999), 'A Better Method for Analyzing the Costs and Benefits of Fundraising at Universities', *Nonprofit Management & Leadership*, Fall, 39–56.

Rose-Ackerman, Susan (1982), 'Charitable Giving and "Excessive" Fundraising', *The Quarterly Journal of Economics*, 97(2), 193–212.

Rose-Ackerman, Susan (1987), 'Ideals versus Dollars: Donors, Charity Managers, and Government Grants', *Journal of Political Economy*, 95(4), 810–823.

Rose-Ackerman, Susan (1996), 'Altruism, Nonprofits and Economic Theory', *Journal of Economic Literature*, 34, 701–28.

Rothschild, M. (1974), 'Searching for the Lowest Price when the Distribution of Prices is Unknown', *Journal of Political Economy*, 82, 689–711.

Rothschild, Michael and Lawrence J. White (1993), 'The University in the Marketplace: Some Insights and Some Puzzles', in Charles T. Clotfelter and Michael Rothschild (eds), *Studies of Supply and Demand in Higher Education*, Chicago: University of Chicago Press (for NBER).

Rothschild, Michael and Lawrence J. White (1995), 'The Analytics of Pricing in Higher Education and Other Services in Which Customers are Inputs', *Journal of Political Economy*, 103, 573–86.

Ruppert, Sandra S. (2003), *Closing the College Participation Gap: A National Summary*, Denver, CO: Education Commission of the States.

Sandy, Jonathan and Kevin Duncan (1996), 'Does Private Education Increase Earnings?', *Eastern Economic Journal*, Summer, 303–12.

Savoka, E. (1991), 'The Effect of Changes in the Composition of Financial Aid on College Enrollment', *Eastern Economic Journal*, 16, 109–21.

Schmalensee, Richard (1972), 'A Note on Monopolistic Competition and Excess Capacity', *Journal of Political Economy*, 80(3), 586–91.

Schmidt, Peter (2003), 'Excluding Some Races From Programs? Expect a Letter From a Lawyer', *The Chronicle of Higher Education*, March 7.

Schultz, T. (1961), 'Investments in Human Capital', *American Economic Review*, March, 1–17.

Schwartz, A. (1988), 'Tenure: Can it be Explained by an Efficiency Wage Argument?', Tel-Aviv University, Working Paper No. 36–88, November.

Sharpe, Russell T. et al. (1946), *Financial Assistance for College Students*, Washington, DC: American Council on Education.

Shea, John (2000), 'Does Parent's Money Matter?', *Journal of Public Economics*, 77, 155–84.

Smith, Adam (1976), *The Wealth of Nations*, Chicago: University of Chicago Press.

Solow, Robert (1956), 'A Contribution to the Theory of Economic Growth', *Quarterly Journal of Economics*, 70, 65–94.

Spence, Michael (2002), 'Signaling in Retrospect and the Informational Structure of Markets', *American Economic Review*, 92(3), 434–59.

Spies, Richard R. (1990), *The Effect of Rising Costs on College Choice*, Princeton, NJ: Princeton University.

Stanley, Marcus (2003), 'College Education and the Midcentury GI Bills', *Quarterly Journal of Economics*, May.

Stecklow, Steve (1995), 'Cheat Sheets: Colleges Inflate SATs and Graduation Rates in Popular Guidebook', *Wall Street Journal*, April 5, A1.

Stecklow, Steve (1996), 'Expensive Lesson: Colleges Manipulate Financial-Aid Offers, Shortchanging Many', *Wall Street Journal*, April 1, A1, A6.

Stiroh, Kevin J. (1998), 'Computers, Productivity, and Input Substitution', *Economic Inquiry*, 36, 175–91.

Strout, Erin (2004), 'Colleges Should Become More Accountable, Smith's Leader Says, or Face the Legislative Consequences', *The Chronicle of Higher Education*, July 13.

Sykes, Charles J. (1988), *Profscam*, Washington, DC: Regency Gateway.

Symonds, William C. (2003), 'Colleges in Crisis', *Business Week*, April 28, 72–8.

Thernstrom, Stephen and Abigail Thernstrom (1997), *America in Black and White: One Nation Indivisible*, New York: Simon and Schuster.

TIAA-CREF (2004), *2003 NACUBO Endowment Study*, Washington, DC: National Association of College and University Business Officers.

Tiffany, Frederick G. and Jeff A. Ankrom (1998), 'The Competitive Use of Price Discrimination by Colleges', *Eastern Economic Journal*, 24(1), 99–110.

Tracy, Joseph and Joel Waldfogel (1997), 'The Best Business Schools: A Market-Based Approach', *Journal of Business*, 70, 1–31.

Trostel, Philip A. (1996), 'Should Education be Subsidized?', *Public Finance Quarterly*, 24(1), 3–24.

Tuckman, Howard P. and Cyril F. Chang (1998), 'How Pervasive are Abuses in Fundraising Among Nonprofits?', *Nonprofit Management & Leadership*, 9(2), 211–21.

Van Der Werf, Martin (2002), 'Mount Senario's Final Act', *Chronicle of Higher Education*, June 14.

Varian, H. R. (1994), 'The Sequential Provision of Public Goods', *Journal of Public Economics*, 53, 165–86.

Veblen, Thorstein (1973), *The Theory of the Leisure Class*, Boston: Houghton Mifflin Co.

Vesterlund, Lise (2003), 'The Informational Value of Sequential Fundraising', *Journal of Public Economics*, 87, 627–57.

Webster, David S. (1992), 'Rankings of Undergraduate Education In *US News & World Report* and *Money*: Are They Any Good?', *Change*, March/April, 19–31.

Weiler, William C. (1996), 'Factors Influencing the Matriculation Choices of High Ability Students', *Economics of Education Review*, 15(1), 23–36.

Weisbrod, Burton A. and Nestor D. Dominguez (1986), 'Demand for Collective Goods in Private Nonprofit Markets: Can Fundraising Expenditures Help Overcome Free-riding Behavior?', *Journal of Public Economics*, 30, 83–95.

Williamson, Oliver E. (1975), *Markets and Hierarchies: Analysis and Antitrust Implications*, New York: Free Press.

Winston, Gordon (1992), 'Hostility, Maximization and the Public Trust', *Change*, July/August, 20–27.

Winston, Gordon (1996), 'The Economic Structure of Higher Education: Subsidies, Customer-Inputs, and Hierarchy', working paper, Williams Project on the Economics of Higher Education, November.

Winston, Gordon (1997), 'Why Can't a College be More Like a Firm?', *Change*, 29, 32–8.

Winston, Gordon (1999), 'Subsidies, Hierarchy, and Peers: The Awkward Economics of Higher Education', *Journal of Economic Perspectives*, 13, 13–36.

Winston, Gordon and David J. Zimmerman (2004), 'Peer Effects in Higher Education', in Caroline M. Hoxby (ed.), *College Choices: The Economics of Where to Go, When to Go, and How to Pay for It*, Chicago: The University of Chicago Press.

Zhang, Jie (1996), 'Optimal Public Investments in Education and Endogenous Growth', *Scandinavian Journal of Economics*, 98(3), 387–404.

Zimmer, R. W. and E. F. Toma (2000), 'Peer Effects in Private and Public Schools Across Countries', *Journal of Policy Analysis and Management*, 75–92.

Index